Fairness in Adaptation to

Fairness in Adaptation to Climate Change

edited by W. Neil Adger, Jouni Paavola, Saleemul Huq, and M. J. Mace

The MIT Press
Cambridge, Massachusetts
London, England

MIT Press books may be purchased at special quantity discounts for business or sales promotional use. For information, please e-mail special_sales@ mitpress.mit.edu or write to Special Sales Department, The MIT Press, 55 Hayward Street, Cambridge, MA 02142.

This book was set in Sabon by SNP Best-set Typesetter Ltd., Hong Kong and was printed and bound in the United States of America.
Printed on recycled paper.

Library of Congress Cataloging-in-Publication Data

Fairness in adaptation to climate change / edited by W. Neil Adger . . . [et al.].
   p. cm.
Includes bibliographical references and index.
ISBN 0-262-01227-8 (alk. paper)—ISBN 0-262-51193-2 (pbk. : alk. paper)
1. Climatic changes—Political aspects. 2. Environmental justice. I. Adger, W. Neil.

QC981.8.C5F345   2006
363.738′74—dc22   2005056246

10 9 8 7 6 5 4 3 2 1

Contents

Foreword by Bo Kjellén   vii

Preface   xi

Contributors   xv

1   Toward Justice in Adaptation to Climate Change   1
    W. Neil Adger, Jouni Paavola, and Saleemul Huq

I   Politics, Science, and Law in Justice Debates   20

2   Dangers and Thresholds in Climate Change and the
    Implications for Justice   23
    Stephen H. Schneider and Janica Lane

3   Adaptation under the UN Framework Convention on Climate
    Change: The International Legal Framework   53
    M. J. Mace

II Aspects of Fairness in Adaptation   77

4   Exploring the Social Justice Implications of Adaptation and
    Vulnerability   79
    Kirstin Dow, Roger E. Kasperson, and Maria Bohn

5   Is It Appropriate to Identify Winners and Losers?   97
    Robin Leichenko and Karen O'Brien

6   Climate Change, Insecurity, and Injustice   115
    Jon Barnett

7   Adaptation: Who Pays Whom?   131
Paul Baer

8   A Welfare Theoretic Analysis of Climate Change Inequities   155
Neil A. Leary

III Fairness in Adaptation Responses   179

9   Equity in National Adaptation Programs of Action (NAPAs): The
Case of Bangladesh   181
Saleemul Huq and Mizan R. Khan

10 Justice in Adaptation to Climate Change in Tanzania   201
Jouni Paavola

11 Adaptation and Equity in Resource Dependent Societies   223
David S. G. Thomas and Chasca Twyman

12 Extreme Weather and Burden Sharing in Hungary   229
Joanne Linnerooth-Bayer and Anna Vári

IV Conclusion   261

13 Multifaceted Justice in Adaptation to Climate Change   263
Jouni Paavola, W. Neil Adger, and Saleemul Huq

References   279
Index   311

Foreword

We live in confusing and uncertain times, with unprecedented change occurring at a rate never experienced before. New information and communication technologies challenge the established patterns of production and administration; and globalization has become a living reality, modifying long-established principles of national independence and control.

To this revolutionary pattern has been added global environmental change. There are six billion people on the planet, and there are expected to be around nine billion in fifty years' time—to be compared with a total world population of 1.6 billion in 1900. Added to technological progress and improved living standards, this means that humankind has now a decisive influence on the whole global system; the Nobel Prize laureate Paul Crutzen has suggested that we now live in the Anthropocene Era.

These global dimensions were certainly instrumental when the Rio process and the climate negotiations were launched in the early 1990s, but even for leading negotiators the full scale and scope of the challenge were still obscure. It slowly dawned upon us that we were entering into new territory, a new type of international problem-solving, a new diplomacy for sustainable development, trying to recognize the needs of the Anthropocene. But as history has shown, the coexistence of traditional power politics and tremendously strong economic interests work to reduce the impact of the Framework Convention on Climate Change.

We are now entering crucial years for international action on climate change. The odds against effective action over the next decade may seem overwhelming, if the "realists" have their way. But what is "realistic" in the face of anthropogenic impacts on large global systems, which will strike back on future generations and which already today threaten the livelihoods of the most vulnerable?

That is why this book is so important. The interests of the unborn and the unseen, the people far from the venues of international conferences, can only be defended in applying the concepts of equity and justice. Those essential elements of a decent world are indispensable for the establishment and effective implementation of a global climate change regime. National self-interest is simply not enough.

As recognized in the climate convention, mitigation efforts have to be based on the principle of common but differentiated responsibility. The developed countries have to take the lead, because the increase in carbon dioxide concentration in the atmosphere since 1800 is mainly a result of their industrialization. Furthermore, they have the technology and the resources to act. But the rapidly growing powers in the South cannot be exempt from effective mitigation efforts within the framework of the future climate regime.

The history of the climate negotiations shows that such commitments for developing countries, even for the most powerful and resource-rich of them, can only be within reach if they are perceived as fair and just. This is a political fact. The concept of contraction and convergence may be very difficult to give concrete shape, but the idea needs to be present in the future structures of an international climate regime. Principles of justice must, however, also be reflected at the national level where they raise difficult problems of equality, with potentially far-reaching political connotations.

In looking toward the negotiations for the long-term climate regime, it is easy to feel discouraged by the sheer complexity of the problems and by the slowness of the process. Tackling climate change forces us to go straight into the heartland of our industrial civilization: energy and transport. Powerful interests are challenged at all levels; basic infrastructures in our societies have to be modified. In a world with so many other problems, it will take time for emission reductions to have a real impact, though this ultimately needs to happen.

Therefore, adaptation will be a major component of the climate change regime. So far, more attention has been paid to mitigation than to adaptation. This is changing, as more and more people become convinced that climate change is already occurring, with unforeseeable consequences and risks. But some countries might consider their national costs of adaptation to be so much lower than the costs of mitigation that "no mitigation action" could be seen as a tempting prospect. This would be an extreme position, but it illustrates the dilemma of reconciling national interest with the global interest, and the close relationship between mitigation and adaptation.

In this perspective, there is special strength in the argument that a society is just only if it enables improvement in the position of the least advantaged. Furthermore, one may argue that the risks inherent in global climate change will spare no one and that it is an illusion to believe that there will really be both "winners" and "losers" in the long term. But at this stage, adaptation has to be focused on the most vulnerable. As this book points out, there is a risk that present adaptation strategies may reinforce vulnerability, if not properly conceived and legitimately implemented.

I have no doubt that over the next decade adaptation to climate change will become a major issue both in academic discourse and in the political context. It will raise problems that are humanitarian, economic, and social in nature. In terms of international solidarity, the rich countries will have to channel development assistance to meet the new demands arising out of climatic disasters and increased risks of drought, floods, and desertification. The number of environmental refugees might also increase dramatically.

Vulnerability and inequality in meeting the strains of adaptation are crucial issues that cannot be dealt with adequately without applying principles of fairness and equity. But there will always be a risk that the political discourse will be too shallow, too general.

I have become convinced that the many complicated and politically sensitive issues connected with climate change cannot be solved through traditional interest-based bargaining. There are also other dimensions, such as the global and long-term character, to this new diplomacy. But this requires national governments and public opinion to give their full support to a new approach to solving international problems. To advance the negotiations, the serious academic study of these concepts will be increasingly necessary.

The climate issue, as well as other elements of human-induced global change, raise essential moral and ethical questions. I believe that the changes that will be imposed on us by forces far greater than any super power make it necessary for national policies and the international system to find new bases for their actions, new paradigms of thinking. This is not utopia, it is new realism. And there can be no other way to achieve this than to convince all concerned that reasonable standards of fairness, equity, and justice are fulfilled.

In conclusion, I recall that John F. Kennedy in his inaugural speech in 1961 said that development aid was necessary, not because of the competition with communism, or because it promoted American commercial interests, but because it was right. Solidarity continues to be right, and action to promote fairness and justice in the globalized world continues to be right, and necessary. The work by the team of scholars represented in this book, with the support of the Tyndall Centre for Climate Change Research, is an important step in promoting this development. It gives forceful arguments to all those who realize that business as usual is not an option in the world of today.

Bo Kjellén
Uppsala, Sweden

Preface

In these first years of the twenty-first century, the divide between the North and South appears to be more polarized than ever before as reflected in the conflict over resources, climate change, emerging diseases, and a host of other problems, old and new. In the somewhat surreal world of climate change politics, convention wording and the rhetoric of nation states stand in stark contrast to the news reports of flooding, drought, and continued misery for many of the world's most vulnerable people.

In the middle of this landscape stands the United Nations Framework Convention on Climate Change. Following the Marrakech Accords of 2001, the convention process has begun to build a framework for the governance of adaptation to climate change that encompasses international transfers, support for national planning, and other mechanisms. National governments, businesses, nongovernmental organizations, and households will make their plans for adaptation to climate change within this framework.

The emergence of international discourse on the governance of adaptation presents a number of important questions. How fair are existing global agreements, arrangements, and plans for adaptation? Will adaptation reform or reinforce the status quo of the global distribution of vulnerability, wealth, and power? What does adaptation mean for global security and for avoiding "dangerous" climate change?

This book has a simple but urgent message. Fairness is essential to reaching any meaningful solution to the problem of climate change during this century. The contributions to this volume emphasize that justice must play a central role in addressing climate change impacts.

The contributions trace the causal chain of climate change impacts and discuss solutions that bring our collective resources and efforts to bear on adaptation challenges that we cannot escape.

These analyses demonstrate how justice is critical to establish the legitimacy and resilience of institutions and actions. They also indicate the ways in which justice is relative, contested, and context specific. Even a negotiated international compromise on climate change cannot dramatically shift the power relations between the rich and powerful on one hand and the vulnerable and marginalized on the other.

This book forms part of a program of research on adaptation to climate change within the Tyndall Centre for Climate Change Research at the University of East Anglia. Under the adaptation theme of the center, cross-disciplinary teams seek to analyze how adaptation will take place and what could and should be done about it. One central question asked is: what are the justice implications of adaptation (see <www.tyndall.ac.uk>)? The Tyndall Centre's adaptation research seeks to move toward both normative and positive theories of adaptation and to further debate in these areas. In this book we hope to make a significant contribution toward that end.

We thank the Tyndall Centre for Climate Change Research for funding two years of empirical work on adaptation planning, participation in the Conferences of the Parties of the Climate Change Convention, and an international seminar during the Third Sustainability Days at University of East Anglia in Norwich in September 2003. The seminar included contributions from internationally prominent scholars and practitioners in law, politics, economics, sociology, geography, and climate science. Many of the contributions to the book come from this seminar. We also thank the Leverhulme Trust for additional research support and the UK Economic and Social Research Council for support of the Centre for Social and Economic Research on the Global Environment in this effort.

Many people at our host institutions provided valuable support for the 2003 Justice in Adaptation Review and to our research efforts. We thank in particular Esteve Corbera, Jona Razzaque, Hannah Reid, Dawn Turnbull, John Turnpenny, and Alexandra Winkels for their help. We also thank Mike Hulme, Benito Müller, Marisa Goulden, Patricia

Iturregui, Mark Pelling, Lasse Ringius, Agus Sari, Steve Rayner, Andrew Simms, Tom Tanner, Emma Tompkins, Roda Verheyen, and Diana Wilkins for their contribution to the success of our seminar and for stimulating the findings in this book. Special thanks are due to Jürgen Lefevere, who was instrumental in the initial collaboration between the core partners during his time at FIELD. He can rightly claim some responsibility (or credit) for this initiative.

The contributions to this book have also benefited from a review process that engaged many leading researchers in commenting and developing the arguments. Our sincerest thanks are due to Nigel Arnell, Declan Conway, Suraje Dessai, Geoffrey Dabelko, Andrew Dlugolecki, Tom Downing, Sam Fankhauser, Tim Forsyth, Joyeeta Gupta, Michael Huber, Jonathon Köhler, Monirul Mirza, Eric Neumayer, John O'Neill, Matthew Patterson, Mark Pelling, John Schellnhuber, Dave Thomas, Chasca Twyman, Roda Verheyen, Katharine Vincent, and Coleen Vogel. We thank the editors and reviewers from MIT Press for constructive and timely comments.

We believe this book will shed light on the issue of justice in adapting to climate change that we know has been overlooked for so long to the detriment of so many.

Contributors

Neil Adger is with the Tyndall Centre for Climate Change Research and the Centre for Social and Economic Research on the Global Environment at the University of East Anglia, Norwich, UK.

Paul Baer is a postdoctoral scholar in the Center for Environmental Science and Policy at Stanford University, San Francisco. He is also the cofounder of EcoEquity.

Jon Barnett is an Australian Research Council Fellow in the School of Anthropology, Geography and Environmental Studies at Melbourne University, Australia.

Maria Teresia Bohn is with the Stockholm Environment Institute, Stockholm, Sweden.

Kirstin Dow is with the Stockholm Environment Institute and an associate professor in the Department of Geography at the University of South Carolina.

Saleemul Huq heads the Climate Change Program of the International Institute for Environment and Development in London.

Roger E. Kasperson is Research Professor and Distinguished Scientist, Clark University, Worcester, Massachusetts.

Bo Kjellén is former chair of the Swedish Research Council on Environment, Agricultural Sciences, and Spatial Planning. He held various chairmanships in the Rio process as the chief negotiator for the Swedish Ministry of Environment during 1990–1998.

Mizan R. Khan is head of the Environmental Studies Department at the North South University in Dhaka, Bangladesh.

Janica Lane is a student in the Graduate School of Business at Stanford University, San Francisco.

Neil Leary is the Science Director of Assessments of Impacts and Adaptations to Climate Change (AIACC) with the International START Secretariat, Washington, DC.

Robin M. Leichenko   is Associate Professor of Geography at Rutgers University, New Jersey.

Joanne Linnerooth-Bayer   is leader of the Risk and Vulnerability Program at the International Institute for Applied Systems Analysis in Laxenberg, Austria.

M. J. Mace   is Director of the Climate Change and Energy Programme at the Foundation for International Environmental Law and Development (FIELD) in London.

Karen L. O'Brien   is Associate Professor in the Department of Sociology and Human Geography at the University of Oslo, Norway.

Jouni Paavola   is a senior research associate at the Centre for Social and Economic Research on the Global Environment at the University of East Anglia, Norwich, UK.

Stephen H. Schneider   is a professor in the Department of Biological Sciences at Stanford University and a senior fellow at the Stanford Institute for International Studies, San Francisco.

David Thomas   is a professor of Geography at the University of Oxford.

Chasca Twyman   is in the Department of Geography at the University of Sheffield, UK.

Anna Vári   is in the Hungarian Academy of Sciences Institute of Sociology and the Department of Environmental Management at the Budapest University of Technical and Economic Sciences, Hungary.

1

Toward Justice in Adaptation to Climate Change

W. Neil Adger, Jouni Paavola, and Saleemul Huq

Changing river flows, retreating glaciers, altered ecosystems, and new patterns of extreme weather events indicate that we are already experiencing global climate change: one of the most serious challenges of the twenty-first century. Climate change is a challenge to the nonhuman world, to sustainability, and to governance and decision making. Some commentators argue that climate change poses a more serious threat than that of terrorism (King 2004, 176). Global collective action is needed to prevent potentially catastrophic impacts of our unprecedented experiment with the planetary climate system and to adapt to unavoidable climate change.

Adaptation to climate change is increasingly the focus of policy action and concern in both industrialized and developing countries that feel under threat. Most literature on adaptation to climate change explores adaptation options (see Smithers and Smit 1997; Smit et al. 2000) and the costs and benefits of adaptation (Fankhauser, Smith, and Tol 1999; Tol et al. 1998; Tol et al. 2004). But to date, relatively little attention has been paid to the social justice aspects of adaptation to climate change. This is somewhat surprising considering the intense research on equity issues in mitigation of climate change (see Arler 2001; Azar 2000; Jamieson 2001; Müller 2001; Ringius, Asjdorn, and Underdal 2002; Rose et al. 1998; Toth 1999). But research on equity in the environmental arena largely stems from the realms of political action over "environmental justice" dilemmas (see Light and de-Shalit 2003; Schlosberg 1999) and from discussions of citizenship and sustainability (Dobson 2003), and fails to address the multiscale and multifaceted issues produced by climate change and its impacts. This book brings together, for the first time, perspectives on justice in adaptation to global environmental change that address both processes and outcomes and that provide signposts for action on these issues in the crucial implementation of international and local action on climate change.

We tackle these issues because we believe they are timely and important. The Kyoto Protocol came into effect in 2005, and the prospect of an agreement for international action after 2012, when the Kyoto commitments end, is likely to be bound up with perceptions of both fair process and outcome. Equity is a core principle of the Framework Convention on Climate Change and, naturally, of all international law. Yet most of the debate has addressed fairness in mitigation (that is, in allocating the right to emit greenhouse gases), rather than adaptation. But perceptions of inequity in vulnerability and in the burden of adaptation are driving many developing country parties to the convention. Consideration of the fairness of adaptation strategies is, we argue, central to the future of international action, as well as to legitimate and timely action in regions and countries.

Large parts of the world's population already confront significant risks from climate variability in the face of pressing needs for survival, and in the face of insecurity, globalization, and global financial crises. Many of the people who are vulnerable to climate change today live in the developing world. The world's changing climate and our responses to it threaten to exacerbate precisely those trends and pressures that cause present insecurities and that are likely to lead to increased insecurity in the future. The old, the young, the poor, and those dependent on climate-sensitive resources, including all of the world's farmers and fishers, are at the greatest risk. Food insecurity, the scarcity of fresh water, and exposure to droughts and floods are all part of a landscape where both the vulnerable and the "better insulated" must learn to live in the future.

Vulnerable groups are also likely to be at the sharp end of the policy responses to climate change. They have not been given a choice as to whether they would like to adapt to climate change. They face increased exposure to climate risks yet are ignored when policy decisions regarding mitigation (reducing emissions of greenhouse gases) and adaptation (adjusting to the risk of climate change impacts) are made. We live in a world where future climate injustices are likely to compound past injustices, such as underdevelopment and colonialism, that themselves have resulted in the uneven patterns of development in today's world.

Fairness in response to climate change involves both processes and outcomes. These are known as procedural and distributive justice. Justice is intimately intertwined with the institutions and procedures of collective action at different levels of decision making. Who makes the crucial decisions on climate change? Is climate change in effect the result of a lack of decision making and institutional failure? In this book we examine the international climate change regime and how it handles the issues of impacts and adaptation in order to answer these questions. We argue that there are both ethical and instrumental reasons for ensuring that adaptation to climate change does not exacerbate existing vulnerabilities. The ethical reason is that climate justice requires the consideration of principles such as precaution and the protection of the most vulnerable because of the uncertainties and irreversibilities inherent in the climate system and climate science. The instrumental reason for sensitivity to justice considerations is that the legitimacy of all political solutions to the problem of climate change among diverse sovereign nations rests on fairness.

We also argue that human life and health, security, and the integrity of the earth system are important justice concerns in their own right. Hence a broad-based analysis of justice in vulnerability and adaptation to climate change must acknowledge the social justice significance of recognition, participation, and legitimate distribution and use of power. These justice concerns have to be addressed simultaneously because of the multilevel nature of adaptation to climate change and because of the multiple objectives of the Climate Change Convention.

In terms of distributive justice, the first key observation of this book is that the distribution of climate change impacts is likely to be unjust and that climate change impacts are likely to create new vulnerabilities, the causes and distribution of which are unfair. Unjust distribution of climate change impacts has two sides. First, physical processes distribute climate change impacts unevenly across the world. As a result, some people, particularly those in the South, will be injured, whereas others (mainly in the North) face smaller impacts or may even benefit from climate change. Second, vulnerability to climate change is unevenly distributed. Some people, again particularly those in the South, are more vulnerable than others because of unequal distribution of wealth, capacity, and power, for example. This dynamic raises questions of responsibility for causing climate change and highlights the duty of those responsible and able to assist adaptation by those who are vulnerable and who have little capacity to adapt to climatic changes for which they are not responsible.

The second key observation is that actions taken to adapt to climate change can themselves have important justice implications because their benefits and costs are frequently distributed in ways that consolidate or exacerbate current vulnerabilities rather than reduce them. That is, adaptation strategies and measures create their own winners and losers depending on the choice of solutions for the governance of collective and individual responses to climate risks.

All of the dilemmas of climate justice are generated by temporal, scale, and power relations related to global climate change and its impacts. They are also related to wider social and political issues of security, global economic order, and the integrity of the earth system.

The remainder of this chapter outlines the broad landscapes of adaptation and vulnerability to climate change, and of climate justice, as they are understood and used throughout this book. The chapter elaborates upon the distinction outlined above between fairness of the decision-making process and its outcomes. These issues and the framing of justice the chapter outlines are discussed at length in subsequent parts of the book. We summarize the major issues covered in the chapters that follow and point to our conclusions.

Contested Ideas of Vulnerability and Adaptation

The earth's surface is warming at a rate that has been unprecedented in the past thousand years (IPCC 2001a). The globally averaged warming of nearly 1°C over the past century has taken place along with changes in patterns of extreme weather. The IPCC (2001a) suggests that warming will accelerate in the future and that climate change will be experienced primarily as increased frequency and intensity of extreme weather events such as droughts, floods, heat waves, and storms. Observations from around the world have already firmly established reduced diurnal temperature ranges, higher minimum temperatures, and a greater number of frost free days in many places. There is less certainty on whether extreme weather events such as hurricanes have become more intense or frequent during the past century. There also remains uncertainty regarding the rate at which extreme weather events will change in the future. But, as Schneider and Lane argue in chapter 2, uncertainty is hardly a reason for complacency.

Places, ecosystems, and people are all vulnerable to the threats imposed by climate change. Vulnerability has become a key concept in debates and scholarship on coping with global environmental change, natural hazards, food security, globalization, uneven development, and financial crises (Moser 1998; Bohle, Downing, and Watts 1994; Cutter 1996; Wisner et al. 2004). The concept is used to refer to the fact that households, communities, and societies are differentially at risk from current climate variability and future climate change. Yet the meaning of vulnerability has remained contested (see, e.g., Cutter 2003).

O'Brien and colleagues (2004a) distinguish between "end point" and "starting point" views of vulnerability. The end point view defines vulnerability as "climate change impacts minus adaptation," effectively identifying vulnerability with residual impacts. In contrast, the starting point view defines vulnerability as a set of attributes generated by social and environmental processes, including climate change, which limit the ability to cope with climatic and other stress. The chapters in this book hold the latter view, according to which vulnerability does not exist in isolation from the wider political economy (see especially chapter 4, by Dow and colleagues, and chapter 5, by Leichenko and O'Brien). This view also understands vulnerability as a relative lack of adaptive capacity, thereby underlining that some households and communities are more vulnerable than others in the face of current climate variability and future climate change.

Both local and global forces shape vulnerability to climate change and other stresses. In this book, the chapters by Thomas and Twyman (chapter 10), Paavola (chapter 11), and O'Brien and Leichenko (chapter 5) suggest that the integration of developing economies into world markets can increase the income insecurity of the poor by exposing them to vagaries and price fluctuations of global markets, making them more vulnerable to other shocks and stresses. Coping with market instability requires resilience and adaptive capacity, as does coping with the vagaries of a variable and unpredictable physical environment.

Climate change impacts will burden especially those populations that are already vulnerable and struggle with current climate variability and extreme weather events. Differential impacts of present-day extreme weather events illustrate this point. Older black males who were living alone and had poor health status made up a disproportionate share of the excess deaths caused by the 1996 heat wave in Chicago (Klinenberg 2002). The 2003 heat wave in Europe caused 20,000–35,000 premature deaths, most of them among the elderly (Schär and Jendritzky 2004). In developing countries, economic effects of weather-related disasters can reach up to a quarter of GDP (Gurenko 2003) and result in thousands of premature deaths. Hurricane Mitch in Honduras in 1998, the hurricanes of 2004 in Haiti and the Caribbean, and extensive flooding in Mozambique in 2000 and Bangladesh in 2004 are only some of the more-publicized events of this kind. In developing countries, economic losses fall on vulnerable households that are uninsured and dependent on risky agriculture and other natural resource based livelihoods. Ultimately, climate change is a threat to the world we have become accustomed to. That is, we have already irreversibly bequeathed a more dangerous world to our grandchildren. Adaptation to climate change will be required from all of us, whether we want it or not.

Many adaptive responses will involve changes in public policies or institutional arrangements. Examples include policies that foster adaptation of food production to changing climate, making insurance available to those at risk, and redistributing burdens of adaptation or residual climate impacts. A second important subset of adaptive responses will include public and private investments in infrastructure and technologies such as water storage capacity, flood protection, and improved buildings. A third subset of adaptive responses includes behavioral changes, such as changes in agricultural practices or migration so as to better cope with climate change impacts. To understand the justice implications of adaptation, it is important to identify how decisions on adaptive responses are made, how adaptive responses are timed with respect to climate change impacts, and what the consequences are of adaptation decisions in terms of welfare changes and disease burden.

From a decision-making viewpoint, there are, in effect, two main adaptation strategies. First, individuals, firms, and other organizations can undertake adaptation actions and measures on their own without mutual coordination. However, they can only do so by employing the alternatives that are available to them and within the constraints of the resources they have at their own disposal. Second, agents can take collective action to alter the set of adaptation alternatives and to redistribute the burden of adaptive responses or residual climate change impacts. Adaptation can be based on collective choice and action at the local, national, and international levels, as well as at many intermediate and multiple levels (see table 1.1). It is important to note that inaction at higher levels of collective action effectively transfers responsibility for adaptive responses to lower levels of collective action or to individual actors such as firms or households, with attendant consequences for the range of available alternatives and burden sharing. This underlines that individual or private adaptation is not autonomous—it always takes place within the constraints and opportunities engendered by antecedent collective action and collective inaction. All adaptation decisions have justice implications because they alter the set of alternatives or "room for maneuver" (see Thomas and Twyman, chapter 12) available for collective and individual actors.

From the viewpoint of timing, there are three distinct ways to undertake adaptive responses (see table 1.1). Proactive responses involve anticipation and planning so as to best deal with climate change impacts before they are realized. Reactive responses, such as burden sharing and rebuilding infrastructure after flood damage, are taken after climate change impacts are realized but they are not necessarily ad hoc. Sometimes uncertainty and cost considerations prevent effective proactive responses, and at other times postponing adaptive responses may be the most feasible alternative. Finally, inaction may be chosen as a response to climate change impacts, implicitly or explicitly. Proactive and reactive

Table 1.1
A typology of adaptive responses: examples from food production and security

Response	Proactive	Reactive	Inaction
International	Guidelines for national adaptation strategies, development of new crops	Food aid measures	No responses are taken to instigate context-specific behavioral responses
National	Grain storage; agricultural policies to change crops and practices	Changes in tariffs and spending to augment food imports and disaster relief	No small infrastructure investments that would confer local benefits
Local	Investment in rainwater harvesting, irrigation and flood protection; local seed banks; local coordination	Mutual help	Migration ignored as an adaptive response
Individual	Livelihood diversification, investment in human and physical capital; alteration of agricultural practices	Migration	Adjustment to increased vulnerability and reduced welfare

responses frequently complement one another—for example, building additional water storage capacity complements and facilitates water rationing. Yet proactive and reactive measures are not likely to result in perfect adaptation; some residual impacts are inevitable.

Contested Ideas of Justice

Adaptation to climate change will be governed by a multilevel solution based on the United Nations Framework Convention for Climate Change (UNFCCC). The convention goal is the stabilization of greenhouse gas emissions at a level and within a timeframe that makes it possible for natural ecosystems, food production systems, and economic systems to adapt. The convention also establishes the duty of developed countries to assist vulnerable developing countries in adapting to climate change and in meeting the costs of adaptation. But these and many other already existing provisions have not been implemented. In 2001, when the Marrakech Accords created mechanisms for funding adaptation and established guidelines for national adaptation planning in the least developed countries (see chapter 3, by Mace, and chapter 9, by Huq and Khan). Still, this governance framework has important gaps. The convention avoids taking up the issue of responsibility for climate change impacts (see Baer, chapter 7) and it has failed to establish a burden sharing scheme that would ensure an adequate and predictable flow of funding for adaptation from developed countries to vulnerable developing countries (see Mace, chapter 3).

It is thus not surprising that climate justice is contested and means different things for different actors, from parties to the convention to national policy constituents and other stakeholders. Much of the debate on climate justice has focused on responsibility for greenhouse gas emissions and has revolved around the issues of contribution, knowledge of the climate change impacts of greenhouse gas emissions, and the nature of atmospheric sinks as a global commons. These issues are also relevant for and relate to debates about greenhouse gas reduction targets, historical responsibility (whether to count nineteenth- and twentieth-century emissions as part of a country's responsibility to the future, or "climate debt"), underdevelopment, and carbon-based economic growth (Jamieson 2001; Paterson 2001; Grubb 1995).

The prominence of debates on rights to emit greenhouse gases has drawn attention away from questions on justice in climate change impacts and adaptation. As the subsequent chapters indicate, views on these issues revolve around the absence of consent to exposure to climate change impacts, as well as differential vulnerability, and compensation. Sovereignty, self-determination, representation, and participation are also frequently evoked in the debates because climate change impacts are experienced and adaptation takes place at the local level, whereas most decisions about them are made at national and international levels.

The contested nature of climate justice can be seen particularly in the international discussions, debates, and negotiations on articles 2 and 4.8. of the UNFCCC. Article 2 identifies the prevention of "dangerous" anthropogenic interference with the climate system as the "ultimate objective" of the convention. Article 4.8 focuses on the concerns of developing country parties arising from the "adverse affects of climate change and/or the impact of the implementation of response measures." Article 2 of the convention provides that

The ultimate objective of this Convention . . . is to achieve . . . stabilization of greenhouse gas concentrations in the atmosphere at a level that would prevent dangerous anthropogenic interference with the climate system.

Article 2 further qualifies that

Such a level should be achieved within a time frame sufficient to allow ecosystems to adapt naturally to climate change, to ensure that food production is not threatened, and to enable economic development to proceed in a sustainable manner.

Article 2 has led to contested discussions on how countries that have not yet benefited from a century and half of carbon emissions can have an equitable chance for development. Although article 2 refers directly only to adaptation of ecosystems, adaptation may also be needed to sustain food production systems and economic systems. Accordingly, scientific assessments have sought to estimate the impacts of climate change on food production (Parry et al. 2001) and to assess what extent climate change impacts could jeopardize the attainment of international development targets such as the Millennium Development Goals. These issues have also been discussed in the context of adaptation funds created by the Marrakech Accords in 2001. Here the debate has been about the extent to which additional funds for adaptation need to be "mainstreamed" into regular development plans and efforts. Some level of agreement on the level and allocation of funding is urgently needed as the least developed countries (LDCs) are already preparing National Adaptation Programs of Action (NAPAs) to integrate adaptation to climate change into their national development plans (see Mace, chapter 3, and Huq and Khan, chapter 9).

Article 4.8 of the convention provides that

the Parties shall give full consideration to what actions are necessary . . . to meet the specific needs and concerns of developing country Parties arising from the adverse effects of climate change and/or the impact of the implementation of response measures, especially on:

(a) Small island countries;

(b) Countries with low-lying coastal areas;

(c) Countries with arid and semi-arid areas, forested areas and areas liable to forest decay;

(d) Countries with areas prone to natural disasters;

(e) Countries with areas liable to drought and desertification;

(f) Countries with areas of high urban atmospheric pollution;

(g) Countries with areas with fragile ecosystems, including mountainous ecosystems;

(h) Countries whose economies are highly dependent on income generated from the production, processing and export, and/or on consumption of fossil fuels and associated energy-intensive products; and

(i) Land-locked and transit countries.

As used in article 4.8, "adverse effects of climate change" refers to the impacts of climate change (see Mace, chapter 3). Oil-producing countries have pushed for an interpretation of this article that would give equal emphasis to the impacts of climate change mitigation policies such as global carbon taxes on fossil fuel–dependent countries (Barnett and Dessai 2002). In recent negotiations, oil-producing countries have also argued that "adaptation" should be construed to include adaptation to the impacts of mitigation measures by fossil-fuel dependent economies. In contrast, the Alliance of Small Island States (AOSIS) and the least developed countries (LDCs) do not consider the impacts of climate change and the impacts of response measures to be on an equal footing. Barnett and Dessai argue that "OPEC's demands for assistance to compensate for lost oil revenues and their strategy of equal progress on all issues under negotiation impedes progress on adaptation in developing and Least Developed Countries" (2002, 238). Thus the fact that even the interests of developing countries conflict in some areas can form an obstacle for the advancement of their shared interests (see Gupta 2002).

This book does not seek to provide a blueprint for achieving justice in the debates on climate justice. Rather, it maps different conceptions of justice and their implications for action on climate change. We explore how international policy debates, national adaptation planning, and other contexts use, misuse, and confuse notions of justice. Moreover, climate justice is not just a matter of contested views and perceptions. All adaptation decisions have justice implications because they influence the alternatives that are available and chosen in the society and because they realize a particular incidence of beneficial and adverse consequences and confirm a particular set of decision-making procedures. In this book we seek to contribute to the identification and analysis of these justice dilemmas.

The importance of justice analysis can perhaps be best illustrated by examining a widely shared view in adaptation research. Uncoordinated adaptation of households, communities, and firms to current climate variability is frequently celebrated as an example of how future adaptation to climate change could take place without the involvement of the state or the international community. But private adaptation measures are undertaken by those who have the knowledge and resources to do so and who typically are not particularly vulnerable to climate change impacts. The aggregate outcome of private adaptation is that a society's resources are allocated to adaptation by the less vulnerable, for purposes they find beneficial for themselves. This is likely to accentuate inequality and vulnerability in the society. A good example is provided by resource-dependent societies dealing with drought. Vulnerable households typically seek to cope by selling off productive assets such as livestock. Other households actually benefit from the situation because they can take advantage of vulnerable households selling livestock at low prices (Roncoli, Ingram, and Kirshen 2001; Little et al. 2001).

Many collective adaptation decisions made at the local and national levels end up protecting vested interests and the interests of the less vulnerable. For example, reconstruction following weather-related hazards often reinforces the status quo in terms of wealth and access to decision making, possibly accentuating the vulnerability of the most at-risk people (see Wisner 2001; Glantz and Jamieson 2000). Collective adaptation measures often have unjust outcomes because access to decision making is not equal—marginalized groups remain vulnerable because they cannot participate in and influence decisions and structures that create their vulnerability.

We also shed light on how different takes on social justice can have quite different implications for adaptation measures and their outcomes. Hence it matters which approach to social justice informs the choice of adaptation measures. To give an example, a utilitarian approach would suggest that adaptation policy is fair if it promotes the greatest good for the greatest numbers. Another approach might instead suggest that the hallmark of fairness is assisting the most vulnerable because they are in the greatest need (see Dow and colleagues, chapter 4). Here a comparison of affluent owners of holiday homes and poor farmers in the same country provides a good example. In coastal areas, owners of holiday homes are exposed to storm and sea level rise risks and are, in one sense of the word, vulnerable to the impacts of climate change. The utilitarian approach could suggest that priority should be given to public investments that protect the holiday homes over measures protecting vulnerable farmers from rising temperatures and more erratic rainfall patterns. The other approach would result in the reverse ranking of adaptation measures because there is a difference between the most exposed and the most vulnerable to climate change impacts. Both of these approaches omit a prior question: whether the most vulnerable groups could be argued to have a right not to be exposed to dangerous climate change impacts. This right would entail a duty of others to see that dangerous climate change impacts are not created.

To summarize, certain actions can be deemed fair (or unfair) from different standpoints. Climate justice is multifaceted and merits serious attention because it is the foundation for relationships within global community. In this book we hope to shed new light on the justice dilemmas involved in adaptation to climate change and to offer insights into their implications.

Toward an Integration of Justice with Adaptation to Climate Change

As we have indicated, from the viewpoint of social justice, adaptation to climate change involves both issues of fair processes and fair outcomes. We use the term procedural justice to refer to the degree of recognition and participation (see Anand 2001). Distributive justice, on the other hand, refers to the distribution of the beneficial and adverse effects of climate change and adaptation. This distribution is between people and occurs across time (see Elster 1992). Although we distinguish between procedural and distributive justice, the two are frequently interdependent in practice. Without fair decision-making procedures, fair outcomes will only ever be coincidental. In effect, those who are disadvantaged in terms of distribution also tend to lack voice in decision making that affects them.

Some theories insist that only a fair process is needed for social justice. For example, libertarian theories of Nozick (1974) and Hayek (1976) suggest that social justice is attained as long as possessions and wealth are acquired and transferred legitimately. This narrow understanding of procedural justice as fair participation in markets is clearly not satisfactory for environmental decision making. First, it is unable to address long-standing inequalities that characterize many environmental issues due to their spatial distribution. Second, environmental decision making takes place mostly outside of markets and, as a result, a market-centered view of justice cannot shed adequate light on social justice in adaptation. Yet fair processes are certainly important for the legitimacy of environmental decisions, and thus procedural justice has to be taken into account in climate change.

As we understand and use the term, procedural justice relates to fairness in access to democratic decision making by individuals, groups, or nations (Young, 1990). Or, to borrow Iris Marion Young's words, procedural justice concerns "democratic decision-making procedures as an element and condition of social justice" (1990, 23). Procedural justice is important in adaptation to climate change because it underpins the legitimacy of the convention—it enjoys legitimacy among the parties to the extent that diverse voices are heard and accounted for in the deliberations. The legitimacy of national and local governments in planning and implementing adaptation strategies similarly rests on procedural justice (see chapter 10 for a discussion on conditions of procedural justice in national adaptation planning in Bangladesh).

Distributive justice can also be based on different foundations. Some approaches argue for the use of one overarching, universal value metric, such as utility or welfare when resolving justice dilemmas. Social justice can also be framed in terms of universal principles such as equality. Communitarian approaches would argue against universal metrics and principles and suggest that justice is specific to particular communities. Still other approaches, such as that of complex equality (Walzer 1983), would argue for the existence of multiple realms or spheres of justice and that justice has to be achieved in each of them simultaneously.

We argue that an approach that does not reduce issues of distributive justice to fair distribution of one overarching good such as utility is particularly relevant in adaptation to climate change. Article 2 of the UNFCCC itself suggests that international action should aim to avoid dangerous human interference with the climate system and makes a clear distinction between concerns for ecosystems, human food security (and, as a result, human life), and economic welfare in this context. This suggests that these issues are distinct and irreducible aspects of climate justice. A set of principles that address different aspects of climate justice are also attractive for many practical reasons, which we will elaborate on in greater detail in the concluding chapter of this book.

To sum up the foregoing discussion, we believe that all adaptation decisions, including failures to act, have justice implications, both distributive and procedural. The existing framework for governance of adaptation to climate change addresses a number of them and ignores others, some of which we present in table 1.2. We argue that justice dilemmas involved in adaptation to climate change can be condensed to four main issues (see also Paavola and Adger 2006):

1. What is the responsibility of developed countries for climate change impacts caused by their greenhouse gas emissions?

Table 1.2
Observations of justice outcomes in local and international scales of adaptation decisions

	Private adaptation	International action
Distributive justice	Risks and hazards are not evenly distributed.	Duty to assist developing countries in implementing the UNFCCC
	Adaptation reduces the vulnerability of the wealthy and vested interests at the expense of the marginalized.	Duty to assist the most vulnerable countries in adapting to climate change
	Reactive responses such as rebuilding of infrastructure often reinforce inequality.	The establishment of mechanisms for assisting adaptation
Procedural justice	Adaptation is based on decision making that weighs interests according to ability and willingness to pay for adaptation measures.	Participation in the UNFCCC process is unequal because of background inequalities
	Marginalized groups are made more vulnerable because their participation in decision making is limited.	Establishment of the Least Developed Countries Expert Group
		NAPA process requiring public consultation (but not participation)

2. How much assistance should developed countries make available for developing countries and how should developed countries share the burden of assistance?

3. How should assistance be distributed between countries and adaptive measures?

4. How should planning and decisions regarding adaptation be made at different levels?

An Outline of the Book

This introductory chapter has located the book in the broader terrain of climate change and justice scholarship and has outlined its broad-based approach to social justice in adaptation to climate change. The subsequent chapters paint a rich, interdisciplinary picture of justice in vulnerability and adaptation to climate change, and set out arguments that will inform the future research agenda in this area. In the first part of the book, two chapters outline the cornerstones of climate justice in science and law. In chapter 2, Stephen Schneider and Janica Lane examine the contribution of climate science to understanding the role of justice in adaptation to climate change. They argue that the "five numeraires"—the cost of a ton of carbon in terms of (1) money, (2) human lives, (3) extinct species, (4) redistribution, and (5) quality of life—offer a more robust approach for addressing questions of climate justice than many other currently used approaches, such as cost-benefit analysis. They also advocate the use of enhanced probability-based approaches to assist political decision making on key value judgments regarding climate change. Chapter 3, by M. J. Mace, outlines the international legal framework for adaptation to climate change, highlighting both positive developments in the international legal framework for adaptation and serious challenges that remain, including the availability and accessibility of funding to assist developing countries in adapting to climate change.

The second part of the book includes five complementary contributions that address broader aspects of justice in adaptation to climate change. In chapter 4, Kristin Dow, Roger Kasperson, and Maria Bohn argue that uncertainties should not be used as excuses not to act and that justice in adaptation requires putting the most vulnerable first when planning and deciding on adaptation measures. They also highlight the social nature and multiple sources of vulnerability. Chapter 5, by Robin Leichenko and Karen O'Brien, critically examines whether it is useful to seek to identify winners and losers from climate change. They indicate how a "winners and losers" framework helps to bring up justice issues involved in adaptation to climate change but also point out how it hides their complexity and can misguide public responses. In chapter 6, Jon Barnett examines the implications of conflict and post-conflict situations for social justice, vulnerability, and adaptation to climate change. He argues that climate change, like environmental change in general, is unlikely to be a direct source of conflicts, but that conflicts themselves create insecurity that makes certain populations particularly vulnerable to climate change and environmental change in general. Chapter 7, by Paul Baer, argues that countries presently emitting significant amounts of greenhouse gases should take responsibility for climate change impacts and provides an estimate of the distribution of such climate change liability. Baer demonstrates that responsibility is not just a North-South issue: the lowest income groups in the North have very low levels of responsibility, and the highest income groups in the South are clearly responsible, too. In chapter 8, Neil Leary outlines how contemporary welfare economics can contribute to the analysis of social justice aspects of climate change and adaptation to climate change. He indicates how adaptation to predicted climate changes is likely to increase inequality in the United States, because its redistributive effects are of the same magnitude as its cost implications.

The third part of the book presents four case studies that situate many of the general arguments presented earlier in the book to specific empirical contexts. Chapter 9, by Saleemul Huq and Mizan Khan, examines the way in which Bangladesh is generating a National Adaptation Program of Action (NAPA), outlining its challenges against the background of present vulnerability and predicted climate change impacts in the country. They argue that the participation of most impacted and vulnerable groups is vital for national adaptation planning in all developing countries. In chapter 10, Jouni Paavola examines the implications of vulnerability for national adaptation planning and action in Tanzania. He argues that the inclusion of rural people, women, children, and pastoralists has to be given attention in national adaptation planning and decision making, and that adaptation measures should include effective environmental governance, improvement of market access, and maintenance and augmentation of human capital. Chapter 11, by David Thomas and Chasca Twyman, highlights that households and local communities in Botswana and Namibia often have significant adaptive capacity and that public measures often hinder, rather than facilitate, its exercise. They advocate international and national measures that enhance flexibility and options for households and communities. In Chapter 12, Joanne Linnerooth-Bayer and Anna Vári explore solutions for sharing the burden of flood impacts in Hungary, indicating how stakeholders are demanding a collective solution while acknowledging the functional role of increased individual responsibility. They also suggest that the Turkish Catastrophic Insurance Pool, a privately managed public insurance system with national cross-subsidies, that transfers part of its risks to the World Bank, may provide a burden-sharing model that is applicable to sharing the burden of climate related damages in developing countries.

In the concluding chapter, we outline and elaborate upon the main contributions of the book. We argue that an acceptance of responsibility for climate change impacts, the duty to assist vulnerable developing countries to adapt, the principle of putting the most vulnerable first, and the principle of universal participation are the four cornerstones of justice in adaptation to climate change. Implementation of these four elements, we argue, would take us a step closer to climate justice.

In many senses, climate change is a specter in discussions of politics and the governance of international affairs: it is an issue that threatens progress in making the world more secure and habitable for all people. Climate change threatens the achievement of the Millennium Development Goals through its impacts on health, water, and agriculture in the coming decades and further threatens the continuation of recognizable security and trust between nations. We believe that the key to addressing the climate change problem lies in recognizing the equity and justice issues inherent in its causes and in appropriate human responses. Finding fair solutions, in the words of Low and Gleeson (1998), gives politics and law their purpose. Politics and law can ultimately have no higher purpose than seeking fair outcomes for the survival of the natural world.

I

Politics, Science, and Law in Justice Debates

2

Dangers and Thresholds in Climate Change and the Implications for Justice

Stephen H. Schneider and Janica Lane

What is the probability of dangerous climate change? What are the justice implications of acting or not acting to prevent or facilitate adaptation to it? To address these questions, we examine climate change scenarios including low-probability, high-impact events and consider the damages they may cause. We also consider the distributional implications of these impacts and surprises and their relations to justice.

We then ask, what is "dangerous" climate change, and how are scientists and policymakers assessing it? Though what constitutes dangerous is ultimately a value-laden decision of policymakers, we make suggestions on how to avoid surprises and other potentially dangerous climate changes, or at least limit their effects, through policies designed to bring about abatement and adaptation. We consider whether there is a fair way to implement such policies and conclude by proposing future courses of action. Our discussion maps the landscape of climate change science, decision making, and governance that subsequent chapters examine in detail. The justice implications of climate change adaptations must, we argue, embrace the nature of scientific uncertainty and policy uncertainty in formulating what is fair.

Climate Change Scenarios

Scientists and policy analysts have invested considerable effort in projecting demographic, economic, political, and technological futures on which a range of emissions scenarios can be based. The best-known of these is the Intergovernmental Panel on Climate Change's (IPCC) Special

Report on Emissions Scenarios (SRES; IPCC 2000). On the one extreme, the SRES introduced the A1 storyline and scenario family, which describes a future world of rapid economic growth, global population that peaks in mid century and declines thereafter, and rapid introduction of new, more efficient technologies. This family of scenarios also presumes capacity building and increased cultural and social interactions that bring about a substantial reduction in regional differences in per capita income. The A1 family of scenarios is subdivided into A1FI (fossil intensive), A1T (high technology), and A1B (balanced), with AIF1 generating the most carbon dioxide (CO_2) emissions in the family and A1T the least. But even in the A1T world, CO_2 still doubles over pre-industrial levels by 2100, as is true for all of the SRES scenarios.

This family of scenarios raises serious justice issues. It is likely that the least privileged groups across the world will be harmed more by the climate change these scenarios imply, while at the same time reaping fewer rewards from the projected rapid growth. As is often the case, environmental injustice is but an aspect of deeper socioeconomic injustice.

SRES offers the B1 family of scenarios as an alternative vision of social and technological futures. These scenarios portray a converging world with the same global population as A1, peaking in mid century and declining thereafter, but with faster change in economic structures toward service and information economies. The B1 scenarios also project efficient ways of increasing economic output with less material, cleaner resources, and more efficient technologies. This is assumed to decrease energy intensity and to bring about the (marginally) lowest emissions of all the IPCC's scenarios. Scenario family B1 assumes that there will be global solutions to economic, social, and environmental sustainability issues and that these solutions will be shared worldwide, providing improved equity everywhere.

Although the B1 scenario appears more just, it is likely that economic and climatic winners and losers would still emerge. Again, the most marginalized countries and groups within nations would benefit the least. In addition, many scientists and policymakers alike have doubted whether a transition to a B1 world is realistic and whether it can be considered as likely as the A1 family.

Climate Change Impacts

Climate change did not take on major international policy significance until 1995, when the IPCC announced in its Second Assessment Report (SAR) that human activities were having a "discernible" impact on climate. That 1997 and 1998 were the warmest years on record up to that time and storm damage increased between the 1960s and 1990s seemed to lend credibility to the finding.[1] In its Third Assessment Report (TAR) in 2001, the IPCC estimated that the planet would warm by between 1.4° and 5.8°C by 2100 (IPCC 2001a), up from 1.0° to 3.5°C that had been estimated in the SAR. Although warming of, say 1.5°C, would likely be less stressful, it would still be significant for some "unique and valuable systems" (IPCC 2001b). Mastrandrea and Schneider (2004) note that the high end of projection in the Third Assessment Report—based on the IPCC's "Reasons for Concern" figure (fig. 2.1)—is likely to exceed dangerous climate thresholds. Warming of nearly 6°C could have catastrophic consequences, as ice ages and inter-glacial periods have involved a change of 5° to 7°C in the global average temperature (Azar and Rodhe 1997). The IPCC projections would also entail a global average rate of temperature change that for the next century or two would exceed the rates sustained over the last 10,000 years (Schneider and Root 2001, 6).

The IPCC has produced a list of likely effects of climate change that includes more frequent heat waves and less frequent cold spells; more intense storms, including hurricanes, tropical cyclones, and a surge in weather-related damage; increased intensity of floods and droughts; warmer surface temperatures, especially at higher latitudes; more rapid spread of disease; loss of farming productivity and movement of farming to other regions, most at higher latitudes; rising sea levels, which could inundate coastal areas and small island nations; and species extinction and loss of biodiversity (see IPCC 2001b).

Surprises

The IPCC also suggested that climate change could trigger rapid, non-linear responses of the climate system to anthropogenic forcing when

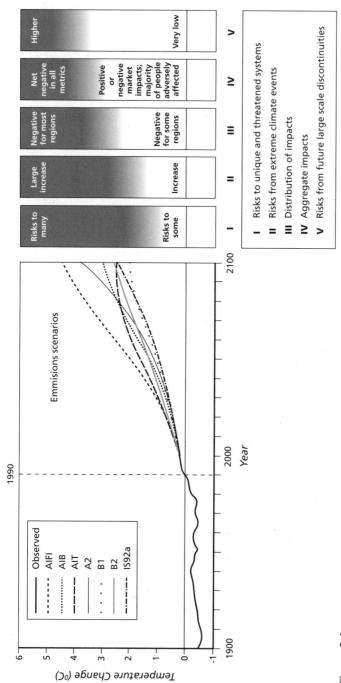

Figure 2.1
Reasons for concern about climate change impacts. The risks of adverse impacts from climate change increase with the magnitude of the climate change itself. The left part of the figure displays the observed temperature increase from 1900 to 1990 and the range of possible increase after 1990. The right panel displays conceptualizations of "five reasons for concern" regarding climate change risks evolving through 2100. White indicates neutral or minimal negative or positive impacts/risks, light gray shading indicates negative impacts for some systems, and dark gray shading represents widespread adverse impacts. The transitions from medium to dark gray shading on the figure have major implications for defining percentile thresholds of "dangerous anthropogenic interference with the climate system," as demonstrated quantitatively in Mastrandrea and Schneider 2004. *Source:* IPCC 2001b.

environmental thresholds are crossed. Schneider, Turner, and Garriga (1998) have identified "imaginable surprises," such as the collapse of the North Atlantic thermohaline circulation (THC) system, which could cause significant cooling in the North Atlantic region, and deglaciation of Greenland or the West Antarctic (which would cause many meters of additional sea level rise) (Schneider 2004). There is also the possibility of *true* surprises (Schneider, Turner, and Garriga 1998). Global environmental change is replete with both types of surprises because of the enormous complexities of the processes and interrelationships involved and our insufficient understanding of them individually and collectively.

Figure 2.1, also known as the "burning embers diagram," graphically represents the range of climate change impacts. The figure shows that the potentially most dangerous climate change impacts (the darker sections on the right of the figure) typically occur after only a few degrees Celsius of warming. What it does not fully depict, except in the third "reason for concern," is how those impacts will be distributed across specific countries and societies. Mastrandrea and Schneider (2004) note that some who focus on equity and justice will consider the third reason for concern, distribution of impacts, to be most important and want to weigh it most heavily, whereas those focusing on market-tradable commodities will put the largest weight on the fourth reason, aggregate impacts. Conservationists worried about species extinctions and ecosystems disruptions might weight the first "burning ember," risks to unique and threatened systems, most heavily. These value judgments are inherent to analysis that seeks to provide weights that reflect different conceptions of justice.

In this chapter we focus on a different set of metrics for impact assessment—the "five numeraires." Of course, they have not been as well analyzed as the IPCC "reasons for concern," which were formulated by dozens of authors and hundreds of reviewers, but we think they have an advantage in being more explicit about market, nonmarket, and justice issues.

Dimensions of Equity in Climate Change Impacts

Developed versus Developing Worlds

Although developed nations have been responsible for most of the greenhouse gases emitted into the atmosphere thus far, the poorer, warmer nations of the world will experience more and more severe climate change impacts than their rich, higher latitude counterparts. Some industrialized nations may even benefit from climate change as a result of having more arable land and longer growing seasons. In contrast, the developing nations will most likely experience predominantly detrimental effects. Situations in which the countries inflicting the damage (through greenhouse gas emissions) are not harmed to the same extent as those countries who contribute minimally to the problem are clearly rife with injustice and have the potential to increase the tension between the political "North" and "South."

Socioeconomic conditions driving emissions also influence adaptive and mitigative capacities (Yohe 2000), and thus there is an imbalance between rich and poor nations' ability to cope with climate change impacts. The countries that have contributed the most to global emissions are likely to cope better with the effects of climate change. Conversely, less developed countries tend to have lower adaptive capacities, as they are often limited by financial, technological, and governmental constraints (IPCC 2001b, 84). Barnett argues in chapter 6 that many countries have been impoverished by coups, wars, and other destabilizing events and have few resources to devote to preventive or adaptive measures concerning climate change. The uneven distribution of climate change impacts leaves the hotter, poorer nations—the countries that have less adaptive capacity—more vulnerable and more in need of adaptation. These countries are not well equipped to deal with natural disasters such as storms, flooding, and droughts that exact high tolls in lives, fractions of GDP, and quality of life in developing countries. It will be difficult enough for them to cope with moderate and gradual climate change; "surprises" could devastate them in both absolute and relative terms. However, embedded in this generalization that the poor are typically more vulnerable, there are exceptions: for example, the European 2003 heat wave and the vulnerability of the U.S. Gulf Coast to increased hurricane intensity.

Intergenerational Equity

If mitigation is postponed and income gaps between populations increase, climate change is likely to increase inequity within the present generation and between present and future generations (IPCC 2001b, 85). Moreover, short-term policies and behaviors could trigger abrupt or irreversible events. We explore the extent to which short-term activities that carry the potential to damage future generations of humans or other species is a question concerning intergenerational equity in greater detail later in the chapter.

Inter-Species Equity

Thus far, the discussion of climate change effects has focused on humans. However, other species are also affected by global warming. In some ways, this is more concerning, as natural systems have limited adaptive capacity and are expected to be less resilient than human systems— particularly in the case of rapid changes for which all but microspecies have no evolutionary mechanisms to adapt quickly. In addition, natural systems will likely be the most undeserving victims of future climate change, as they have no influence on policymaking, except to the extent that humans value their services and survival.

Scientists have already detected that the approximate 0.7°C of warming that has occurred on Earth since the mid 1800s is having a discernible impact on ecosystems. Root and Schneider (2001) reported that the ranges of the species they studied were moving poleward, up mountain slopes, or both. They also found that many of the investigated species had consistently shifted toward earlier spring activities. These findings have been supported by more recent results (Root et al. 2003). Parmesan and Yohe (2003), after analyzing over seventeen hundred species, also detected habitat shifts toward the poles (or higher altitudes) averaging about 6.1 km per decade, as well as the advancement of typical spring activities by 2.3 days per decade. Furthermore, scientists have identified "geoboundaries" such as coastlines and mountaintops that are more prone than other areas to irreversible losses. If these areas become unsuitable for their present occupants, many of the plant and animal species that dwell there will be unable to find suitable alternative habitats, making extinction much more probable (e.g., Thomas et al. 2004).

The severity of climate change impacts will vary among species and may result in the dismantling of existing plant and animal communities as individual species' responses to climate unfold. This could create disruptions in what Daily (1997) calls ecosystem goods (seafood, fodder, fuel wood, timber, pharmaceutical products) and services (air and water purification, waste detoxification and decomposition, climate moderation, and soil fertility regeneration). The more rapidly climate changes, the more likely there will be "no-analogue" communities (see Overpeck, Webb, and Webb 1992; Schneider and Root 1998).

Five Numeraires

We have discussed some of the indicators Schneider, Kuntz-Duriseti, and Azar (2000) labeled "the five numeraires": market system costs in dollars per ton carbon (C); human lives lost in persons per ton C; species lost per ton C; distributional effects in changes in income differentials between rich and poor per ton C; and quality of life changes, such as heritage sites lost per ton C or refugees created per ton C (see table 2.1). It is the belief of those authors that one must consider all of these factors to arrive at a fair and accurate assessment of climate change damages. However, it is difficult to assign a monetary value to nonmarket categories of damages. Can we, for example, place a dollar value on a human life and the quality of that life? How do we value ecosystem goods and services (see Daily 1997, and discussion above)?

Economists usually focus on impacts that can be easily quantified monetarily and ignore others. Nordhaus (1994), who surveyed conventional economists, environmental economists, atmospheric scientists, and ecologists about estimated climate damages, gathered evidence of this. His study indicates a striking cultural divide across surveyed natural and social scientists. Conventional economists believed that even extreme climate change (i.e., 6°C of warming by 2090) would not likely impose severe economic losses and hence considered it cheaper to emit more in the near term and worry about cutting back later, using additional wealth from emitting to fund adaptation. Natural scientists

Table 2.1
Five numeraires for judging the significance of climate change impacts

Vulnerability to climate change	Numeraire
Market impact	$ per ton C
Human lives lost	Persons per ton C
Biodiversity loss	Species per ton C
Distributional impacts	Income redistribution per ton C
Quality of life	Loss of heritage sites; forced migration; disturbed cultural amenities; etc., per ton C

Note: Multiple metrics for the valuation of climatic impacts are suggested. Typically in economic cost-benefit calculations, only the first numeraire—market sector elements—is included. Different individuals, cultures, and governments might have very different weights on these five—or other—numeraires, and thus it is suggested that analysis of climatic impacts be first disaggregated into such dimensions and that any re-aggregation provide a traceable account of the aggregation process so that decision makers can apply their own valuations to various methods of analysis.
Source: Schneider, Kuntz-Duriseti, and Azar 2000.

estimated the total economic impact of extreme climate change to be twenty to thirty times higher than conventional economists' projections and were much less optimistic that humans could invent acceptable substitutes for lost climatic services. Neither the economists nor the ecologists surveyed touched upon the other three numeraires, which could be said to be more directly related to equity and justice concerns.

Traditional cost-benefit analysis (CBA), such as that used by most of the economists in the Nordhaus survey, tends to consider a sole numeraire, market values, and is often viewed as unjust (e.g., Jenkins 1998; and Huq and Khan in chapter 9) because nature and distributional aspects are rarely explicitly treated. In a traditional CBA, the ethical principle is not even classical Benthamite utilitarianism (greatest good for the greatest number of people), but an aggregated market power form of utilitarianism (greatest good for the greatest number of dollars in benefit-cost ratios). Thus, an industrialized country with a large economy that suffered the same climate damages as an unindustrialized nation with a less robust economy would be considered to have suffered more and would be more important to "rescue" or rehabilitate. Even more problematic, what if an industrial Northern country experienced a monetary gain from global warming due to longer growing seasons, while at the same time less developed southern countries suffered from excessive heating that amounted to a monetary loss of the same dollar value as the gain in the North? This could hardly be viewed as a "neutral" outcome despite a net welfare change of zero (derived from summing the monetary gain in the North and the loss in the South). Very few would view a market valuation of impacts in which the rich get richer and the poor get poorer as ethically neutral. In international negotiations, members of the political South often challenge supporters of the use of aggregated market damages as the only numeraire for impacts analysis.

Under the framework of the five numeraires, the interests of developing countries and the less privileged within those nations would be given a greater weight on the basis of the threats to nonmarket entities such as biodiversity, human life, and cultural heritage sites. Take the example of Bangladesh. Assume that rising sea levels caused by climate change lead to the destruction of lives, property, and ecosystems equivalent to about 80 percent of the country's GDP. Although the losses would be indisputably catastrophic for Bangladesh, they would amount to an inconsequential 0.1 percent of global GDP (IPCC 2001b, 97), causing a market-aggregation-only analysis to classify the damage as relatively insignificant. Those considering multiple numeraires, on the other hand, would argue that this is clearly unfair: the loss of life, degraded quality of life, and potential loss of biodiversity is at least as important as aggregate market impacts.

"Dangerous" Climate Change

What Is "Dangerous"?

Article 2 of the United Nations Framework Convention on Climate Change (UNFCCC) calls for stabilization of greenhouse gases to "prevent dangerous anthropogenic interference with the climate system"

(UNFCCC 1992). Although it seems that some of the impacts of climate change discussed thus far suggest that dangerous levels of climate change may occur, the UNFCCC never actually defined what it meant by "dangerous." What we do know is that dangerous climate change is a concept that cannot simply be inferred from a set of observations or calculated by a model. It can be argued that any climate change that impacts more upon those who contributed the least to the problem is less just and thus arguably more dangerous—and could have repercussions that extend beyond environmental damages to, for example, security, health, and economy.

Dessai and colleagues (2004) have distinguished between two kinds of definitions of danger: those derived from top-down research processes and those derived from bottom-up methods. The more commonly used top-down approach determines physical vulnerability based on hierarchical models and different scenarios of socioeconomic change. In contrast, the bottom-up approach focuses on the vulnerability and adaptive capacity of individuals or groups, which leads to social indications of potential danger such as poverty, lack of access to healthcare, or ineffective political institutions.

Although the bottom-up approach seems to provide a more equitable framework for assessing what is dangerous, it is a common view of most natural and social scientists that it is not the task of the scientific community to define what "dangerous" means. It is a political question resting on *value judgments* about the relative salience of various impacts and how to face climate change-related risks and form norms for defining what is "acceptable" (Schneider and Azar 2001, 87; Mastrandrea and Schneider 2004).

The Role of Scientists

Although scientists are not responsible for interpreting what is dangerous, they must help policymakers evaluate what dangerous climate change entails by laying out the elements of risk—traditionally defined as probability × consequence. They should also help decision makers by identifying thresholds and possible surprises, as well as estimates of how long it might take to resolve uncertainties that plague climate assessments.

There is a host of information available about the possible consequences of climate change, including the SRES scenarios. However, they
do not have probabilities assigned to them,[2] which complicates risk
management. Some argue that scenarios based on social trends and
norms should not be assigned probabilities (Grübler and Nakicenovic
2001), as scenarios are used when probabilities cannot be estimated.
Indeed, models do not calculate objective probabilities for future outcomes as the future has not yet unfolded and "objective statistics" are
impossible to obtain. However, modelers can assign subjective confidence levels to their results by discussing how well established the processes underlying a model are, or by comparing their results to observational data for past events, or elaborating on other consistency tests
of their performance (Giles 2002, 476). It is our belief that qualified
assessment of clearly admitted, subjective probabilities in every aspect
of projections of climatic changes and impacts would improve climate
change impact assessments. Subjective probabilities help complete the
risk equation and give policymakers some idea of the likelihood of threat
associated with various scenarios, aiding effective decision making and
illuminating the equity dimensions of risk.

A full assessment of climate change impacts and their probabilities
involves a cascade of uncertainties in emissions, carbon cycle response,
climate response, and impacts. We must estimate future populations,
levels of economic development, and potential technological props spur-
ring that economic development, all of which will influence the radiative
forcing of the atmosphere via emissions of greenhouse gases and other
radiatively active constituents. At the same time, we also must deal with
the uncertainties associated with probabilities generated with carbon
cycle modeling, and confront uncertainties surrounding climate sensitivity estimated from climate models tested on paleoclimatic situations, as
well as perform other "validation" exercises. Schneider (2001) showed
that one could arrive at very different estimates of the probability of
"dangerous" climate changes in 2100 because of the lack of specification
by the IPCC of the independence of various scenarios or climate model
sensitivities or their respective probabilities.

Figure 2.2 shows the "explosion" that occurs as the different elements
of uncertainty are combined. This should not be interpreted as a sign

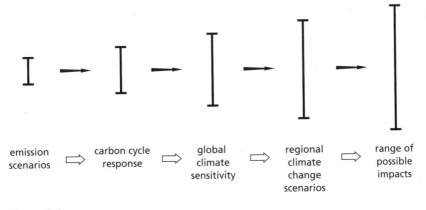

emission scenarios ⟹ carbon cycle response ⟹ global climate sensitivity ⟹ regional climate change scenarios ⟹ range of possible impacts

Figure 2.2
Range of major uncertainties typical in impact assessments showing the "uncertainty explosion."
  These ranges are multiplied to encompass a comprehensive range of future consequences, including physical, economic, social, and political impacts and policy responses. The only policy response implicit on this figure is adaptation, because the processes shown stop at impacts. In reality, perceptions of "unacceptable" risks could create abatement policies that would narrow the range of emission scenarios, thus reducing the final impacts range. In that case, awareness of the large range of impacts might feed back on policies, thus altering the emission scenarios so the cascade would be less "explosive." *Source:* Modified after Jones 2000, and the "cascading pyramid of uncertainties" in Schneider 1983.

that scientists cannot assign a high degree of confidence to *any* of the projected climate change impacts, but rather that the scope of possible consequences is quite wide. There are many projected effects, on both global and regional scales, that carry high confidence estimates, but figure 2.2 suggests that there still are many impacts to which we can only assign low confidence ratings and others that have not yet been postulated—that is, "surprises" and irreversible impacts.
  Estimating climatic risk requires combining many factors, all of which carry their own uncertainties. We need to calculate joint probabilities of, say, climate scenarios and climate sensitivity. Sensitivity in this context means the amount global average temperature will rise for a specific increase in CO_2 levels. We present a simple example below of approaching the joint probability of temperature rise to 2100 and the possibility of crossing "dangerous" warming thresholds. Instead of using two prob-

ability distributions, we pick a high, medium, and low range for each factor. For example, a glance at the cumulative probability density function of Andronova and Schlesinger (2001) reproduced in figure 2.3, shows that the tenth percentile value for climate sensitivity is 1.1°C for a doubling of CO_2 (i.e., 4 W/m² of radiative forcing). 1.1°C is, of course, below the 1.5°C lower limit of the IPCC's estimate of climate sensitivity and the temperature projection for 2100. But this tenth percentile value merely means that there is a 10 percent chance climate sensitivity will be 1.1°C or less—that is, a 90 percent chance climate sensitivity will be 1.1°C or higher. The fiftieth percentile result—that is, the value that climate sensitivity is as likely to be above as below—is 2.0°C. The ninetieth percentile value is 6.8°C, meaning there is a 90 percent chance climate sensitivity is 6.8°C or less, but there is still a very uncomfortable 10 percent chance it is even higher than 6.8°C.

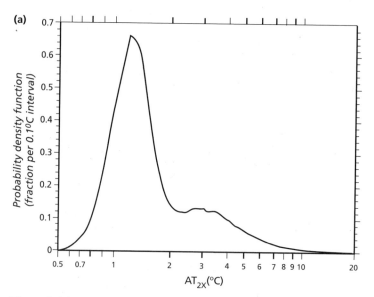

Figure 2.3
Probability density function (*a*) and cumulative density function (*b*) for climate sensitivity to a doubling of CO_2. Climate sensitivity is estimated by matching a range of possible human radiative forcings to the climate system over the past several decades to the observed temperature changes. About half the values for climate sensitivity fall outside of the "canonical" 1.5–4.5°C range used in most assessments. The cumulative density function (the lower panel) suggests about

These three values (6.8°C, 2.0°C, and 1.1°C) for high, medium, and low climate sensitivity help produce three projections of temperature over time, once an emissions scenario is given. In the example below, we combine these three climate sensitivities with two of the SRES storylines: the fossil fuel intensive scenario (A1FI) and the high-technology scenario (A1T), where development and deployment of advanced lower carbon-emitting technologies dramatically reduces the long-term emissions. These are a good pair of scenarios to compare. They capture the high and low ends of cumulative emissions of the six SRES scenarios to 2100. The only major difference between the two scenarios is the technology component—an aspect decision makers have the capacity to influence via policies and other measures. Asking how different the projected climate change to 2100 is for the two different scenarios is a very instructive exercise in exploring in a partial way the likelihood of crossing "dangerous" warming thresholds.

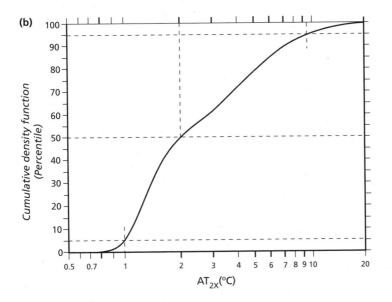

a 15 percent chance that CO_2 doubling in equilibrium would cause warming less than the lower limit used in most assessments and about a 20 percent chance of warming above the 4.5°C upper limit. Thus, uncertainties in this one factor, the climate sensitivity, contribute significantly to the cascades featured in figure 2.2, suggesting climate impacts ranging from negligible to truly catastrophic. *Source*: Andronova and Schlesinger 2001.

We use a conservative estimate of 3.5°C for this "dangerous" threshold because 3.5°C was the highest number projected for the 2100 temperature rise in the SAR and because the IPCC Working Group 2 TAR suggested that after "a few degrees" serious climate change impacts could be anticipated. However, the IPCC noted that some "unique and valuable" systems could be lost if warming is any higher than 1–1.5°C. In essence, the threshold for what is dangerous depends not only on the probabilities of factors such as climate sensitivity or adaptive capacity, but on value judgments as to what is acceptable given any specific level of warming or damage—and who suffers the damage or pays the adaptation costs. Figure 2.4 presents the results.

The most striking feature of both figures 2.4a (upper panel) and 2.4b (lower panel) (A is for the A1FI scenario and B the A1T) is the ninetieth percentile line, which rises very steeply above the other two lines below it. That is because of the peculiar shape of the probability density function for climate sensitivity in figure 2.3—it has a long tail to the right due to the possibility that aerosols have been holding back not-yet-realized heating of the climate system.

This simple pair of figures 2.4a and 2.4b shows the amount of temperature change over time for three climate sensitivity probabilities (tenth, fiftieth, and ninetieth percentile). However, it does not give probabilities for the emissions scenarios themselves; only two are used

Figure 2.4
Global mean temperature change to 2100 of two global emissions scenarios with a range of climate sensitivities: Panel (a) emissions scenario is A1F1 from IPCC (2000); Panel (b) emissions scenario is A1T from IPCC (2000).
Three climate sensitivities—10th, 50th, and 90th percentiles—are read off the Andronova and Schlesinger estimate (fig. 2.3) and combined with the radiative forcings for two SRES scenarios, A1FI, and A1T. These produce similar projections of warming for the first four to five decades of the twenty-first century, but diverge considerably—especially in the high-sensitivity 90th percentile case—after mid century. Two of the three A1FI lines exceed the threshold of 3.5°C warming, indicated by the dashed horizontal line and the shaded area. Notice the shaded area is much more dramatic in the fossil intensive scenario than the technological innovation scenario. In fact, at 2100, when the A1T curves are stabilizing, the A1FI curves are still upwardly sloped—implying yet greater warming in the twenty-second century. *Source*: Climate model used to prepare graphs described in Schneider 1992.

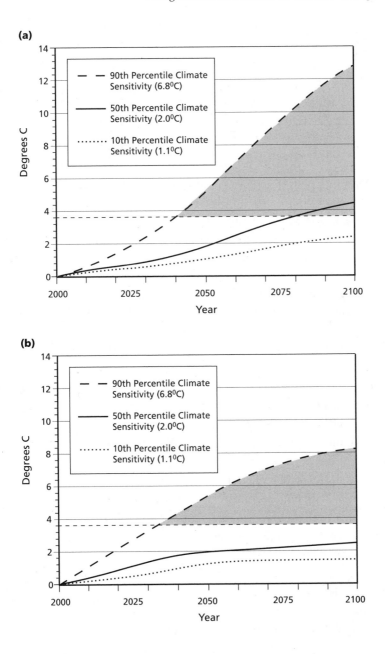

to "bracket uncertainty," and thus one can glean no joint probability from this exercise. That is the next step that the IPCC needs to consider, although a group at MIT has already made an effort at it (Webster et al. 2003), as have Mastrandrea and Schneider (2004). These probabilistic approaches are likely to become more common in the future, but given the heavy model-dependence of results, individual answers will remain controversial and assumption-bound for a considerable time to come. A lively debate over methods of scenario constructions is ongoing, and SRES will certainly be updated.

The likelihood of crossing thresholds is thus sensitive to the selection of scenarios and climate sensitivities and to what is "dangerous." This adds urgency to assessing the relative likelihood of scenarios and sensitivities so that the joint distribution is consistent with the underlying probabilistic assessment of the components. Arbitrary scenarios and sensitivities generate distributions that could easily be misinterpreted as containing subjective probabilistic analysis by experts when they do not do so.

For this reason, Moss and Schneider (2000) call for a "traceable account" of why any particular selections of climate sensitivities or emissions scenarios are made and recommend the use of consistently defined confidence bands. Moss and Schneider also argue that when scientists describe their results, they should assign one of five confidence ratings, ranging from "very low confidence" to "very high confidence." When lack of direct observations prevents the calculation of probabilities, Moss and Schneider suggest that experts assign subjective probabilities to important conclusions by taking into account their knowledge of the models and the data behind them. Although confidence levels for future events are subjective, they can be updated when more data becomes available (see Schneider 2002).

The Value Judgment

Despite the uncertainties surrounding climate change impacts and their probabilities, policymakers must judge what climate change risks to face and what to avoid. They must use all expert information available to decide how to allocate funds on climate change versus healthcare versus education versus a host of other worthy causes.

From a justice perspective, this means that justice issues in climate change become part of the value judgments made by an individual or group of decision makers after examining risks in many numeraires, for which different policymakers might have different concerns attached.

Equity in Policy Challenges

This section examines possible policy responses to climate change in order to demonstrate their justice and equity challenges. These responses range from mitigation to adaptation, but the two are not substitutes. More specifically, we outline arguments for no-regrets actions and precautionary hedging and their implications for equity.

The "No Regrets" Approach to Climate Change Policy

Many policymakers have remained in the "do nothing," "wait and see," and "more research is needed" camps, but some have supported "no regrets" policies that entail eliminating existing "market failures" such as inefficient energy systems, which would pay for themselves with or without climate abatement benefits. A few countries have also sought to internalize the "externalities" of carbon emissions. In Norway, a US$50 per ton tax is levied on carbon emissions. However, the lack of policies among the world's biggest emitters is concerning, as delay is likely to breed further delay (Schneider and Azar 2001, 119). The unwillingness of many decision makers to implement anything other than "no regrets" policies is also unjust, as it will likely lead to greater harm to the developing nations, who have contributed less to the problem!

Hedging

Hesitation to implement climate change policies seems curious given that many other risk management decisions are based on strategic hedging against low-probability, high-cost events (IPCC 2001b, 96). The Bush administration experimented with hedging strategies, often referred to as the "precautionary principle," against the threat of weapons of mass destruction based on little established evidence by starting the war with Iraq. Yet the same administration demands high levels of certainty before it will consider hedging against threats to environmental security. This inconsistency has not gone unnoticed by the nations who have ratified the Kyoto Protocol, a treaty the Bush administration and its allies in the fossil fuel and automobile industries strongly oppose, claiming it runs contrary to their economic interests. Bush decided in March 2001 that the United States would not be a signatory while his administration was in power.

Courses of Policy Action—Abatement

Thus far, most decision makers have focused on mitigation actions, of which the Kyoto Protocol is the most obvious example. Under the Kyoto Protocol, the developed (Annex I) signatory countries agreed to reduce their emissions by 5.2 percent below 1990 levels between 2008 and 2012. Developing countries were not assigned emissions targets or timetables. Yet in order to slow down climate change, policymakers will need to adopt much greater emission reductions than envisioned in the Kyoto Protocol. Eventually, all emitters, developed and developing countries alike, will need to participate. Decisions on abatement levels and other actions could be aided by better information on the risks of "dangerous climatic interference" (as calculated in Mastrandrea and Schneider 2004 or Schneider and Mastrandrea 2005).

Any international agreement on mitigation has significant justice considerations. Rich nations have contributed 80 percent of anthropogenic CO_2 in the atmosphere to become rich and enjoy a tenfold advantage in emissions per capita. Their emissions also affect poor nations disproportionately. But if developing nations insist on a right to "catch up" in per capita emissions, the atmospheric burden, when multiplied by the population of developing countries (about four times that of the developed world), could more than triple CO_2 concentrations after the twenty-first century and cause "dangerous" climate change (see Azar and Rodhe 1997; Schneider 2002; Oppenheimer and O'Neill 2002). Thus, it is important for all nations to participate in mitigation, as a ton of CO_2 emitted in Beijing has the same impact as a ton emitted in Boston or Brussels.

Although participation of the developing world in mitigation is essential for the stabilization of planetary climate below a few degrees of warming, it is not necessary that the costs of mitigation should be equally shared. The "playing field" is so tilted in favor of the developed countries that the distribution of "who plays" can be very different from the distribution of "who pays." This is why the Conference of the Parties (COP) process has called for "common, but differentiated responsibilities" in burden-sharing (see chapter 3, by Mace). This idea is included in the Kyoto Protocol's Clean Development Mechanism (CDM) and Joint Implementation (JI) initiatives. They have been designed to help rich nations reach their targets under the Kyoto Protocol more cost effectively, but also to provide incentives for developing nations to become venues for low-cost, clean technologies for emissions abatement. The strategy of encouraging the developing world not to mimic the Victorian industrial revolution on their road to development by increasing coal burning and the use of internal combustion engines, but to jump over these dated technologies and pursue more efficient, high-technology solutions, has been called "technology leapfrogging."

It will be economically, politically, and ethically difficult to fashion fair, affordable, and acceptable mitigation and leapfrogging schemes in all sectors and regions. One prerequisite is a spirit of international cooperation and a recognition of the common planetary destiny. Hopefully, the efforts to fashion a cooperative international negotiation process based on cost effectiveness and fairness over a past decade can be extended into new and more climatically "safe" agreements in the decades ahead.

The utilization of the "sustainability approach" of the five numeraires, rather than a traditional cost benefit analysis, would likely help to achieve this goal. The sustainability approach attributes more importance to damages in places such as Bangladesh. It is also more capable of valuing low-probability and far-off catastrophic events such as a shutdown of thermohaline circulation in the North Atlantic or the melting of Greenland and West Antarctic ice sheets and the consequent sea level rise. Cost-benefit analyses discount these "surprises" and make future catastrophes only marginally significant for present cost considerations. Cost-benefit analyses are also devoid of equity considerations, based on the notion that benefits in one part of the world might compensate for damages somewhere else, regardless of who benefited from the activities that caused the impacts and how the impacts are differentially distributed.

Is It Too Expensive to Mitigate CO₂ Emissions?

Many policymakers seem unconvinced to implement abatement policies on the basis of risk avoidance and equity considerations, claiming that economic costs could be severe (see Linden 1996). It may, therefore, be worth pointing out that substantial reductions in carbon emissions and several-fold increases in economic welfare *are* compatible goals. Using a simple model, Azar and Schneider (2002) estimated the present value (discounted to 1990 and expressed in 1990 USD) of the global costs to stabilize atmospheric CO_2 at 350 ppm, 450 ppm, and 550 ppm over the next 100 years at $18 trillion, $5 trillion, and $2 trillion, respectively. The World Bank estimates that worldwide GDP in 2002 was about $32 trillion, which makes spending $18 trillion, or 56 percent of 2002 GDP, to stabilize CO_2 seem unthinkable. However, what is often forgotten is that a CO_2 stabilization cost of $10–20 trillion represents the *present value* of spending that would be done *over the entire period of the next 100 years*. Most recent economic models calculating CO_2 abatement costs assume that growth in population and the productivity of labor will drive about a 2 percent annual growth rate in the worldwide economy, which amounts to a GDP-doubling time of about thirty-five years, meaning global GDP will likely reach about $240 trillion per annum by 2100. In that light, a present value of $20 trillion over the *entire century* seems relatively low in cost. In fact, if conventional economic models are remotely accurate in their 2 percent per year growth rate projection, then even if we were to spend those trillions of dollars on CO_2 stabilization over the next 100 years, global income levels around 2100 (some 500 percent higher per capita than today) would be delayed less than a decade (Schneider 1993), and probably only a couple years (Azar and Schneider 2002), behind the no-abatement-spending scenario, as figure 2.5 illustrates.

The question is not *whether* to abate—that seems essential to avoid a substantial risk of dangerous climatic change (Mastrandrea and Schneider 2004)—but how to fashion cost-effective incentives and fair burden sharing among nations and groups within nations, not all of which contribute equally to the greenhouse gas concentrations in the

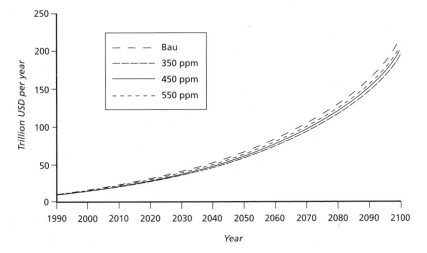

Figure 2.5
Global income trajectories under business as usual emissions scenario and in the case of stabilizing the atmosphere at 350 ppm, 450 ppm, and 550 ppm of CO_2.

Observe that we have assumed rather pessimistic estimates of the cost of atmospheric stabilization (average costs to the economy assumed here are $200/tC for 550 ppm target, $300/tC for 450 ppm, and $400/tC for 350 ppm) and that the environmental benefits of meeting various stabilization targets have not been included. *Source*: Azar and Schneider 2002.

atmosphere or share equal adaptive capacities and vulnerabilities to climatic changes. Paul Baer discusses these issues in greater detail in chapter 10.

Can Adaptation Be "Traded off" against Abatement?

Unlike mitigation, adaptation is a *response to* rather than a *slowing of* global warming. The IPCC has identified two types of adaptation, autonomous and planned. An autonomous adaptation is a non-policy-driven reactive response to a climatic stimulus that occurs after the initial impacts of climate change are felt (IPCC 2001a, 88). Planned adaptation comes in passive and anticipatory forms, as Schneider and Thompson (1985) describe. Passive adaptation is reactive in nature and could involve buying additional water rights to offset the impacts of a drying climate, for example. Schneider, Easterling, and Mearns (2000) use farming examples to illustrate that passive adaptation cannot be assumed to occur automatically, questioning whether farmers will invest heavily in new crops or improved irrigation to adapt before climate change occurs. Although some have argued that farmers *do* adapt to changes in markets, technology, and climatic conditions, others have contended that this neglects problems such as resistance to unfamiliar practices, problems with new technologies, unexpected pest outbreaks, and the high degree of natural variability of weather (Schneider, Easterling, and Mearns 2000). Any passive adaptation will almost certainly not be smooth or instantaneous, as autonomous adaptation is often assumed to be. Rather, adaptations to slowly evolving trends embedded in a noisy background of inherent variability are likely to be delayed by decades, as farmers attempt to sort out true climate change from random climatic fluctuations. In fact, if by dint of poor luck, there was a sequence of weather anomalies that were the opposite of slowly building climatic trends, misperception of these as the new climatic regime could actually lead to maladaptations. Even in the face of policies to facilitate passive adjustment such regulations on sharing losses, changes in land use, changes in location, retreat from rising sea levels (see West, Dowlatabadi, and Small 1998), maladaptation can occur. Such actions can be more damaging than not adapting at all to developing countries and marginalized groups, who have limited financial and other resources. For them, even one round of successful adaptations will be taxing, let alone multiple rounds when the early measures prove to be maladaptations.

Anticipatory or proactive adaptation has considerable policy potential. It could include such technical actions as purchasing more efficient irrigation equipment, building higher bridges and dams, and engineering seeds to make them cope better with altered climates. It could also include political actions such as setting up networks to disseminate climate information and suggest potential adaptive actions, and creating insurance mechanisms or transfering payments to disadvantaged groups. Some of these actions would also be a cobenefit toward sustainable development.

With well-defined central policy coordination on a wide range of proactive measures, maladaptation is more likely to be avoided. However, this is not as simple as it seems. Proactive adaptation is part of a complex cycle: human behavior within physical, biological, and social systems causes disturbances that propagate through natural systems and create responses that, in turn, feed back on human behavior in the form of policies for adaptation or mitigation to the human-induced disturbances (Root and Schneider 2001, 41). In addition, most studies of anticipatory adaptation assume that countries and groups will be able to afford it, which is unlikely to be universally true.

Several funds have been established to aid developing countries in adaptation, the most well known being the Marrakech Funds (established at the seventh Conference of the Parties meeting—COP 7—in Marrakech, Morocco, in 2001) and the Global Environmental Facility's (GEF) climate change operational program. However, there are still no clear guidelines for determining which adaptation projects are worthy of funding. The GEF requires such projects to show "global environmental benefits" and the Marrakech Funds try to assure funding of adaptation to long-term climate change rather than to short-term climate variability. Yet it is difficult to assess adaptation projects on these grounds because they are local (and therefore bring local, rather than global, benefits) and will likely improve an area's ability to adapt to climate change *and* climate variability (Huq and Burton 2003). The rules for eligibility are in need of clarification and standardization. Huq and Burton (2003) suggest that once an adaptation effort has been selected for funding, both the GEF and Marrakech resources should serve as incremental financing for adaptation activities that are already underway, and preferably activities that have other benefits such as biodiversity conservation.

It is often considered that one can view mitigation and adaptation as competing strategies to deal with climate change. However, doing so would have considerable equity implications. Suppose it were cheaper for a rich, high-emitting nation in the North to adapt than to mitigate. If the rich nation chose only to adapt, it would likely be detrimental to a poorer, less adaptable country in the south. Simply comparing mitigation and adaptation costs and aggregating the values across all nations is a "one dollar, one vote" aggregate prescription, and it clearly has serious equity implications.

The mitigation-adaptation trade-off is not meaningful even in the cost-benefit framework, because mitigation costs should be compared with the benefits of avoided climate damages and not with adaptation costs. Adaptation can reduce climate damages. However, adaptation costs are likely to be low at low levels of climate change, whereas first mitigation steps may be costly (presuming perfect markets and the absence of "no regrets" options). As greenhouse gas concentrations increase, adaptation costs will likely rise and adaptation may not even be feasible when climate changes are large or irreversible. Economic modeling studies suggest marginal abatement costs are much lower for higher values of greenhouse gas concentrations (see the IPCC Synthesis Report—IPCC 2001d). Thus, as greenhouse gas concentrations increase, the current situation in developed countries of potentially low marginal adaptation costs and relatively high abatement costs will reverse. But the justice implications of such trade-offs are substantial and the low-cost option for one country is most likely not synonymous with the low-cost option for the world.

Who Wins? Who Loses?

Marginalized Groups—Excluded from the Policy Process?
Even if an "optimal" combination of mitigation and adaptation is chosen, it may not be as just as it could or should be. As Adger and colleagues argue in chapter 1, climate change policy decisions do not always benefit those countries or groups within countries who are most vulnerable. The most marginalized groups tend to have little political and economic power and hence have little influence in the decision-making processes. Conversely, those with political and economic power tend to be less vulnerable to climate change damages and to have influence over policy decisions. This is why policies often cater to special interests such as the coal industry or countries such as the United States at the expense of more needy groups or nations. As Dow and colleagues show in chapter 4, differential vulnerability is intimately intertwined with social justice and adaptation.

Can Marginalized Groups Be Treated Fairly?
In order to avoid overlooking and subjugating marginalized groups when formulating climate policies at the local, national, and interna-

tional levels, decision makers must consider not only the economic costs and benefits of actions, but the effects these actions (or lack thereof) will have on the well-being of people and other species around the world. In most frameworks of distributive justice, it is argued that disadvantaged countries and groups should be given the highest priority when climate change policy decisions are made. Under such distributive justice, setting the level of "dangerous" climatic change to be prevented is both a technical risk assessment (what can happen and what are the odds?) and a social value assessment (what level of risk is acceptable, and to whom, and what policies are fair for abatement or to compensate "losers" who are forced to adapt to the actions of others?).

Conclusion

Let us return to the issue of intergenerational equity and sustainability over centuries. As figure 2.6 illustrates, our actions over the next few generations can precondition climatic changes and impacts over the next millennium.

The figure shows a "cartoon" of effects that can play themselves out over a millennium, even for decisions taken within the next century. Such long-term potential irreversibilities as significant increases in global annual average surface temperature and sea level rise from thermal expansion and melting glaciers are precisely the kinds of nonlinear events that would likely qualify as "dangerous anthropogenic interference with the climate system." Whether a few dominant countries and a few generations of people demanding higher material standards of living and consequently using the atmosphere as an unpriced sewer to achieve such growth-oriented goals is "ethical" is a value-laden debate that will no doubt heat up as increases in greenhouse gas concentrations continue.

Our personal value position, given the vast uncertainties in both the climate science and impacts estimations, is that we should fashion policies and measures to slow down the rate at which we disturb the climate system. This can both buy time to better understand what may happen—a process that will take many more decades, at least—and help to develop lower-cost decarbonization options (as abatement policies will

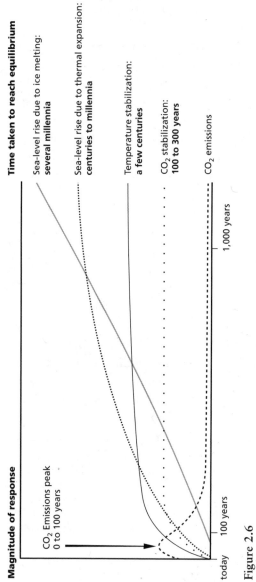

Figure 2.6
CO$_2$ concentration, temperature, and sea-level rise. *Source:* IPCC 2001d.

provide incentives to invent cleaner, cheaper technologies) so that the costs of mitigation can be reduced. Slowing down the pressure on the climate system and addressing the needs of marginalized countries and groups are the "insurance policies" we have against abrupt and dangerous climate change and the injustices they entail. These measures will also help us move toward the goals of the UNFCCC to stabilize greenhouse concentrations so as to allow ecosystems to adapt naturally to climate change, ensure that food production is not threatened, and enable economic development to proceed in a sustainable manner. Policies to slow down the rate at which we disturb the climate system are also justified, in the context of this book, as they are fundamentally fair.

Acknowledgments

Special thanks to the two reviewers of this chapter and to the Winslow Foundation for partial support.

Notes

1. The World Meteorological Organization has since reported that both 2002 and 2003 were warmer than 1997 but cooler than 1998. However, 2005 is estimated to be the first or second warmest year on record. Schneider (2002) reports that losses from weather-related disasters in the 1990s were eight times higher than in the 1960s. Vellinga et al. (2001) acknowledge various influences on climate damages and recognize the difficulty in attribution. In contrast, Pielke Jr. and Landsea (1998) dismiss any effect of climate change on hurricane damage, explaining increased damages as a result of richer people moving into harm's way. However, Pielke Jr. and Downton (2000) suggest that climate is a partial factor for noncoastal weather-related casualties. Recent studies show that tropical cyclone intensities are significantly correlated with ocean warming since 1970.

2. The IPCC described all of its scenarios as "equally sound," offering no assessment of which scenarios are more or less likely. This implies that the probability of an A1 business-as-usual scenario is the same as that of the egalitarian B1 world, when it is doubtful that most analysts would really agree those were equally likely worlds given current trends and value systems. See Schneider and Kuntz-Duriseti 2002, 72.

3

Adaptation under the UN Framework Convention on Climate Change: The International Legal Framework

M. J. Mace

It is now inevitable that human-induced climate change will result in sea level rise, changes in the intensity and frequency of extreme weather events, and alterations in patterns of biodiversity. These events will have significant but varied social, economic, ecological, and public health consequences in different countries. Many countries with little historical responsibility for greenhouse gas (GHG) emissions, such as small island developing states in the Pacific and Caribbean, face daunting challenges in addressing climate change impacts. Their access to financial resources, know-how, and technology for adaptation will determine their ability to minimize loss of life and productive land, and disruptions to their natural, social, and economic systems.

Through the United Nations Framework Convention on Climate Change (UNFCCC),[1] countries with diverse interests in climate change and diverse vulnerabilities to it have agreed to work cooperatively to reduce and stabilize greenhouse gas emissions and adapt to anthropogenic climate change. Against this backdrop, this chapter explores the international legal framework on adaptation, to highlight present challenges for distributive and procedural justice in adaptation at the international level through the UNFCCC process.

Equity and Differentiation in Adaptation

The UNFCCC uses differentiation among parties to respond to challenges of equity in adaptation, much as it does in the context of the mitigation of GHG emissions. The convention distinguishes among "developed," "developing," and "least developed countries"; between "vulnerable" and "particularly vulnerable" countries; and among "Annex I," "Annex II" countries, and "economies in transition." The convention also distinguishes among countries with different physical characteristics, highlighting the needs of small island countries, countries with low-lying coastal areas, countries prone to floods, droughts, and desertification, and countries with fragile ecosystems.

This differentiation is used to allocate responsibilities between groups. For example, Annex II parties, and those Annex I parties that are able, are responsible for providing financial assistance to developing countries that are "vulnerable" and "particularly vulnerable" to the impacts of climate change. But this framework, which is intended to respond to differing abilities and levels of vulnerabilities among parties, also raises many other equity issues.

Equity *among developing countries* is implicated in the identification of "particular vulnerability," the prioritization of adaptation activities under the convention process, and the elaboration of rules for accessing funding and technology transfer to meet these needs. Issues of equity are also implicated *among developed countries* in sharing the burden of financial assistance and technology transfer for adaptation—particularly as some convention parties engage in aggressive measures to reduce greenhouse gas emissions, while the reluctance of others compounds the global adaptation challenge.

Procedural justice among the differently situated convention parties is sought through the UNFCCC's governance structures and procedures. These include the Conference of the Parties (COP), its subsidiary bodies, its financial mechanism, and its expert groups. Procedural justice requires the effective participation of parties in these bodies and in the negotiating process itself. I argue that although many of the convention's procedural provisions appear impartial, it is increasingly difficult for developing countries to participate effectively and on an equal footing—with predictable consequences for the achievement of distributive justice.

The convention's achievement of distributive justice will be measured by its success in seeing that the needs of the most vulnerable parties are adequately identified and addressed, and that the costs of doing so are borne by those most financially able and most responsible for causing climate change. We are far from that point. The convention process has so far had only limited success in strengthening developing country capacity to identify and respond to adaptation needs in key sectors. It has also failed to create an institutionalized, equitable, and adequate burden-sharing arrangement for addressing the costs of adaptation.

Convention Framework on Adaptation

One of the most challenging aspects of the convention's framework for adaptation is that adaptation is not addressed in any single article in a comprehensive way. Many articles bear upon the issue, creating a web of interlinking responsibilities, approaches, and mechanisms for addressing adaptation needs. The term "adaptation" is often used in the convention but never defined.[2] Thus we must understand the term in relation to terms such as "climate change" and the "adverse effects of climate change" that are defined. Article 1 of the convention defines "climate change" as "a change of climate which is attributed directly or indirectly to human activity that alters the composition of the global atmosphere and which is in addition to natural climate variability observed over comparable time periods." Thus "climate change" is limited to anthropogenic change—a limitation that has important implications for understanding the "effects" of climate change to be addressed by the convention process, and for determining the role of the convention process in fashioning an equitable response.

"Adverse effects of climate change" is defined as "changes in the physical environment or biota resulting from climate change which have significant deleterious effects on the composition, resilience or productivity of natural and managed ecosystems or on the operation of a socio-economic systems or on human health and welfare." This definition recognizes that ecosystems, socioeconomic systems, health, and welfare are all anticipated to be negatively impacted by climate change. Although the term "significant" is not defined, the breadth of the terms "composition," "resilience," and "productivity" draw in a wide range of climate change impacts to which adaptation efforts may be properly directed under the convention.

Article 2 defines the "ultimate objective" of the convention as the "stabilization of greenhouse gas concentrations in the atmosphere at a level that would prevent dangerous anthropogenic interference with the climate system" (without defining the term "dangerous"). These concentrations "should be achieved within a time-frame sufficient to allow ecosystems to adapt naturally to climate change, to ensure that food production is not threatened and to enable economic development to proceed in a sustainable manner." The length of time taken to stabilize emissions, and the level at which emissions are stabilized in the atmosphere, will directly affect the form and magnitude of adaptation that is required.

Article 3 then identifies principles to guide convention implementation, including the principles of intergenerational equity, common but differentiated responsibilities and respective capabilities, and the precautionary principle (see Bodansky 1993). Developed countries are to "take the lead" in combating climate change and its adverse effects, and the "specific needs and special circumstances of developing country parties, especially those that are particularly vulnerable to the adverse effects of climate change . . . should be given full consideration." The parties are to take "precautionary measures to anticipate, prevent or minimize the causes of climate change and mitigate its adverse effects" and "[w]here there are threats of serious or irreversible damage, lack of full scientific uncertainty should not be used as a reason for postponing such measures."

Article 4 sets forth commitments on adaptation, including commitments to formulate and implement national programmes to facilitate adequate adaptation (4.1(b)); cooperate in preparing for adaptation (4.1(e)); employ methods to minimize the impact of measures taken to adapt (4.1(f)); provide funding for adaptation (4.3, 4.4); promote and finance technology transfer (4.5); and consider actions to meet the needs and concerns of developing countries and the special situations of least developed countries (4.8, 4.9).

Articles 5 and 6 elaborate upon article 4.1(g) commitments regarding research and systematic observation related to the effects of climate change, and article 4.1(i) commitments regarding education, training, and public awareness.

Article 9 creates a Subsidiary Body for Scientific and Technical Advice (SBSTA) to advise the COP on scientific knowledge relating to the effects of climate change. Article 10 creates a Subsidiary Body for Implementation (SBI) to assist the COP in reviewing the effectiveness to support convention implementation. Article 11 creates a financial mechanism for convention implementation on a grant or concessional basis. Finally, article 12 creates a system of national reporting for the communication of adaptation needs and strategies to the COP.

The convention also includes processes for the elaboration of existing obligations. Article 7 establishes the COP, which meets annually to make decisions to clarify the role and meaning of previously agreed provisions and encourage and reflect input from the SBSTA, the SBI, the UNFCCC Secretariat, the Intergovernmental Panel on Climate Change (IPCC), and other intergovernmental conventions and processes. The convention contains further structural mechanisms for the expansion of party commitments on adaptation through amendments (article 15), annexes (article 16), and protocols (article 17), as well as through the creation of new subsidiary bodies for convention implementation (article 7.2(i)).

The following sections will examine this legal framework in greater detail, focusing on actions to address adaptation, funding for adaptation, transfer of technologies to support adaptation, and mechanisms to report on adaptation needs through national communications. Conclusions then discuss and highlight key challenges for the elaboration of this framework in a fair and equitable manner.

Actions to Address Adaptation

Central convention articles addressing adaptation in developing countries include articles 4.8 and 4.9. Under article 4.8, all parties are to give full consideration to "what actions are necessary," including actions related to *funding, insurance,*[3] and the *transfer of technology,* to meet the specific needs and concerns of developing country parties "arising from the adverse effects of climate change and/or the impact of the implementation of response measures." The parties are to look "especially" at these effects and impacts on:

(a) Small island countries;

(b) Countries with low-lying coastal areas;

(c) Countries with arid and semi-arid areas; forested areas and areas liable to forest decay;

(d) Countries with areas prone to natural disasters;

(e) Countries with areas liable to drought and desertification;

(f) Countries with areas of high urban atmospheric pollution;

(g) Countries with areas with fragile ecosystems, including mountainous ecosystems;

(h) Countries whose economies are highly dependent on income generated from the production, processing and export, and/or on consumption of fossil fuels and associated energy-intensive products; and

(i) land-locked and transit countries.

Article 4.8 is problematic in its linkage, in a single article, of the "adverse effects of climate change" and "the impact of the implementation of response measures" (measures taken to mitigate GHG emissions). These effects and impacts have different causes, nature, and timing. The affected groups have also different vulnerabilities and interests. Since the convention was agreed in 1992, this linkage has proven challenging for subsequent negotiations on ways to address adaptation to adverse effects of climate change.

Article 4.9 addresses the needs of the least developed countries (LDCs), providing that "the Parties shall take full account of the specific needs and special situations of the least developed countries in their actions with regard to *funding* and *transfer of technology*" (emphasis added).

The COP has moved slowly in elaborating "necessary" actions under articles 4.8 and 4.9. At COP 4 in Buenos Aires, the parties recognized that several information gaps needed to be filled. Decision 5/CP.4[4] adopted a work program to identify the adverse effects of climate change, the impacts of the implementation of response measures under the convention, the specific needs and concerns of developing country parties, and actions related to funding, insurance, and technology transfer to meet these needs. This process was to culminate at COP 6. However, agreement was not reached on a package of decisions until COP 7, in 2001, when the Marrakech Accords advanced a range of adaptation actions and funding through a series of related decisions.[5]

Marrakech Decision 5/CP.7

The central Marrakech decision on adaptation activities (5/CP.7) has four parts: I) adverse effects of climate change; II) implementation of article 4.9; III) impact of the implementation of response measures; and IV) further multilateral work relating to articles 4.8 and 4.9.

Section I, on the adverse effects of climate change, lists activities to be supported by the convention's financial mechanism, the Global Environment Facility (GEF), and other multilateral and bilateral sources. It also lists activities to be supported by a new Special Climate Change Fund "and/or" a new Adaptation Fund. Finally, it provides that insurance-related actions will be considered at COP 8.

Although decision 5/CP.7 expands the scope of adaptation activities previously supported through the GEF,[6] it does not set out adaptation measures that go beyond capacity building, assessments, and planning—such as the retrofitting of coastal infrastructure to withstand sea level rise and extreme weather events and the relocation of vulnerable populations threatened by droughts, floods, or sea level rise. The listed actions are also to be supported "in accordance with" the guidance given to the GEF in decision 6/CP.7. Decision 6/CP.7 does request the GEF to fund "pilot or demonstration projects to show how adaptation planning and assessment can be practically translated into projects that will provide real benefits"—but to do so by the staged approach endorsed by COP decision 11/CP.1. This limits fundable activities to measures to *prepare* for adaptation, as envisaged in article 4.1(e).[7]

Decision 5/CP.7 also provides that the Special Climate Change Fund and the Adaptation Fund may be used for "*starting* to implement adaptation activities *promptly* where sufficient information is available to warrant, in the areas of water resource management, land management, agriculture, health, infrastructure development, fragile ecosystems and integrated coastal zone management" (emphasis added). However, this language has been limited in its impact by the pace and content of subsequent negotiations over the operationalization of the Special Climate Change Fund.

Section II of decision 5/CP.7 creates a work program for LDCs and a mechanism for identifying the urgent and immediate needs of LDCs that may not be expressed through national communications, due to lack of capacity or the absence of a timeframe for LDC national communications (article 12.5). This includes strengthening national climate change secretariats and focal points to enable convention and protocol implementation, and training in negotiating skills and language for LDC negotiators. But most significantly, it includes the development, preparation, and implementation of National Adaptation Programs of Action (NAPAs) "to serve as a simplified and direct channel of communication of information relating to the vulnerabilities and adaptation needs of the least developed countries." Related Marrakęch decisions establish a Least Developed Country Fund to support this work program (27/CP.7), an LDC Expert Group to assist with its implementation (29/CP.7), and guidelines for the NAPA process (28/CP.7).

The NAPA process is a country-driven, bottom-up process to generate a list of priority activities for adaptation in LDCs "whose further delay could increase vulnerability, or lead to increased costs at a later stage." It includes the assembly of a national multidisciplinary team, composed of a lead agency and stakeholder representatives. The NAPA team synthesizes available information on adverse effects of climate change and coping strategies, assesses vulnerability to current climate variability and extreme weather events, determines where climate change is causing increases in associated risks, and identifies key adaptation measures.[8] Each NAPA is to be exposed to public review and comment, endorsed by the relevant national government, and published. The NAPA guidelines also propose a list of criteria for the selection process, and an outline for the NAPA document to allow for a consistent NAPA format. What the guidelines lack, however, is a mechanism for the implementation of these priority projects once they are identified. Although NAPA priorities are to be "made available" to the GEF and to other sources of funding, there is presently no guarantee that any of the activities identified as priorities will be funded.

To summarize, the NAPA process addresses several concerns related to procedural justice. It is a bottom-up, stakeholder-driven, and country-driven process. However, although concerns of procedural justice may be satisfied at the country level, distributive justice concerns remain largely unaddressed (see Huq and Khan, chapter 9). One concern is the limited amount of funding available in the LDC fund to carry out the work program. A second is the absence of a developed country burden sharing mechanism to support the costs of the LDC work program and NAPA implementation. The LDC fund is funded only by nonmandatory contributions from developed country parties; certain major emitters of GHGs, such as the United States, have chosen not to contribute. A third key concern is the absence of detailed, agreed criteria for the allocation of LDC fund resources. These criteria will affect the distribution of limited LDC fund resources among countries, and among priority activities.

Finally, section IV of decision 5/CP.7 provides for workshops to identify further actions under articles 4.8 and 4.9, including actions on integrated assessments, synergies between conventions, modeling, economic diversification, and insurance. In the years following decision 5/CP.7, negotiations have continued over the terms of reference of these workshops and how to take their outcomes forward.

Buenos Aires Decision 1/CP.10

A further milestone in adaptation came at COP 10, when the parties agreed the "Buenos Aires programme of work on adaptation and response measures" (decision 1/CP.10). This decision incorporates the results of many SBI negotiating sessions on "Progress in the Implementation of Decision 5/CP.7," and SBSTA negotiations on the scientific and technical aspects of adaptation. The decision has four parts: I) adverse effects of climate change, II) impact of the implementation of response measures, III) further multilateral work, and IV) SBSTA program of work on impacts, vulnerability, and adaptation to climate change. LDC issues were negotiated separately.

Section I, relating to the adverse effects of climate change, further elaborates on decision 5/CP.7 activities. Among other things, it requests the UNFCCC secretariat to organize three regional workshops, as well as an expert meeting for small island developing states on their priorities, to enable further consideration of needs and concerns. Although the word does not explicitly appear in the decision, it is understood that "insurance" will be addressed at some of these events.[9] The lack of an express reference to insurance has resulted from the United States' resistance to any linkage between extreme weather events and climate change, and the efforts of many parties to resist OPEC claims for compensation through "insurance" mechanisms in section II of the decision.

In section IV, the parties request SBSTA to develop a structured five-year work program on the "scientific, technical and socio-economic aspects of impacts, vulnerability and adaptation to climate change." This decision merely initiates another discussion, with no timetable agreed for the commencement of the SBSTA work program, or its completion. The status of the implementation of article 4.8, decision 5/CP.7, and decision 1/CP.10 will be assessed at COP 14 in 2008.

The net result is that more than ten years after the convention was agreed upon, little concrete action has been taken under article 4.8 or 4.9 to move beyond planning, assessment, and workshops to address the distinct needs of vulnerable countries. Several factors have contributed to this slow progress. Industrialized countries have pointed to scientific uncertainties regarding the magnitude and incidence of climate change impacts, and to difficulties in isolating the effects of natural climate variability from anthropogenic climate change. They have called for further studies, raised concerns about the possibility of maladaptation, and called for the mainstreaming of adaptation activities into development planning as a condition for funding adaptation projects. These positions have been perceived as delaying tactics by developing countries who face pressing adaptation needs and are eager to advance to concrete projects to address these needs.

At the same time, the diversity of national circumstances and interests within the Group of 77 and China (the developing country negotiating bloc) presents its own challenges. Differences in institutional capacity, bargaining power, and negotiating skill all affect the prioritization of issues that emerge from the group. This can be seen in the success oil-producing countries have had in hitching their economic concerns for the "impacts of response measures," to the needs of vulnerable countries arising from "the adverse effects of climate change."[10] This has often been reflected in the parallel treatment of these issues in G-77 negotiating texts—which makes agreement with developed country parties very difficult to achieve. This linkage has persisted, despite vivid differences in the nature and urgency of these issues, and the vulnerability of their advocates. This is a measure of the strength of the OPEC bloc within the group, and the challenges faced by many developing country delegations, rather than any equivalence of these issues from the perspective of equity. OPEC countries' opportunistic use of the G-77 bloc to advance their agenda, often at the expense of progress on issues that affect the most vulnerable, underscores the uneven playing field of climate negotiations. It also highlights the need for the greater empowerment of vulnerable countries within the negotiating process to support the fairness of the process as a whole.

Funding for Adaptation

Financial transfers to developing country parties were proposed in the negotiation of the convention for two reasons: 1) to offset the cost of implementing the convention's general commitments; and 2) to aid developing countries in adapting to the adverse effects of climate change if the convention failed to abate global warming adequately (Bodansky 1993). The convention anticipates financial transfers from Annex II parties to developing country parties under article 4.3 and to developing country parties that are "particularly vulnerable" to the adverse effects of climate change under article 4.4.

Under article 4.3, Annex II parties agree to provide new and additional funding to meet the agreed full costs of developing countries' national communication obligations under article 12.1. This includes the full costs of activities related to the formulation of national communications—such as studies of possible impacts of climate change, identification of options for implementing article 4.1(b) and 4.1(e) obligations, and relevant capacity building.[11] Annex II parties further agree to provide the funding needed by developing countries to meet the "agreed full incremental costs" of implementing measures covered by article 4.1. For article 4.3, "new and additional" means additional to expected flows of development assistance. "Agreed" means as agreed between the developing country party and the convention's financial mechanism—entrusted to the Global Environment Facility (GEF). "Incremental cost" refers to the cost differential between a baseline action to address a national need and the additional cost of an action that generates "global benefits."[12]

In contrast to article 4.3, article 4.4 provides simply that Annex II parties "shall also assist the developing country Parties that are *particularly vulnerable* to the adverse effects of climate change in meeting costs of adaptation to those adverse effects" (emphasis added).

Article 4.3's "incremental cost" and "global benefits" criteria are extremely problematic in the context of adaptation within the GEF's climate change focal area. First, it is difficult to establish a baseline for adaptation measures, given the varied nature of these measures. Second, the incremental cost formulation assumes that a baseline measure would have been undertaken to address a particular national need.[13] However, some adaptation measures (e.g., planting mangrove swamps [which may mitigate emissions, yielding "global benefits"] or erecting sea walls [which will not]) might not be considered at all, if it were not for the need to address climate change impacts. Third, adaptation measures are necessarily adopted for their local benefits. The *need* for adaptation arises from a global cause, but the *remedy* must yield local benefits. Thus the requirement of global benefits is an absurd limitation in the adaptation context. These criteria, as they are presently interpreted, have severely constrained parties' ability to access funding to address adaptation needs.[14]

Some have argued that article 4.4's mandatory nature and broad language may signal virtually unlimited liability for the costs of adaptation in particularly vulnerable developing country parties (Verheyen 2002). But this of course raises the question of which countries are particularly vulnerable and who decides. Although the convention's preamble recognizes a number of groups as particularly vulnerable, this preambular language is not binding (Verheyen 2002).[15] It has also not yet been clarified whether "particular vulnerability" will be limited to physical vulnerability, or be understood to extend more broadly to vulnerability resulting from lack of financial, social, or institutional adaptive capacity.

Over the years, developing countries have expressed dissatisfaction with the GEF. In response to this mounting frustration,[16] in Marrakech, the COP acknowledged the need for new and additional funds beyond those contributed to the GEF. The following three new funds were created for the purpose:

• an LDC Fund, under the convention, to address the LDC work program (27/CP.7);

• a Special Climate Change Fund (SCCF), under the convention, to finance adaptation, technology transfer, climate change mitigation, and economic diversification (7/CP.7); and

• an Adaptation Fund, under the Kyoto Protocol, to support concrete adaptation projects and programs (10/CP.7, 17/CP.7).

The Marrakech Accords identified certain activities to be addressed by the new funds. However, the specific allocation of these activities among these funding mechanisms, the scope of the measures to be funded by each mechanism, and the operational criteria for each fund were left to be decided by future COPs. The need for an equitable burden sharing arrangement was also acknowledged but left unaddressed (7/CP.7). The LDC Fund and SCCF are supported by nonmandatory developed country contributions. The Adaptation Fund will be supported in part by a 2 percent share of the proceeds of Clean Development Mechanism project activities.

Guidance on the LDC and SCCF

Lengthy negotiations have continued since Marrakech on how to operationalize the LDC Fund and SCCF. When, near the end of COP 9, the parties could not reach full agreement on criteria for funding NAPA implementation, by decision 6/CP.9 they requested the GEF to develop operational guidelines based on agreed elements. These included "cost-effectiveness," "complementarity with other funding sources," equitable access by LDCs to funding for implementation, "criteria for supporting activities on an agreed full-cost basis, taking account of the level of funds available," the "urgency and immediacy of adapting to the adverse effects of climate change" and "prioritization of activities."[17] Similarly, when no detailed agreement could be reached on guidelines for SCCF funding, the GEF was tasked to arrange for expedited access to the SCCF, in keeping with existing GEF practices, in view of the partial agreement reached on the fund's priorities under decision 5/CP.9. That decision had agreed that adaptation was the SCCF's top priority, and technology transfer was also essential.

Thus, despite the continuing difficulties developing countries had had in accessing convention funding through the GEF, and despite their success in obtaining new, potentially more flexible funding sources in Marrakech, much of this momentum was lost at COP 9 with the ceding back to the GEF of responsibility for the development of guidelines for these funds. One motivation for developing countries' agreement to this course of action was their desire for an early start to funding for concrete adaptation projects.

Not surprisingly, given the influence of LDC Fund donor countries within the GEF, at COP 10 the GEF presented programming elements for the fund that relied heavily on established GEF practice.[18] Of particular offense to LDCs was the GEF's handling of their request for full cost funding for NAPA implementation. LDCs also strenuously objected to GEF proposals requiring cofinancing, noting that they would make funding in practice inaccessible to many LDCs. Further guidance to the GEF resolving these issues could not be agreed at COP 10 and the fund remained unavailable for the implementation of NAPA priorities.

With respect to the SCCF, at COP 10 developing countries challenged what they viewed as the GEF's creation of new conditionalities for accessing the SCCF, beyond those adopted by the COP.[19] These included further reports, additional criteria, and burdensome cofinancing requirements. AOSIS, the LDC Group, and the African Group highlighted the difficulty these elements would pose for vulnerable countries in accessing funding, stressing that under article 11 of the convention, it is for the COP, rather than the GEF, to decide on the GEF's "policies, program priorities and eligibility criteria."[20]

The trajectory of negotiations on the SCCF and LDC Fund underscores the challenges developing countries face in negotiations with the better equipped developed country contributors to these funds. It is clear that the achievement of favorable substantive outcomes depends upon bargaining power and negotiating ability that developing countries often lack, even when their urgent and immediate needs are directly at stake, and even when funds have been created for their benefit.

The Marrakech Accords package, which included the creation of three new funds, was achieved when developing country buy-in was needed to permit adoption of rules for the use of the Kyoto Protocol flexible mechanisms—to aid developed country parties in meeting their Kyoto commitments at a lower domestic cost. In the absence of similar leverage at COP 9 and COP 10, developing countries failed to obtain more flexible funding guidelines to address adaptation needs under the LDC and SCCF.

Equally problematic is the fact that many significant decisions for adaptation funding are taken outside the UNFCCC negotiating arena and within the GEF itself. Under article 11, the UNFCCC's financial mechanism is required to have "an equitable and balanced representation of all Parties within a transparent system of governance." The GEF Council, which has primary responsibility for developing, adopting, and evaluating GEF programs, consists of 32 members: 16 from developing countries, 14 from developed countries and two from economies in transition.[21] Decisions of the GEF Council are taken by consensus. However, if "no consensus appears attainable," any council member may require a formal vote. Decisions requiring formal votes are generally taken by a double weighted majority, which requires an affirmative vote representing both a 60 percent majority of the total number of participants and a 60 percent majority of total contributions.[22] This means that GEF Council members from countries that make the largest contributions carry the most weight (Streck 2001). Therefore, although procedural justice is reflected in the composition of the GEF Council, major donor countries are nevertheless the most influential under the GEF's voting rules. This has implications for the GEF's decisions and for distributive justice within the UNFCCC process.

Technology Transfer

Article 4.5 directs developed country parties to take steps to promote, facilitate, and finance the transfer of environmentally sound technologies and know-how to enable convention implementation, and to support the development and enhancement of the endogenous capacities and technologies of developing country parties. This is understood to include technologies for adaptation.

At COP 1, the parties requested that the secretariat prepare an inventory and assessment of technologies and know-how conducive to mitigating and adapting to climate change, as well as a progress report on "concrete measures" taken by developed country parties with respect to their commitments on technology transfer to "facilitate adequate adaptation to climate change."[23] At COP 3, the secretariat presented progress reports addressing adaptation technologies and technology transfer.[24]

At COP 7, the parties agreed on a framework for technology transfer and established an Expert Group on Technology Transfer (EGTT) to identify ways to facilitate and advance technology transfer activities (4/CP.7). Since that time, the secretariat has presented a progress report on activities under decision 4/CP.7,[25] and released a working paper listing activities it has undertaken on technology transfer under various COP decisions.[26] At SBSTA's request, a number of technical reports relevant to adaptive technologies also have been prepared.[27] Yet little tangible progress has been made on the development and transfer of adaptive technologies.

At COP 9, a senior level round-table discussion on enabling environments for technology transfer noted that although attention has focused on mitigation technologies, this must be complemented by the transfer of adaptation technologies.[28] It also acknowledged that most adaptation research is carried out in industrialized countries, and that joint research and development with receiving countries may therefore be useful.[29] At COP 10, however, parties were merely encouraged to explore opportunities for joint research and development programs on technology transfer, with no express reference to adaptive technologies.

As part of the EGTT's work program, the UNFCCC secretariat continues to focus on issues and activities around technology transfer for adaptation and environmentally sound technologies for adaptation to climate change. These efforts may draw further attention to these aspects of articles 4.8 and 4.5.

National Communications

Article 12 creates a process for the exchange of information among the parties on the implementation of convention commitments, including those on adaptation. Guidelines for reporting have been developed separately for Annex I and non-Annex I parties, based on the different commitments of each group. The focus on mitigation to date has led to very detailed reporting requirements on greenhouse gas sources and sinks, and far less detailed reporting requirements on adaptation.

The timetable for the submission of national communications, the contents of these reports, and the level of scrutiny of these communications differ for Annex I and non-Annex I parties. However, reporting guidelines for both sets of countries request information on vulnerability and adaptation to the impacts of climate change.

Annex I parties are to include "information on the expected impacts of climate change and an outline of the actions taken to implement Article 4.1(b) and (e) with regard to adaptation."[30] Annex II parties are to also provide details of measures taken to give effect to their commitments under articles 4.3, 4.4, and 4.5. They are required to indicate what "new and additional financial resources" they have provided under article 4.3, and provide detailed information on the assistance provided "to assist developing countries that are particularly vulnerable to the adverse effects of climate change in meeting the costs of adaptation to those adverse effects," including through bilateral, regional, and other multinational channels. Reporting on financial contributions is required on an annual basis, for COP review.[31]

Although this appears transparent, in reality it is difficult for developing country parties to determine how developed countries are implementing their convention obligations on adaptation funding and technology transfer. For example, although parties are asked to note their contributions to the GEF, this figure is not broken down between climate change activities and other UN convention activities addressed by the GEF.[32] In reporting on assistance given to "developing countries that are particularly vulnerable," the question of how "particular vulnerability" is determined has been left to each reporting government. These factors make it difficult to assess burden-sharing for adaptation costs among developed countries within the UNFCCC process, and to review the distribution of these efforts across developing country party beneficiaries.

For non-Annex I countries, national communication guidelines (set out in decision 10/CP.2) invited information on specific needs and concerns arising from the adverse effects of climate change, using numerical indicators where possible, such as affected percentage of land area,

population, and gross domestic product.[33] Developing countries were
are also encouraged to provide a description of steps taken to implement
the convention, including policy options, planning frameworks, and
financial and technical needs for implementing adaptation measures and
response strategies.[34]

The UNFCCC secretariat's fourth synthesis of thirty-one developing
country national communications that had been submitted noted that
many non-Annex I parties had had difficulty in identifying their climate
change impacts and adaptation needs due to a lack of financial resources
and technical support for research and systematic observation, a lack of
downscaled models to suit national circumstances in assessing impacts,
and a lack of human capacity and capabilities in collecting, archiving,
and managing data needed for national communications.[35]

The fifth synthesis report, a year later, reviewed sixteen additional
national communications. It reported difficulty in use of the IPCC
Guidelines for Assessing Climate Change Impacts and Adaptations; lack
of capacities to conduct the kinds of vulnerability assessments that
would generate reliable results for incorporation into the national development planning process; lack of data arising from inadequacies in data
collection and monitoring, and access to existing databases; lack of
institutional capacity and financial resources; and a lack of in-depth
studies in various sectors, including agriculture, biodiversity, forestry,
health, and tourism.[36] All sixteen communications indicated that adaptation was a major issue, but adaptation options were not evaluated,
prioritized, or costed.[37]

It is clear that initial national communications from developing
country parties have not generated information in a format that requests
or allows for the systematic prioritization of adaptation needs either
within countries, or between countries through the UNFCCC process.
Existing syntheses do not group by region, geography, particular vulnerability, or economic status, and the process of aggregating information
from countries as small as Niue, with countries as large and populous
as Bangladesh, only serves to obscure challenges identified at the country
level.

At COP 8, new guidelines were adopted for developing country
national communications (17/CP.8). These guidelines require more

detailed vulnerability and adaptation assessments and aim to collect information in a more transparent, consistent, and comparable manner. Countries are requested to identify their most critical vulnerable areas, provide information on strategies and measures for adapting to climate change in these key areas including those of highest priority, provide information on projects for financing under article 12.4 and opportunities for pilot or demonstration adaptation projects, and identify barriers to adaptation projects. However, the revised guidelines raise issues of capacity, and the adequacy of funding for the national communication process itself.

Second national communications from non-Annex I parties are now in preparation. National communications are the primary vehicle for conducting vulnerability and adaptation studies for many developing countries. Yet little funding is available for these communications,[38] which are expected to facilitate the identification, prioritization, and costing of adaptation activities with a sufficient degree of confidence to guide and attract adaptation funding. If adequate funding and technical assistance for in-depth vulnerability and adaptation studies in priority sectors is not provided, the systems created through the convention process to identify, address, and fund adaptation needs will fail to assist the most vulnerable communities and countries.

Conclusion

Recent decisions of the COP have created new institutional arrangements and work programs that address many aspects of adaptation related to procedural justice. The LDC work program and NAPA process are particularly notable examples. The COP has also created expert groups that may address certain obstacles facing the most vulnerable countries in communicating their needs, by providing assistance in assessing and prioritizing these needs in country, from the bottom up, and outside the problematic top-down formal negotiating process. New funds have been created that may ultimately provide funding for pressing adaptation needs outside article 4.3 of the convention.

These are promising developments. However, many of these mechanisms and initiatives have themselves sprung from difficulties developing countries have had in expressing and advancing their needs through the convention process. It is critical that these tools do not fall victim to the same lack of developing country voice and influence that has necessitated their creation. This exclusion could occur through a lack of financial support for the efforts of expert groups, a failure to institutionalize support for the LDC work program, or a failure to create a stable, predictable, and accessible source of funding to address adaptation needs once identified.

The central challenge for the achievement of procedural and distributive justice in adaptation must be to ensure that the needs of developing countries drive adaptation actions and funding, rather than the other way around. To do this, the convention's adaptation framework must evolve in a manner that not only assists developing country parties in determining and expressing their adaptation needs, but then responds to these prioritized needs in an organized manner, recognizing key differences between groups of developing country needs, based on transparent and equitable criteria.

Many challenges remain for the achievement of procedural and distributive justice through the convention's framework on adaptation. The most critical are inequities in the negotiating process, the development of mechanisms for financing adaptation, and the political will to address the needs of the most vulnerable by those most responsible and able.

The developing country parties that are most vulnerable to the impacts of climate change, and have contributed the least to global emissions, should present the most compelling case for assistance. Nevertheless, they are also frequently the most disadvantaged in negotiations. Many have small delegations, which presents a major challenge when negotiations relevant to adaptation proceed in parallel. Eleven distinct agenda items addressed aspects of adaptation at COP 9; at COP 10, there were ten such agenda items.[39] Additional challenges include the lack of translating services in contact group and "informal" working group sessions—where most contentious issues are settled; the lack of funding for regional preparatory meetings in advance of negotiations to formulate group positions; the growing complexity of negotiations; and the number of past COP decisions upon which new decisions build. Many countries lack institutional and technical capacity to prioritize their adaptation needs, which complicates the identification of forward-looking negotiating strategies. Often developing country parties lack funding even to attend the sessions that affect their interests. At SB 18, in June 2003, for example, some parties went completely without representation, and others suffered reduced representation, due to a shortage of GEF Trust Fund support for their attendance. Although some of these issues cannot be addressed through the convention process, others can and must be in order to maintain its legitimacy.

The development of mechanisms for funding adaptation presents many hurdles. These include the GEF's incremental cost and global benefits criteria, GEF's lack of a formal operating program on adaptation within its climate change focal area, its emphasis on enabling activities when many countries are prepared to commence projects, and the preference of its implementing agencies for larger projects. Many countries have to bundle themselves into regional projects, despite COP decisions underscoring the importance of country-driven approaches. The GEF's cumbersome application procedure and cofinancing requirements further deter countries from seeking funding. Within the GEF itself, there is a need to address differences in power, finance, institutional capacity and knowledge, and to provide support to weaker actors (Streck 2001, 17). The dynamic of the recent LDC Fund and SCCF negotiations underscore the need for closer interaction and understanding between the GEF and the needs of the countries it serves.

The absence of an institutionalized, equitable, and adequate burden-sharing arrangement to address the costs of adaptation presents a challenge for both developed and developing countries. A system will have to be devised to share this burden, through funding streams that draw upon the resources of all Annex II convention parties, including those outside the Kyoto Protocol, and that more directly operationalize the polluter pays principle.

Finally, the strong resistance of oil producing countries and the United States to forward momentum in the climate negotiations has to be addressed. The convention's adaptation framework will be slow to evolve without the political will to address the causes of climate change and the needs of the most vulnerable, by those most responsible and most able. Initiatives external to the convention process are likely to play a role in creating this momentum. These include scientific advancements in determining the causal link between GHGs and specific climate change impacts, and the corresponding attribution of responsibility for these impacts.[40] They also include the use of complementary legal processes to encourage responsible action by major emitters. For example, using domestic law, cases have been brought against the U.S. Environmental Protection Agency for failure to regulate carbon dioxide as a pollutant under the Clean Air Act; against development banks for failing to conduct environmental assessments before financing natural gas and petroleum projects in developing nations; and against U.S. power companies, for creating a public nuisance through greenhouse gas emissions.[41] Using public international law, in December 2005 the Inuit filed a petition before the Inter-American Human Rights Commission, highlighting the impacts of human-induced climate change in the Artic on their environmental, subsistence, and human rights.[42] Under the UNESCO Convention, petitions have been submitted to place glaciers and coral reefs on the List of World Heritage in Danger as a result of climate change.[43]

These and other initiatives will assist in focusing attention on the needs of the most vulnerable, and support the elaboration of a just international legal framework on adaptation.

Notes

1. Available online at <http://www.unfccc.int>.

2. The scientific literature uses several definitions of adaptation. See FCCC/TP/1997/3 p. 3; IPCC 2001b:982.

3. The Alliance of Small Island States (AOSIS) proposed the creation of an international insurance pool or fund to provide compensation for damages suffered as a result of sea level rise. The result of this effort was article 4.8's reference to insurance (see Linnerooth-Bayer, Mace, and Verheyen 2003).

4. Decisions of the COP are available online at <http://www.unfccc.int>.

5. The Marrakech Accords include decisions of the COP 7 and are referred to in the form __/CP.7.

6. See GEF/C.23/Inf. 8, "GEF Assistance to Address Adaptation," April 28, 2004, GEF Council, 19–21 May, 2004 at 16–17.

7. COP decision 11/CP.1 gave guidance to the GEF that adaptation strategies should be implemented in a staged approach. Stage I includes planning, such

as studies of possible impacts of climate change, to identify particularly vulnerable countries or regions and policy options for adaptation and appropriate capacity building. Stage II includes measures such as capacity building, which may be taken to prepare for adaptation, as envisaged by article 4.1(e). Stage III includes measures to facilitate adequate adaptation, including insurance, and other adaptation measures as envisaged by article 4.1(b) and 4.4. Decision 2/CP.4, taken at COP 4, permitted Stage II measures to be funded in particularly vulnerable countries and regions identified in Stage I.

8. Verheyen (2002) points to the NAPA process as a relaxation of the convention's limitation on adaptation funding to impacts of anthropogenic climate change.

9. See FCCC/SBI/2004/L.11. See also SBI Conclusions from SB 22 regarding article 4.9. For background on the issue of insurance, see Linnerooth-Bayer, Mace, and Verheyen 2003.

10. See Barnett and Dessai 2002, for an explanation of why OPEC country negotiating tactics obstruct progress on assistance to developing countries for adaptation.

11. Decision 11/CP.1 and note 7.

12. See GEF's guidelines. Available online at <http://www.gefweb.org/Operational_Policies/Eligibility_Criteria/Incremental_Costs/IncreCostsLand.pdf>.

13. GEF Council Paper on Incremental Costs, GEF/C.7/Inf.5.

14. The GEF is experimenting with the concept of an "adaptation increment" to address the global "dis-benefit" of climate change, but this approach is still evolving and overly complex. GEF/C.23/Inf.8/Rev. 1, fig. 1.

15. Verheyen (2002) cites the Vienna Convention on the Law of Treaties for the proposition that the preamble may only be used as an interpretative aid and not as an authoritative rule.

16. See, for example, decision 2/CP.4; FCCC/SBI/2002/Misc.9.

17. FCCC/CP/2003/6/Add.1.

18. Elements to be Taken into Account in Funding the Implementation of NAPAs Under the LDC Fund, GEF/C.24/Inf.7, October 26, 2004. Available online at <http://www.gefweb.org>.

19. Programming to Implement the Guidance for the Special Climate Change Fund Adopted by the Conference of the Parties to the United National Framework Convention on Climate Change at its Ninth Session, GEF/C.24/12, October 15, 2004. Available online at <http://www.gefweb.org>.

20. Earth Negotiations Bulletin, vol. 12, nos. 250, 251. 2004. Available online at <http://www.iisd.ca/climate/cop10/>.

21. GEF Council Rules of Procedure <www.gefweb.org>.

22. GEF Instrument, para. 25(c) <www.gefweb.org>.

23. Decision 13/CP.1, FCCC/CP/1995/7/Add.1, pp. 40–41.

24. Decision 9/CP.3, FCCC/CP/1997/7/Add.1, pp. 39–40. See FCCC/SB/1997/1, 3 and 4, FCCC/SBSTA/1997/10.

25. FCCC/SBSTA/2002/10.

26. UNFCCC (2003, 6 para. 27).

27. UNFCCC (2003, para. 28).

28. FCCC/SBSTA/2004/2, para. 10.

29. FCCC/SBSTA/2004/2, para. 40.

30. Decision 9/CP.2, FCCC/CP/1996/15/Add.1, pp. 26–27; decision 4/CP.5, FCCC/CP/1999/7, pp. 91–98.

31. Decision 7/CP.7, FCCC/CP/2001/13/Add.1, p. 44.

32. Decision 4/CP.5, FCCC/CP/1997, p. 93.

33. Decision 10/CP.2, FCCC/CP/1996/15/Add.1, Annex at p. 46.

34. Id. at 47–48.

35. Synthesis reports are available online at <http://www.unfccc.int/national_ reports/non-annex_i_natcom/compilation_and_synthesis_reports/items/2709. php>.

36. Fifth Synthesis Report, paras. 128, 160, 162.

37. Id., para. 128.

38. For initial national communications, a maximium of US $130,000 out of a total of US $350,000 was available to each non-Annex I party for assessing both mitigation and vulnerability under the GEF's expedited procedures. For second national communications, a ceiling of US $150,000 out of a total of US $420,000 is available for assessing mitigation, vulnerability, and adaptation. See GEF/C.23/Inf.8, paras. 12–13; FCCC/SBI/2004/18 at 9.

39. See UNFCCC 2003, 3. Prior to COP 10, the UNFCCC website listed ten agenda items for negotiation relevant to adaptation.

40. See Allen and Lord 2004.

41. See <http://www.climatelaw.org/cases>.

42. Id.; see also Revkin 2004.

43. <www.climatelaw.org/cases>.

II

Aspects of Fairness in Adaptation

4

Exploring the Social Justice Implications of Adaptation and Vulnerability

Kirstin Dow, Roger E. Kasperson, and Maria Bohn

A complicated array of equity and social justice issues besets efforts to fashion global responses to climate change. They include specific questions as to who bears the responsibility for the legacy of accumulated greenhouse gas emissions, and whether such emissions were essential for livelihood support or resulted primarily from the growing affluence of populations. Climate justice also involves issues of how climate change is associated with other broad inequalities in wealth and well being, dissociations between those who will benefit from and those who will bear the burdens and damage associated with climate change, procedural justice issues as to how decisions have been made in structuring international approaches to assess scientific issues and creating the institutions of the global climate change regime to address the problems, and how equity issues and adaptation strategies may interact (Boehmer-Christiansen 2003; Brown 2003; Baer et al. 2000; Helm and Simonis 2001; Kasperson and Dow 1991; Metz et al. 2002; O'Brien and Leichenko 2003; Sagar 2000, and chapters in this book).

Among these complex issues, the differential vulnerability of populations to climate change stands out as being of fundamental importance. Differential vulnerability and the differences in exposure, sensitivity, and resilience in responding to changes is intimately intertwined with social justice and adaptation questions and occupies a central place in these debates. We focus in this chapter on the most vulnerable peoples and places, arguing that they deserve special attention and consideration in our efforts to reduce the human drivers of climate change and to ameliorate the human harm and suffering that will come in its wake. In doing so, we ask whether the most vulnerable people merit special attention? And if so, why? We then consider whether highly vulnerable people and places can actually be adequately identified and the causes of their vulnerability reasonably profiled and understood. Finally, we wrestle with the questions of how potential injustices can be addressed by mitigation and adaptation and to what extent such injustices can be avoided or redressed.

What is the Moral Imperative for Giving the Most Vulnerable Special Attention?

We know from many other risky situations and technologies that risk and harm are often highly concentrated in those who are most exposed and susceptible to risk (Kasperson et al. 1995). Farmers applying pesticides often receive doses dramatically higher than the general population. Children have been at high risk from exposure to lead in the ambient environment. Subsistence farmers in food-insecure places are at particular risk from drought. In the case of climate change, as detailed below, a number of populations are at particular risk from sea level rise, increasing water scarcity, and riverine and coastal flooding.

Many regulations and protective standards are constructed so as to protect the most susceptible, including those on the "tails" of risk distributions, even at considerable increased cost to society. Support exists in many theoretical conceptions of social justice for the contention that the most vulnerable ought to be given special attention in adaptation to climate change. Several different principles have been suggested to be *the* single principle or *one of* the principles according to which distribution in society should occur to make the distribution just. Some of these principles are equality, desert, liberty, and need, as Adger and colleagues discussed in chapter 1. There are, of course, also different ideas about the relevance of the content of the distribution, such as, what should be distributed in this or that way? It should be noted that some question also exists as to whether *distribution* is at all relevant for a conception of justice. Despite the differences and disagreements among different conceptions of justice, many can be used to generate reasons why the most vulnerable to climate change ought to be given special attention. Looking at conceptions of justice centered around one principle only, as well as a contextualist approach to justice, we will attempt to shed light on this reasoning. The present and future situation of life threatening risks can be said to be unfair in many different ways. People holding different views on justice may be able to come to agreement on the condemnation of this situation and the need to devote special attention to the most vulnerable.

Rawls, in his seminal work *A Theory of Justice*, writes that the subject matter of justice is "the way in which the major social institutions distribute fundamental rights and duties and determine the division of advantages from social co-operation" (1972, 7). The distributive principles are those to which a person would consent if all he or she knew about his or her life was that he or she would want to choose and pursue some goals, would have some values and desires, and would rather have a larger than a smaller share of the primary social goods comprised of rights, liberties, powers, opportunities, income and wealth, and basis of self respect. Rawls (1972, 302) argues that the principles thus consented to would be:

1. Each person is to have an equal right to the most extensive total system of liberties compatible with a similar system for all.
2. Social and economic inequalities are to be arranged so that they are both (a) to the greatest benefit of the least advantaged, and (b) attached to offices and positions open to all under conditions of fair equality of opportunity.

Taking the second of these two principles, a society is just only if it is arranged in such a way that the position of the least advantaged is optimized. One can see social and economic inequalities in the world as being partly expressed in differential greenhouse gas emissions and in differential incidence of climate change impacts. Often the most vulnerable to climate change are those with poor social and economic conditions that often affect negatively sensitivity and resilience (African Development Bank et al. 2003). The most vulnerable hence suffer some of the consequences of the actions of the more advantaged as these latter have exercised, and continue to exercise, this advantage. This arrangement of social and economic inequalities is clearly not to the greatest benefit of the least advantaged—the most vulnerable.

One should note that both benefits and risks will occur as a result of climate change. But the relationship between the most adaptive and resilient and those who are most vulnerable will be asymmetrical. The ability to reap benefits from climate change will be closely linked to the extent of adaptive capacities and resources. Those with strong abilities to anticipate climate change and to institute timely and rapid adaptations will be the primary beneficiaries. Those who lack adaptive capacities, namely the most vulnerable, will not only experience the greatest risk and damage but also realize the fewest opportunities for improving their situations. This further asymmetry adds to the imperative for special consideration, just as it also broadens the scope of what that consideration needs to include.

Amartya Sen (1982) suggests that distributive justice has to do with the equality of capability, where capability links resources and welfare. Capabilities determine what goods can do to or for people. It can be argued that the risks of climate change will settle primarily upon peoples already beset by other existing or future environmental and economic stresses—people who possess inadequate coping resources and limited adaptive capacities to buffer themselves from the further loss and harm that climate change may bring.

To take a particular case, the low lying islands of the Pacific and the densely populated but poor deltas of Egypt and Bangladesh have limited abilities to assess the risks of climate change and institute protective actions. By comparison, the Netherlands, despite its low-lying elevations, has a high societal capability to assess and implement protective systems in the face of sea level rise. Hence, the most vulnerable ought to be given special attention because there is a differential around the globe in the capabilities or capacities to achieve or maintain welfare in the face of climate change, and the most vulnerable often have the lowest capabilities or capacities.

Turning to the principle of desert, another argument can be made why the most vulnerable ought to be given special attention. It is likely that those who have contributed most to climate change are likely to suffer least from its effects, and that those who are most vulnerable to future effects and have contributed the least are likely to suffer the most. Whether we choose to see desert as depending on natural endowments or as depending on decisions, choice, and effort, the burden of the risks inflicted on the vulnerable is in neither case one that they deserve. The discrepancy between responsibility for the creation of the problem and the vulnerability to the harm likely to emerge adds further to the moral imperative to act on behalf of those at highest risk.

Conceiving of justice as liberty as opposed to equality, it remains possible to argue for special attention for the most vulnerable. In *Anarchy, State and Utopia* (1974), Robert Nozick contends that justice is about individual rights to life, external acquisitions, and bodily integrity. Within this conception, it is the process of acquiring property that is thought to be constitutive of the justice of possessing it, not its distribution. In fact, Nozick argues against the very idea of such a thing as a just distribution. Given that the process of acquiring certain kinds of property result in greenhouse gas emissions (either in their creation or in their transport), and that the consequent climate changes pose threats to bodily integrity and life for some, particularly the most vulnerable, these acquisitions can be interpreted as disrespectful of individual rights and thus unjust. The most vulnerable ought to be given special attention somehow to remedy this injustice.

It may be argued that the differential ability to protect oneself from or adapt to environmental and other perturbations and insults should be a consideration in society's allocation of resources for risk protection (Derr et al. 1983). David Miller suggests a contextual approach to justice, where distributive principles are dependent on the context in which they operate (Miller 1976, 1980). Hence, distribution according to equality is relevant when considering ourselves as citizens or when distributing by default. In the context of community, however, the appropriate principle for distribution is need. In a community, he argues, there is a common idea of what is needed and membership is defined by need and necessary reciprocity. Miller (1976) argues that the context of community is largely one of the nation-state that embodies nonvoluntary and cooperative relationships, and that across these communities of nation-states the principle of need cannot operate. Among states, it is instead then a matter of humanity as opposed to one of justice to distribute to satisfy needs equally.

With the advent of climate change, however, one could argue that all nation-states are interdependent through their influence and dependence on and sensitivity to a global natural system, and that this interdependence has created a greater sense of community among people and states than before (a community that is different from the nation-state in its recognition of global natural systems). Resources for adaptation are a need in the face of risk of harm, because adaptation is a solution to avoiding harm and a way to avoid economic and psychological costs of uncertainty. The most vulnerable therefore ought to be given special attention because they are in need of resources for adaptation. The international community could choose to see this as an opportunity to prevent harm from occurring on a full scale.

Who Are the Most Vulnerable? Do We Know?

An ethically based global effort focused on adaptation by those who are most vulnerable to climate change assumes that, in addition to the financial and political support needed for these efforts, such groups and places can be identified with reasonable accuracy. If these initiatives are to support a broader agenda of development and actions to reduce vulnerability, then there must also be a requisite understanding of the causes of the vulnerability. How sufficient is the knowledge of vulnerability and its dynamics for such a resolve? The answer to this question depends specifically on how one frames the issue of sufficient knowledge.

Levels of Scientific Accuracy and Consensus

If the need is to pinpoint with significant accuracy at subnational and local scales those most vulnerable to climate change at future times, then the answer is negative, for several reasons. First, global climate models lack detailed resolution to profile the types and magnitudes of changes to be expected in particular countries and regions, let alone subregions within those countries. These uncertainties include the direction of change in precipitation (whether it will be wetter or drier) or temperature (whether it will be warmer or cooler) in some regions, as well as the potential for the frequency and magnitude of extreme events (IPCCa 2001; Easterling et al. 2000).

Second, significant limitations also exist to our abilities to assess the human vulnerabilities to those ill-defined stresses (Kelly and Adger 2000). The interaction of multiple, sometimes rapidly fluctuating stresses (such as economic shocks and natural hazards) with chronic stresses (such as malnutrition and other health threats) in shaping vulnerability and the dynamic interactions of these processes across social and geographical scales or levels, means that levels of vulnerability are difficult to predict. Not surprisingly under these challenging analytical circumstances, the scientific and policy communities also lack consensus on the conceptual framework for assessing current levels of vulnerability at a single social level or geographic scale, and disagree on how best to treat the dynamics of vulnerability, though we are making some progress (see Kasperson J. X. and Kasperson R. E. 2001a).

Vulnerability indicators and indices are potentially significant assessment tools, although these indices and their portrayal in maps encounter the same conceptual difficulties reviewed above. Human vulnerability is often taken to include three major dimensions—exposure, sensitivity to the stress (or coping abilities), and longer term resilience to future stresses (and particularly adaptive capacity). Differences in measures of related traits, such as sensitivity, adaptive capacities, and the order of impacts considered contribute to difficulty in comparing analyses.

A variety of efforts have been made to develop indicators and even indexes for measuring vulnerability, but these are primarily at the national level and are as yet unvalidated and their accuracy is unknown (see Lonergan, Gustavson, and Carter 2000; Kaly et al. 1999; Downing et al. 2001). For instance, the UNDP Human Development Indices include measures of longevity, knowledge, standard of living, and in the case of the HDI-2, of participation (UNDP 2002a). These indices are clearly significant in representing the current level of criticality in the absence of climate change (see Downing et al. 2001) and reflect aspects of sensitivity, coping abilities, and adaptive capacities. But their relationship to vulnerability to potential climate impacts such as drought, sea level rise, or changing patterns of vector borne diseases is not sufficient to support accurate comparisons among places or of the value of adaptation efforts.

More detailed data for characterizing each of these vulnerability dimensions are either absent at the needed scale or of questionable accuracy and consistency. For instance, poverty is not synonymous with vulnerability; there are wealthier vulnerable groups, but poverty is nonetheless widely accepted as an important indicator of vulnerability. Although decades of analytical and methodological development have focused on poverty measures and mapping, even these methods for collecting information on and mapping vulnerability remain controversial. It must also be recognized that because vulnerability is place-specific, the ability of the social sciences to predict future social and economic attributes of populations is weak. Thus identifying vulnerable groups in time and space with high levels of accuracy for global comparisons of climate impacts through to some carbon stabilization scenario is simply not possible.

Sufficient Knowledge to Reduce Potential Harm?

We can reframe the question of what is sufficient knowledge to guide action as follows. Do we have knowledge that would be valuable in identifying groups highly vulnerable to climate change and designing efforts for reducing such vulnerability? To that question, the answer is certainly in the affirmative. Although it is clearly not possible to pinpoint the specific groups and local places at highest risk and to quantify the degree of vulnerability, we do know the broad regions likely to experience certain types of climate change and extreme events.

For example, under a variety of combinations of climate change scenarios and definitions of "critical stress," Alcamo and Hendricks (2002) found that a subset of the areas potentially subject to water stress appeared to be consistent across the scenarios: central Mexico, the Middle East, parts of the Indian subcontinent, and stretches of the North African coast. Research on the impacts of climate change on global food production suggests that there will be significant regional variation impacts on yield and the risk of hunger (Parry et al. 1999; Fischer, Shah, and van Velthuizen 2002).

We also know that many of these areas are already under high stress from existing environmental and socioeconomic changes that are likely to continue into the future (UNEP et al. 2000; Gleick 2000; World Economic Forum et al. 2002). These environmental pressures include land degradation, high levels of stress on water resources, and deforestation driven by both basic and affluent consumption demands. The current distribution and likely patterns of spread of the HIV/AIDS epidemic are becoming better understood, as are the long-term consequences for households, communities, and nations (FAO 2003a). Many countries are experiencing violent conflict or the complex recovery process of rebuilding institutions and infrastructure to meet future environmental challenges (Barnett, chapter 6; UNEP 2002a). We further know where coping resources are weak due to patterns of global inequalities, chronic poverty, and persisting poor health (UNDP 2002a; World Bank 2002a; FAO 2002). Past experience with development efforts, natural disasters, climate variability, resource management, and other social problems also indicates that underlying these global patterns are further patterns of social vulnerability, such that women, children, elderly, and minority populations often face more severe challenges in difficult situations.

Examples of major areas highly likely to be adversely affected include such regions as small island states, water scarce regions, marine ecosystems, and food insecure regions (Kasperson and Kasperson 2001b). With high population densities concentrated in coastal areas, specialized island economies, and heavily affected by various globalization phenomena, many small island developing countries are highly vulnerable to future sea level rise (Pelling and Uitto 2001). These islands contain a high proportion of the world's linguistic and cultural diversity, the loss of which would be irreversible and of a value perhaps impossible to calculate. One-third of the world's population now lives in countries that are already water stressed, and that number is expected to reach about five billion people in 2025 (IPCC 2001b). Meanwhile, half of the world's population lacks access to adequate sanitation. Climate change is likely to produce reduced stream flow and increased droughts in many of these areas, particularly central Asia, the Mediterranean, and southern Africa.

Serious future effects from sea level rise are also likely on a variety of marine ecosystems, such as coral reefs, atolls, salt marshes, and mangrove forests. Losses of land and inundation are likely to be particularly severe in the densely populated deltas of the Mekong, the Ganges-Brahmaputra, and the Nile. Finally, adverse effects of climate change on agriculture and food security are likely to be concentrated in a number of developing countries where impacts will interact with other environmental stresses and chronic socioeconomic vulnerabilities (IPCC 2001b). New extremes in both temperature and precipitation are likely to pose formidable problems in areas already food insecure, particularly in Africa.

Within these critical regions and ecosystems, some currently vulnerable livelihoods are closely linked to resources at risk from climate changes (Downing 2002a). Small-scale farmers with limited ability to purchase materials to address changes in rainfall, stream flow, temperature, salinity, or other climate-based resources important to their livelihoods exist within many of these areas. Pastoral livelihoods in water-stressed, food-insecure regions of sub-Saharan Africa are currently under substantial resource competition pressures, which could be worsened under climate change scenarios. In areas where fishing is a major element of livelihoods, losses in fish habitats and reduction in catch may disrupt household incomes as well as the availability of fish protein in the diets of the poor.

This list of regions and livelihoods can easily be expanded to identify a number of broad types and areas likely to be at high risk. But as a first cut on the required knowledge base, it provides an initial qualitative assessment of some broad priorities. It is possible, we argue, to guide interventions aimed at reducing risks to the most vulnerable, by supplementing the broad scientific assessment of risk and vulnerability with participation that draws in the knowledge of those who will bear the risks or are responsible for managing them. Local knowledge can calibrate and deepen the more general knowledge of climate impact and vulnerability assessments.

Such assessment objectives, of course, raise questions as to whether existing data and methodologies allow assessments for future climate change that will be sufficiently robust to guide policy interventions. For the future stresses accompanying climate change—changes in temperature and precipitation regimes, severe storms, sea level rise—the IPCC assessments make clear that only broad regional patterns can be projected, lacking sufficient geographical and temporal specificity to be highly helpful for place-based and subregion-based vulnerability assessment. On the other hand, we know quite a lot about areas that are highly stressed by the scarcity of clean water, flooding, inadequate sanitation, food insecurity, and HIV/AIDS, health threats and scarcity of resources that are almost certain to continue.

Although vulnerability assessment is currently still at an early stage of development, particularly in regard to choice of indicators and availability of place-specific data, again many things are known regarding poverty, lack of social capital, gender inequality, and marginality that point to areas and groups at higher risk of complexes of stresses emanating from climate change and other globalization and regional development processes (Wisner et al. 2004). Indeed, assessments will in any event be made and decisions taken. Although the current state of assessment is clearly not as advanced as it could and needs to be, the state of current assessment and methodologies surely adds to the existing capability.

The Stockholm Environment Institute (SEI) conducted such an analysis in the Mekong Region of Southeast Asia (Stockholm Environment Institute 2001). Though not focused on climate change, the methodology developed is directly applicable to climate change impact analyses. This exploratory study sought to assess the potential effects of developments in the transportation infrastructure and energy system (especially dam building) on vulnerable communities, social groups, highly valued natural resources, and protected environments. SEI (2001) formulated a research plan that included identifying regions at high risk of adverse impacts that were, in short, highly vulnerable to prospective changes. Using geographic information systems, a series of maps depicting relevant data on naturally protected areas, flooding, proposed water dams, poverty, and indigenous groups were assembled and brought into interaction. The study then developed a collaborative process with a "panel of qualified observers" from knowledgeable local experts drawn from government agencies, NGOs, and communities, to identify the high-risk regions and to demarcate their boundaries.

Figure 4.1 shows that the consensus hot spots from the headwaters of the Mekong to Ton Le Sap in Cambodia are geographically diverse and face a wide variety of stresses and elements of vulnerability. The

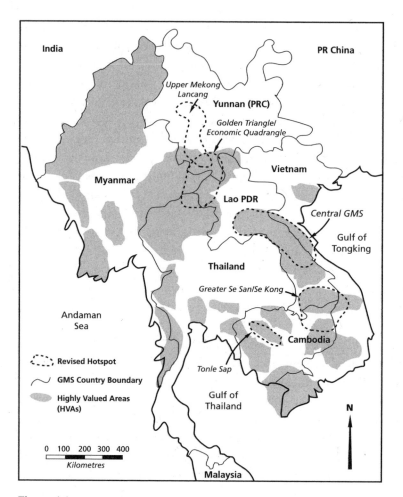

Figure 4.1
High-risk hot-spot regions in the Greater Mekong Region. *Source*: Stockholm
Environment Institute 2001.

exploratory process of expert elicitation needs further development but illustrates how local and other knowledge can be brought together in a participatory process to map high-risk or "hot spot" regions. Such a methodology, further improved and formalized, has high potential for analyses supporting assessment and decision making around climate change issues.

We conclude that current limits to knowledge need not prevent ethically based initiatives on adaptation. At the same time, such approaches need to be sensitive to the limits and uncertainties surrounding the knowledge base.

What Can and Should Be Done?

Recognizing the limitations of current abilities to identify precisely the most vulnerable people does not suspend the ethical obligation to act to avoid harm. Given the mounting evidence of ongoing climate change, adaptation cannot wait for an absolute, and perhaps unattainable, definitive identification of the most vulnerable peoples over the coming decades. Indeed, growing recognition of the coming changes and threats increases the obligation to act sooner. Some of the uncertainties identified above may be resolved over time, whereas others, such as long-term forecasting of social change, are almost guaranteed to endure. So uncertainty cannot be viewed as a barrier to action. Response needs to incorporate constructively current limits to knowledge as guidance into the necessary characteristics of immediate response and the criteria for selecting among adaptation options.

Despite the uncertainties that beset all adaptations to climate change, there are several efforts to scope the range of adaptation options and to offer guidance in adaptation decisions. Smit et al. (1999) identify two roles for adaptation research in the IPCC assessment process—as a part of impact assessment informing the issue of what adaptations are likely, and a normative role in addressing what adaptations are recommended. Table 4.1 summarizes the range of adaptation options and their attributes and addresses the issues of who adapts to what, when, and how, as well as the function or how the risk is handled, and suggests measures of performance.

Table 4.1
A typology of adaptations to climate change

Differentiating concept or attribute	Examples of terms used	
Purposefulness	autonomous	planned
	spontaneous	purposeful
	automatic	intentional
	natural	policy
	passive	active
		strategic
Timing	anticipatory	responsive
	proactive	reactive
	ex ante	*ex post*
Temporal scope	short term	long term
	tactical	strategic
	instantaneous	cumulative
	contingency	
	routine	
Spatial scope	localized	widespread
Function/effects	retreat, accommodate, protect prevent, tolerate, spread, change, restore	
Form	structural, legal, institutional, regulatory, financial, technological	
Performance	cost-effectiveness, efficiency, implementability, equity	

Source: After Smit et al. 1999.

A variety of adaptation options matches at least some of these descriptions, as climate adaptation is not new to human interactions with the environment. Some criteria for evaluation of adaptation options, such as costs, reversibility of impacts, benefits, efficiency, urgency, equity, informing long-term investments and implementability have been put forward (Smith 1997; Fankhauser, Smith, and Tol 1999; Smith et al. 2000, 229; Tol, Fankhauser, and Smith 1998). We seek below to elaborate on the equity considerations for evaluation of the management and performance of adaptation strategies.

Despite the lack of scientific certainty, there are several reasons to act quickly in support of adaptation of the most vulnerable to climate change using known strategies, such as those for natural hazard reduction or enhancing the reliability of water supplies and developing new strategies. Such a precautionary stance can aim to avoid potentially serious and irreversible harm, highly likely to accrue to the most vulnerable, and to types of losses that cannot be replaced or compensated for. Taken sooner, actions to increase adaptation, such as rehabilitation of marginal areas, can open a wider set of opportunities for later adaptation. These early actions are highly likely to be more cost effective than later actions. For example, investing in more protective building standards is generally less expensive than retrofitting a structure.

A precautionary stance to adaptation action is particularly important when the events threaten lives and the costs of total damages are difficult to calculate and perhaps impossible to compensate fully. In addition to the difficulties in comparing the relative and absolute values of loss among different groups, such as the poorer and wealthier, and identifying the near-term sociological consequences, the long-term costs of a climate-related disaster are uncertain. As in the case of Hurricane Mitch in Honduras or the 1998 floods in Bangladesh, for the most vulnerable, personal and household losses can be compounded by the long-term effects of disasters on national development efforts, infrastructure, and economies (IFRC 2002; Lewis 1999). The costs of lost opportunities and setbacks in development may extend over decades, although, over time, measures of their economic and human impact become increasingly difficult to track (IFRC 2002). The full costs of these events are likely to be incalculable.

Within such a precautionary approach, the management system will need systematically to monitor evolving patterns of vulnerability. The monitoring system should encompass both the climate and the societal processes involved in vulnerability, as changes in social circumstances, such as economic shocks, HIV/AIDS epidemics, and conflict, can turn a stable situation into a precarious one. Some current early warning systems, such as the Famine Early Warning System (FEWS), offer examples of effective integration of biophysical and social monitoring. More effort will be needed to understand the processes of recovering from impacts as damaged peoples and areas are likely to be more vulnerable to new events and stresses. Existing natural disaster research, however, provides only limited guidance in this realm.

Management institutions will also need to maintain sufficient flexibility to address the emergence of new scientific knowledge and substantial surprises that are possible within the current context of limited scientific certainty and ongoing social change (Barnett 2001a; Kates and Clark 1996). In coming years, models will improve their projections of climate impacts in terms of spatial distribution and types of changes. Nonetheless, it is likely that some unexpected events will occur. Because the interactions between climate and society are not well understood at present, changes in patterns of climate events are likely to reveal previously unrecognized patterns of dependencies through first, second, and higher order impacts.

Management institutions will also be required to make choices about which adaptive strategies to pursue. Despite current uncertainty, experience with natural disasters, environmental management, and sustainable development planning offers a wide variety of feasible options. Building social capacity, implementing technological solutions, encouraging changes in land use and many other options are potentially useful investments, but the scope of benefits, the relevance to local concerns, the efficiency, and the impacts and other characteristics of adaptation strategies will differ. In reducing vulnerability through adaptation, a key decision will be how to balance efforts to reduce exposure, decrease sensitivity, and increase resilience, or which of these to prioritize in any given situation.

Kates (2000) reviews five analogues to climate change from developing countries' experience in which he examined social costs to the poor (often the most vulnerable) associated with past adaptation strategies—the direct costs of adaptation, the costs of adapting to the adaptation, and the costs of failing to adapt—and found that the costs of these adaptations have been enormous. In summary, he cautions, "the linked tales of poor people and the environment tell of how one group's adaptation is another group's hazard" (p. 15) and that "if the global poor are to adapt to global change, it will be critical to focus on poor people, not on poorer countries" (p. 16), as the interests of these groups are not always the same.

The obligations derived from commitments to ethical principles and human rights point to three sets of characteristics that make some

Table 4.2
Ethical considerations in selecting adaptation strategies

Considerations	Applications in adaptation strategy
Avoiding harm and reducing risks	Timing of implementation—Preference should be given to strategies that aim to avoid harm rather than to compensate after the fact.
	Scope of risk addressed—Preference should be given to strategies that both reduce potential impacts and address the causes of climate change.
	Burden transfer—Preference should be given to strategies that reduce risk rather than transfer it to other places, populations, or the future.
	Liability—Preference should be given to policies that create liability for risks that cannot be eliminated or reduced.
Reducing vulnerability	Scope of social injustice addressed—Preference should be given to strategies that avert harm *and* address social processes contributing to vulnerability.
	Capacity building—Preference should be given to strategies that increase the capacity of the most vulnerable to manage risks on their own.
Supporting human rights and well-being	Human rights—Preferred strategies contribute to securing fundamental human rights and promoting social progress and better standards of life.
	Self determination—Preference should be given to strategies that respect the right to self determination through participatory processes that facilitate input into assessment of the relevance of vulnerability reduction adaptations as well as the range of options developed, offered, and supported.

adaptation options preferable to others as they contribute more broadly to the avoiding of harm and reducing the risk for harm, to increasing people's ability to cope with risks that cannot be avoided, and to reducing the threat of harm or level of vulnerability in ways that support human rights and social progress more generally. Table 4.2 identifies specific attributes of adaptation strategies that strengthen their contributions to social justice. We recognize that it may not be possible to achieve all of these in every situation, and that there will be trade-offs among them in any given case, but that each of them merit consideration as adaptation efforts should be consonant with higher aspirations for sustainable, just development.

Conclusion

Although substantial uncertainty surrounds climate change, we know that the most vulnerable people are also generally the most at risk, the least able to help themselves, the least responsible for the events to come, and the least likely to capitalize on adaptation opportunities in a timely manner. Limits to climate science, vulnerability theory, scale-sensitive indicators, and ability to forecast social changes combine to reduce precision in identifying the most vulnerable over the coming decades. But these limitations do not eliminate the ethical obligation to act to support building adaptive capacity and vulnerability reduction and to take into account what is known. Growing evidence of changes consistent with climate projections is increasing the obligation to act sooner, particularly with interventions that realize multiple goals. Experience of natural disasters warns us of potential human costs that cannot be fairly compensated by post facto responses.

Management systems that incorporate monitoring, early warning, learning, and flexibility can seek to keep pace with the dynamics of uncertainty and identify adaptation opportunities for the most vulnerable. Although we have yet to explore them, there are already a full array of potential adaptation strategies for most foreseeable impacts. Ethical obligations in this area offer further guidance in selecting among adaptation strategies and emphasize the related obligations to ensure access to these options and to the participation of those at highest risk in their selection and development.

Acknowledgments

The authors thank Tom Downing and reviewers for their helpful comments on this manuscript. We also thank Erik Willis of SEI-York for his cartographic contribution. All errors and shortcomings are the responsibility of the authors.

5

Is It Appropriate to Identify Winners and Losers?

Robin Leichenko and Karen O'Brien

The belief that climate change produces winners and losers is widely held. Yet there have been few systematic efforts to define "winners" or "losers" from climate change, and little attention has been given to the implications of the acceptance of the idea of winners and losers for questions of justice and equity in climate adaptation.

The use of a winners and losers framework places equity and justice at the forefront of efforts to develop strategies, mechanisms, and programs for adapting to climate change. It also underlines that some regions are expected to benefit from climate change. Yet identification of winners and losers is fraught with difficulties owing to differences in perceptions of what constitutes a win or loss and disagreements about the appropriate scale, time period, and level of aggregation at which to identify winners and losers. There is also a lack of consensus over the manner in which society as a whole might best address winners and losers, particularly with regard to the issue of compensation of losers.

In this chapter we explore the use of the framework of winners and losers in climate change research and attempt to reconcile its limitations with the need to address equity and justice in the assessment of vulnerability to climate change and in the actions to adapt to climate change. We begin by exploring definitions and theoretical perspectives on winners and losers. We then examine the use of the winners and losers framework in research on climate change impacts, and identify its problems in the context of adaptation. In the concluding section, we raise questions about the applicability of a winners and losers framework in climate change research. We suggest it is useful in highlighting justice and equity in relation to climate change impacts and adaptation, but that it does not ensure the use of equitable or fair procedures for allocating adaptation funds and prioritizing adaptation in one sector or location over another. These tasks require a more comprehensive understanding of what constitutes climate vulnerability and how this vulnerability can be reduced.

Defining Winners and Losers

The use of a winners and losers framework is by no means limited to climate change research. The notion permeates the natural and social sciences, playing a role in disciplines ranging from biology and ecology to history, political science, and economics (O'Brien and Leichenko 2003). Although nuances differ, there is a general understanding across all fields that winners gain something, whereas losers experience disadvantages or deprivations. However, there are many difficulties in defining winners and losers beyond this.

First, there is a need to distinguish between static characterizations of winners and losers that reflect current social, economic, or political inequities, and dynamic interpretations that emphasize identification of winners and losers after an event or longer term environmental processes such as climate change. In static characterizations, the labels of "winner" or "loser" are often used to make judgments that apply to the status quo. For example, nations with high per capita agricultural output may be considered winners, as compared to nations with low levels of output. Such static characterizations do little more than describe existing patterns of differentiation and inequality in the world. Dynamic characterizations, in contrast, express changes over time, as is the case of winners from climate change. Although the emergence of winners and losers in a dynamic context may, of course, reflect prior or existing inequities, the outcome may also exacerbate or ameliorate these inequities, or create new patterns of inequality.

Dynamic characterizations delineate between those winners and losers resulting from a specific, voluntary event from those resulting from larger structural processes. Voluntary winners and losers emerge from a competition or other interaction on the basis of specific rules. No winners or losers exist at the outset and the outcome is more or less undetermined. Participation in an interaction is typically voluntary and based on knowledge of the potential costs and benefits. In contrast, structural winners and losers emerge from larger societal processes, where the distribution of the impacts is unequal and gains and losses accrue differentially to participants. Participants do not typically choose to engage in the processes and do not fully know potential costs and benefits. Most winners and losers from climate change are structural rather than voluntary.

One can also make a distinction between absolute and relative winners and losers (Gruber 2000, 4). Absolute wins or losses are based on comparison of a nation's status prior to and following an event. If a nation is better off after an event, then that nation is considered an absolute winner. Relative wins and losses, in contrast, depend on comparison with the situation of other nations. If two nations are both made better off by an event, the nation that gains more is considered the relative winner; the nation that gains less is considered the relative loser. In the case of climate change, two nations may experience absolute productivity gains in agriculture such that both would be considered winners in absolute terms. In relative terms, however, the nation that gains more would be considered a winner, whereas the nation that gains less would be considered the loser. When it comes to the impact of climate change on biodiversity, all nations may lose in absolute terms, but the nations that lose most would be the relative losers.

A further issue that merits consideration when defining winners and losers is the question of self-identification. A nation-state may determine whether it has been made better or worse off in both relative and absolute terms as the result of climate change. A key advantage of self-identification is that the criteria that determine winning and losing, which may include productivity increases, reduced disaster-related insurance payments, better environmental conditions, and so forth, are based on internal standards, rather than on criteria imposed from outside. However, an important disadvantage of self-identification is the possible sense of victimhood or dominance for political, economic, or other motives. For example, nation-states with industrial policies that result in high levels of greenhouse gas emissions might over-identify as winners for domestic audiences, in order to avoid the short-term political and economic ramifications of acknowledging that these policies are detrimental in the long run, both globally and nationally. It can also be advantageous for a nation to identify itself as a loser from climate change, to enhance its ability to negotiate for advantageous policies, technological assistance, or compensation. For example, the availability of funds for adaptation under the so-called Marrakech Funds and the Global Environment Facility may encourage developing countries to over-identify as losers from climate change. External criteria and the appeal to the principle of impartiality is important in defining winners and losers in these circumstances.

Theoretical Perspectives on Winners and Losers

Although research on the multifaceted concepts and consequences of global change is still in its infancy, many of its notions of winners and losers can be traced to social and scientific theories, including neoclassical economics and political economy, rooted in the writings of Adam Smith, David Ricardo, and Karl Marx, and notions of evolution and "survival of the fittest" based on the work of Charles Darwin and others. Themes from these bodies of literature such as competition, adaptation, and adjustment appear in contemporary discussions about winners and losers under climate change.

Economic Interpretations of Winners and Losers

Two major paradigms explaining the emergence of winners and losers include neoclassical economics and Marxian political economy. Neoclassical interpretations stress the importance of a free market to provide signals to producers about the effects of environmental changes on input and output prices (Mendelsohn, Nordhaus, and Show 1994). Producers respond to these market signals and adjust input usage and output patterns, thus adapting to ongoing environmental changes. In the short term, winners will include the more efficient producers who best adjust to the new competitive environment, and losers will include those producers who are unable to adjust adequately. In the long run, inefficient producers (and the factors of production employed by them) are also expected to adjust to the new competitive environment by increasing their production efficiency, exploiting new niche markets, or finding employment in other sectors.

Theoretical perspectives based on Marxian political economy share a common foundation in the Marxian critique of capitalism, and include world systems theory and dependency theory. In contrast to the neoclassical approach, Marxian political economic perspectives suggest that winners and losers reflect biases inherent in the free market system of capitalism favoring the owners of the means of production. Expansion of capitalism exacerbates inequalities between capitalist and labor classes, as workers are further divested of control of the means of production (Goodall 1987). As capitalism expands, it increasingly transfers "surplus" value from the periphery to the core. Thus, it is not only laborers who lose, but also those living in rural areas, less-developed countries, and the "East," all of whom become increasingly dependent upon urban areas, advanced countries, and the "West" (Marx and Engels 1961, 17). In this perspective of climate change, winners and losers are considered logical outcomes of historical and contemporary social, economic, and political structures.

Ecological Interpretations of Winners and Losers

Social Darwinism and environmental determinism have frequently been used to account for winners and losers. Although both of these theories have been widely criticized, their remnants persist and underlie many contemporary discussions of global environmental change. A somewhat less cohesive paradigm of political ecology emanates from the Marxian political economy perspective described above, offering a contrasting explanation for winners and losers from environmental change.

Social Darwinist perspectives attribute tendencies for winning and losing to genetic and evolutionary explanations. This understanding is inspired by Darwin's theories of evolution and natural selection. Social Darwinism, as developed by Herbert Spencer in the late nineteenth century, argues that, like organisms, societies have evolved by a natural process whereby the fittest members survived and were the most successful. Social Darwinists, and later sociobiologists, thus integrated Darwin's ideas and his concept of "survival of the fittest" into theories about human society (Kaye 1997; Dickens 2000). Darwin's ideas on adaptation, mutation, and selection have been used in the social scientific theories of socioeconomic and sociocultural evolution (Koslowski 1996). The direct transfer of the notion of an inherent biological tendency for winning or losing to human society has also been used as an argument against government intervention to help disadvantaged members of society and as a justification for racism, elitism, and eugenics (Kaye 1997; Dickens 2000).

Environmental determinism is a related paradigm that lingers within contemporary explanations of winners and losers. Environmental determinism, which attributes human social and cultural behaviors exclusively to environmental factors rose to prominence in the early twentieth century (Huntington 1914; see Johnston et al. 2000). According to this paradigm, winners are associated with favorable environments conducive to productivity and efficiency, whereas losers are products of difficult, marginal, or hazardous environments. Environmental determinism informed the writings of early geographers such as Ellen Churchill Semple: "The debilitating effects of heat and humidity, aided by tropical diseases, soon reduce intruding peoples to the dead level of economic inefficiency characteristic of the native races" (Semple 1911). Views such as Semple's were vehemently disputed and eventually disregarded. As Carl Sauer noted, "[e]nvironmental response is the behavior of a given group under a given environment. Such behavior does not depend upon physical stimuli, nor on logical necessity, but on acquired habits, which are its culture" (Sauer 1941). Despite being discredited as a simplistic and racist approach, we shall see below that environmental determinism persists within the climate change literature and policy debates, albeit in a more discrete and sophisticated form.

Unlike social Darwinism or environmental determinism, which use biological or ecological phenomena to explain human conditions, political ecology draws upon social phenomena to explain environmental conditions. Blaikie and Brookfield (1987, 17) define political ecology as an approach that "combines the concerns of ecology and a broadly defined political economy." Although political ecology is not a theory of behavior, it brings together aspects of political economy, human and cultural ecology, and social theory to explore the causes and consequences of environmental and resource issues. Political ecology thus represents a move toward an integrated understanding of how environmental and political forces interact to mediate social and environmental change (Bryant 1992). Similar to the political economy perspective described above, winners and losers are considered a rational outcome of ongoing social and political processes. However, these processes interact with ecological conditions across different spatial and temporal scales to shape winners and losers. Winners and losers from climate change are not considered to be absolute, definitive, or predetermined, but rather are the consequences of nature-society interactions.

Winners and Losers: Naturally or Socially Generated?
Political economy and political ecology not only offer a contrast to neoclassical views but may also be contrasted with sociobiological and environmentally deterministic interpretations. Karl Marx was, in fact, "the first of many to charge that Darwin's theory of evolution was largely a projection of bourgeois competitive relations onto the realm of nature" (Kaye 1997, 23). The various ecological and economic positions discussed above can be distilled into two contrasting views of winners and losers. The first view, found in social Darwinism, environmental determinism, and neoclassical economics, suggests that winners and losers are a natural, inevitable, and evolutionary outcome of either ecological processes or the invisible hand of the free market. We refer to this first position as the NIE (natural, inevitable, and evolutionary) view of global change.

The second view suggests that winners and losers are created through inequitable processes that benefit some at the expense of others. This position, which we term the socially and politically generated (SPG) view, is linked to the Marxian political economy and political ecology views that emphasize the actions of human agents within the context of unequal social and political structures in the determination of winners and losers. Whereas the NIE view regards the "system" as working properly (with winners and losers as a consequence), the SPG position emphasizes that there is room for intervention to alter patterns and identities of winners and losers. As we discuss in the next section, both NIE and SPG interpretations of winners and losers are evident in climate change debates.

Winners and Losers in Climate Change Impacts Studies

The climate impacts literature discusses winners as having improved conditions, opportunities, positive effects, and benefits, whereas losers face negative effects and increasing vulnerability. Although winners and losers are frequently mentioned in discussions and debates, official documents such as the Intergovernmental Panel on Climate Change (IPCC) Assessment Reports avoid explicit reference to them, reflecting the political sensitivity of the topic. Nonetheless, evidence suggests that winners from climate change will include the middle and high latitude regions, which are expected to experience warmer summers and a longer agricultural growing season. Losers from climate change are expected to include marginal lands in Africa, which are likely to experience an increased frequency and magnitude of extreme events, particularly droughts, and countries with low-lying coastal zones, which may be damaged by more frequent storm surges or flooded by rising sea levels (IPCC 2001b; Fischer et al. 2001; Kasperson, J.X. and Kasperson, R. E. 2001b). The least developed countries (LDCs) are considered to be losers due to their higher vulnerability and lower adaptive capacity (Huq et al. 2003).

The perspective that winners and losers are natural, inevitable, and evolutionary (NIE) outcomes of environmental processes underlies many climate impact assessments. This perspective involves a view according to which climate sensitivity and biophysical vulnerability determine who is a winner and who is a loser. Indeed, if environmental determinism can be described as the idea that "the environment controls the course of human action" (Lewthwaite 1966), then examining the direct consequences of physical changes in the climate system for human systems invariably reflects an NIE perspective (Taylor and Buttel 1992; Demeritt 2001). Biophysical approaches to climate impacts based on hydrological models, crop yield models, and other dose-response models also include an NIE understanding of climate change winners and losers.

The concept of adaptation, which plays a prominent role in climate impact assessments, also reflects an NIE interpretation of climate change, particularly when it assumes that adaptation is spontaneous and "just happens." Adaptation refers to adjustments to a system in response to actual or expected physical stimuli, their effects, or impacts (Smit et al. 2000). The notion of adaptation draws upon ecological and evolutionary analogies such as resilience, sensitivity, flexibility, and viability (Smit et al. 2000). Many commentators regard adaptation as providing a possible "win-win" opportunity, in that adaptive responses generally involve actions that improve the environment, regardless of climate change (Carter 1996). For example, making more efficient use of water for irrigation in semi-arid regions would have a positive effect by reducing waterlogging and salinization even in the absence of climate change (Leichenko and Wescoat 1993). Nevertheless, it is possible that adaptation measures will reinforce rather than alleviate uneven distributions of power between and within social groups (see chapter 1). As Kates (2000, 7) notes, "adaptation, even by the invisible hand of the market, is not cost-free and does not yield the same benefits everywhere."

The Second Assessment Report of the Intergovernmental Panel on Climate Change (IPCC 1996) exemplifies the NIE approach. That report focused on assessing the sensitivity and vulnerability of systems to a range of potential climate changes, and then evaluating these systems in the context of future climate change scenarios. The report examined impacts on terrestrial ecosystems, aquatic ecosystems, food and fiber, human infrastructure, and human health. Biophysical impacts form the basis for most of the assessments reviewed in the report, directly determining the socioeconomic impacts. One of the conclusions of the Second Assessment Report was that "[p]eople who live on arid or semi-arid lands, in low-lying coastal areas, in water-limited or flood-prone areas, or on small islands are particularly vulnerable to climate change" (IPCC 1996, 24).

The Second Assessment Report did not explore the factors that contribute to vulnerability and adaptive capacity (Rayner and Malone 2001). This may indicate that these themes were not prevalent in the impacts literature assessed for the report. The Second Assessment Report came up with a general conclusion that "systems are typically more vulnerable in developing countries where economic and institutional circumstances are less favorable" (IPCC 1996, 24). The report did not address who in these countries are most vulnerable, where they are located within the countries (e.g., urban versus rural areas), or why they are vulnerable, aside from disadvantageous economic and institutional circumstances. Kelly (2000), however, challenges the deterministic "truism of global warming" that developing countries will be the greatest losers from climate change and sea level rise, suggesting instead that these countries may be better able to cope or adapt to climate change as a result of high levels of past and present vulnerability to climate hazards. Indeed, vulnerability to climate risks and other factors can be considered a driver for adaptive resource management (Adger et al. 2003b).

The alternative perspective, that winners and losers are socially and politically generated (SPG), is reflected in much of the recent social vulnerability literature (Bohle, Downing, and Watts 1994; Ribot 1995; Handmer, Dovers, and Downing 1999; Kelly and Adger 2000; Adger et al. 2003b). This literature emphasizes the social construction of vulnerability, focusing on the factors that underlie vulnerability to climate change rather than on the direct consequences of biophysical changes. Understanding the structures and causes of present-day climatic vulnerability is seen as critical to identifying and addressing winners and losers under climate change. Bohle, Downing, and Watts (1994) argue that current vulnerability differs widely between countries and social classes, varying over both time and space, and that climate change will have differential impacts on vulnerable groups. Even in arid or semi-arid lands, low-lying coastal areas, and water-limited or flood-prone areas, some will emerge as winners and some as losers, depending on the particular contexts and constellations of vulnerability. Furthermore, it is not adaptation *per se*, but rather the social, economic, and political *capacity* for adaptation that is seen as a key factor in determining winners and losers under climate change (Kelly and Adger 2000; Kates 2000).

A subtle acknowledgment of the social construction of vulnerability appears in the IPCC Third Assessment Report. The report recognizes that the consequences of biophysical impacts "can differ for members of the same community—as when some individuals or groups perceive an opportunity with change, and others experience a loss, thereby changing community dynamics and complicating decisions about how to adapt and the apportionment of costs of adaptation" (IPCC 2001b, 90). In shifting from an NIE to an SPG perspective on winners and losers, the Third Assessment Report also begins to address some of the issues that were lacking in the Second Assessment Report, including questions of equity, differential vulnerability within regions, and differing adaptive capacity (IPCC 2001b).

In terms of equity, the Third Assessment Report distinguishes between utilitarian approaches and other methods for comparing situations in which different people are affected differently. It acknowledges that the utilitarian rule (described in more detail below), which asserts that the rule with the best overall consequences is considered the best, is for the most part insensitive to distributional issues. However, it notes problems with other methods as well, including the difficulties in comparing well being across nations with measures such as GDP and the Human Development Index (HDI). The Third Assessment Report concludes that "economics may be able to highlight a large menu of distributional issues that must be examined, but it has trouble providing broad answers to measuring and accounting for inequality, particularly across nations" (IPCC 2001b, 125).

Assessments of winners and losers in climate change are also complicated by issues related to spatial and temporal scale. National level impact assessments are likely to yield different conclusions regarding winners and losers than regional or local level assessments (O'Brien, Sygna, and Haugen 2004). When results are aggregated across large spatial units, the net impacts can hide social and geographic variations, such that individual or regional winners and losers disappear within the aggregate outcome (Glantz 1995; Jones and Thornton 2003). For example, at the national level, agriculture in the United States is expected to benefit from climate change (Fischer et al. 2001; Reilly et al. 2003). Regional assessments, however, show that agriculture in the southern United States is likely to be adversely affected (Adams, Hurd, and Reilly 1999; Reilly et al. 2003). At the local and individual levels, some communities or farmers in the southern United States may nevertheless emerge as winners, depending on what they grow, how commodity prices are affected by supply changes in other regions or countries, and so forth.

Similarly, with regard to adaptation, the scale of analysis is crucial. At the national level, a country such as Norway is seen as having high adaptive capacity due to high income levels, an extensive natural resource base, good infrastructure, and other factors (O'Brien, Sygna, and Haugen 2004). Yet at the regional and local levels, many of Norway's remote, resource-dependent, northern villages have limited capacity to adapt to negative changes in the natural resource base such as changes in fish stocks that may result from climate change. By contrast, a developing country such as India that is highly dependent on agriculture might be seen to have a lower adaptive capacity to climate change at the national level. Yet across different regions India, some areas are likely to be much more capable of adapting than others depending upon the quality of local infrastructure, human capital endowments, levels of irrigation, and other factors (O'Brien et al. 2004b). Assessments of both the impacts of climate change and adaptation to climate change may thus produce different patterns of winners and losers, depending on the scale of analysis.

Assessments of winners and losers are also dependent upon temporal factors. Vulnerability is a dynamic concept that is subject to change over time, in response to structural economic changes and other external shocks (Leichenko and O'Brien 2002). Economic globalization may, for example, transform some climate change losers into winners if new economic opportunities arise. Alternatively, it may compound the negative effects of climate change and render some regions or groups as "double losers" (O'Brien and Leichenko 2000). In the long run, it is also possible that those assumed to be overall winners under climate change may in fact be or become losers in significant, important respects, as a result of political backlash or political and economic instability stemming from climate-related impacts in other countries or regions of the world. Furthermore, the magnitude of climate change over the long run may surpass critical thresholds of tolerance or trigger catastrophic events, thereby transforming short-term gains into long-term losses.

Finally, the metric or unit of analysis is critical to the conclusions of climate change studies. Tol and colleagues (2001) find that monetary estimates of climate change impacts lead to the conclusion that the world as a whole may win from climate change. By contrast, when aggregate assessments are based on estimates of the number of people that will be positively or negatively affected, the net global effect is negative. Although aggregation may provide policymakers with a single estimate that represents the magnitude of damages expected to occur at a global scale, such aggregation hides many critical issues and value-laden assumptions, which have a wide range of implications at the local level (Tol et al. 2001). For example, human life and health, security, and the continued integrity of the earth system can be considered important independently of human welfare. These impacts do not easily lend themselves to be monetized, which complicates issues of compensation (Müller 2002).

Addressing Winners and Losers

In addition to difficulties associated with identification of winners and losers from climate change, there is also a lack of consensus within the global change literature over the manner to address the winners and losers so identified. Issues of equity and compensation are particularly delicate within debates about climate change mitigation and adaptation, with differing positions often stemming from competing political philosophies and cultural frameworks (see O'Riordan and Jordan 1999). It is beyond the scope of this chapter to provide a comprehensive review of philosophical and cultural viewpoints regarding compensation (see Müller 2002; Rose and Kverndokk 1998, and discussions in chapter 3). The perspectives of utilitarianism and egalitarian liberalism, however, merit brief examination because they play a significant role in debates over how to address the inequitable outcomes of global change.

Utilitarian ideologies, as noted earlier, stress the importance of efficiency and agree that social arrangements should be judged by how they contribute to the sum of satisfactions available to individuals (Anderson 1990). With regard to climate change, winners and losers may be inevitable, but it is the aggregate balance of wins and losses that matters more than individual wins and losses. Abatement and adaptation strategies are thus selected based on criteria that maximize net economic welfare, even if this implies that benefits and costs are unevenly distributed (Nordhaus 1991; Rose and Kverndokk 1998; Rayner and Malone 2001).

Egalitarian liberals, by contrast, stress that the state should secure equal liberties for all citizens and that "inequalities of wealth and authority are just only if they result in compensating benefits for every-one, and in particular for the least advantaged members of society" (Rawls 1972, 15). Recognizing that winners and losers are socially generated, egalitarian liberals contend that it is the responsibility of society to address losers. Accordingly, losers under different abatement or adaptation strategies require some form of compensation or redress for the inequities suffered (Müller 2002).

Philosophical differences related to efficiency versus equity, combined with the differing NIE and SPG perspectives on the origins and defini-tions of winners and losers discussed above, also influence debates over procedures for deciding who receives compensation for climate change impacts and the types of adaptation measures that might be appropriate. Concerning compensation, the UNFCCC, the Kyoto Protocol, and the various decisions framed at Conferences of Parties (COPs) underscore the obligation of developed countries to assist developing countries to adapt, through finance, insurance, and the transfer of technology. For example, article 4.8 of the UN Framework Convention on Climate Change provides:

the Parties shall give full consideration to what actions are necessary under the Convention, including actions related to funding, insurance and the transfer of technology, to meet the specific needs and concerns of developing country Parties arising from the adverse effects of climate change and/or the impact of the implementation of response measures.

Under the UNFCCC, actions are supposed to meet the special needs and concerns of developing countries, particularly small island coun-tries, and countries with low-lying coastal areas; with arid and semi-arid areas; with areas prone to natural disasters; with high urban atmos-pheric pollution; with fragile ecosystems; and with economies that are dependent on income generated from fossil fuels. These criteria favor the NIE understanding of environmentally determined winners and losers, and at the same time emphasize the focus on mitigation in the UNFCCC (see Müller 2002). Although the highlighting of the particu-lar needs and circumstances of these groups reflects the reality of limited resources for addressing climate change, there are other principles that could be used to prioritize the distribution of these resources (Müller 2002).

Under the present political reality, socially and politically generated losers within developed countries are also not considered eligible for compensation. In other words, losers emerging within developed countries do not qualify for compensation, unless such compensation is administered through national-level programs. For example, resource-dependent communities in the United States that have experienced chronic economic distress may have adaptive capacities comparable to some of the LDCs (Rayner and Malone 2001; Glasmeier 2002). If climate change has negative impacts on agriculture and timber-related industries, the losses to these communities are unlikely to be addressed through current international arrangements.

Concerning adaptation measures, those who view winners and losers from an NIE perspective, which emphasizes differential physical impacts of climate change, may favor technological adaptation projects that directly address biophysical vulnerability (e.g., irrigation infrastructure or flood containment). Because winners and losers are often seen as the inevitable consequences of environmental factors, these types of adaptation responses can minimize the physical impacts of climate change and hence the number of losers. By contrast, those who adopt an SPG perspective, which views winners and losers as socially constructed, may place a greater emphasis on the need to address the structural factors that contribute to vulnerability and limit adaptive capacity. Enhancing adaptive capacity through livelihood diversification, land reforms, education, and so on, may be emphasized over concrete adaptation projects that call for technology and investments. This, however, requires more pragmatic rules with respect to funding and supporting adaptation to climate change, and treatment of adaptation more broadly as part of a a strategy for sustainable development (Huq and Burton 2003).

There is a growing mismatch between the international institutions that are evolving to address climate change adaptation as part of a global managerial discourse, and the needs of local communities to respond to present day variability and future climate change (Adger et al. 2001; Burton et al. 2002). Although it is tempting to use the labels of winners and losers as a means for directing or "managing" adaptation to climate change, the confounding factors described earlier in this chapter suggest that a simple binary categorization of winners and losers

may not provide a sound and equitable basis for action, as these categories are themselves fluid, dynamic, and relative, and depend, among
other things, on the level, time frame, and scale of analysis. However,
measures that address vulnerability as a socially, politically, and bio-
physically generated characteristic are likely to promote adaptations
to both present day climate variability and long-term climate change
that take into account issues of outcome and procedural equity (see
chapter 1).

The differing perspectives on adaptation to climate change can be
considered part of what Adger and colleagues (2003b, 180) describe as
the "dilemma at the heart of international action on adaptation to
climate change—the need for reductionist identification of the 'climate'—
related part of global social and economic trends, versus the desire to
see climate change as another important dimension of global environmental threats to development."

Conclusions

Acknowledgement of winners and losers from climate change is a necessary step in addressing equity and justice issues associated with climate
change impacts and adaptation. Recognition of the existence of different
perspectives on how to assess and address winners and losers will also
enhance climate change research in a number of ways. First, the difficulties associated with identifying winners and losers point to a need for
more explicit recognition of the role of scale, time period, and aggregation in considering who benefits and who loses from particular climate
policies at the global, national, regional, and local levels. In order to
avoid viewing winners and losers through a single, static lens, research
should incorporate multiple scales of analysis and should take into
account the possibility that the identities of winners and losers from
global change may shift over time.

Second, in light of the difficulties associated with identifying winners
and losers, there is a need to consider equitable compensation for the
impacts of climate change in a rigorous manner. To date, compensation
has received relatively little direct attention in the climate change literature. As the discussion above revealed, approaches to the challenge of

compensation will likely be influenced by underlying ideological perspectives (e.g., NIE and SPG, utilitarian and egalitarian), which will affect not only whether compensation is given, but also who is compensated and how compensation decisions are made. As the ongoing process of climate change continues, compensation is likely to become a central issue for policy negotiations.

Third, in light of the difficulties and uncertainties associated with the application of a winners and losers approach, it is useful to consider whether this type of binary framework is appropriate for consideration of broader questions related to equity and justice in adaptation to climate change. One advantage of the winners and losers framework is that it emphasizes the possibility of both positive and negative effects of climate change. The positive effects of climate change are often downplayed, yet recognition that winners are likely to emerge from climate change is essential to debates about equity and justice. At the same time, however, a winners and losers approach is inherently divisive, pitting diverse groups into adversarial positions. As such, it may be seen as an example of a dualistic approach that has long been criticized in social sciences. Poststructural critiques, in particular, emphasize the limitations posed by binary classifications (e.g., agriculture-industry, Fordist–post Fordist, North-South), suggesting that such dichotomies provide little insight into the underlying social and political processes that shape different outcomes, and may, in fact, serve to reinforce existing inequities (Sayer and Walker 1992; Goodman and Watts 1994; Jarosz 1996).

Finally, a related problem with the use of a winners and losers binary classification in climate change research is that it risks reifying biophysical interpretations of climate change vulnerability while downplaying the role of social and political factors in influencing differential vulnerability and shaping adaptive capacity. Under a binary approach, nations, regions, and populations are simply categorized as either winners or losers based on a series of biophysical measures such as changes in mean temperatures and rainfall amounts, with little attention to socially and politically generated differences in vulnerabilities to these changes. By the same token, adaptation strategies based on a winners and losers framework may tend to emphasize technological solutions. As shown throughout this volume, such actions tend to reinforce rather than alleviate inequitable distributions of economic and political power between and within social groups.

In light of these issues, Gibson-Graham's (2002, 7) critique of the local-global binary classification is perhaps equally relevant to the winners and losers classification: "Like all distinctions, this categorization enhances visibility but disintegrates upon inspection." Winners and losers are made visible through a binary framework, but this framework provides little basis for action. Without attention to the underlying differences in the socially constructed vulnerabilities of different populations, use of a winners and losers framework risks reducing climate change impacts into a simple accounting of biophysical changes. A winners and losers approach thus shows that there are inequities related to climate impacts, but it does not provide sufficient insight for addressing many issues related to social equity and adaptation to climate change. Equitable responses and adaptation strategies instead require a contextualized understanding of how climate change will affect systems and societies as a function of differential vulnerabilities.

Acknowledgments

Some of the material presented is based on O'Brien and Leichenko 2003. We thank the article's four original reviewers, M. J. Mace, as well as two anonymous reviewers for comments and suggestions on this chapter.

6

Climate Change, Insecurity, and Injustice

Jon Barnett

This chapter, like this book, is premised on five broad insights from research on the causes, consequences, and solutions to climate change. The first insight is that responsibility for climate change is not equally distributed; some people and groups have emitted more greenhouse gases than others and continue to do so and hence are more to blame. Second, climate change will not affect all people equally; some people and groups are more vulnerable than others. Third, this vulnerability is itself determined by political-economic processes that benefit some people and disadvantage others—with the disadvantaged frequently being the most vulnerable to climate change. The fourth insight is that climate change will compound underdevelopment because of these aforementioned reasons. Finally, climate change policies may themselves create unfair outcomes by exacerbating, maintaining, or ignoring existing and future inequalities.

This chapter adds a dimension to these insights about climate change by considering the way violent conflict creates multiple insecurities, including to climate change. So, although it begins by explaining the broad dimensions of climate insecurity, the chapter does not discuss the more popular assumption that climate change may cause violent conflict. Instead, it inverts the climate change-conflict relationship to explain the ways violent conflict is a powerful cause of climate insecurity.

Three main justice issues emerge from the way violent conflicts create climate insecurity. First, there is a political economy to climate insecurities—there are some political processes that have hitherto not been identified as either causes of insecurity or as justice issues. Second, the popular understanding of climate justice as equal distribution of costs and benefits among interdependent parties is about equity proper, rather than justice per se. This common understanding fails to capture many ethical and rights-based issues associated with processes that cause insecurity, and with the risk of irreversible losses. Finally, in terms of procedural justice, the limited capacity of most post-conflict countries, and their understandably different priorities, mean that international efforts to address climate change need to do more to foster the participation of this group of countries. Failure to do so means that their concerns are not taken into account, and that they are excluded in policies and measures designed to facilitate adaptation to climate change.

Climate Change as a Security Issue

Discussions about climate change and security are a subset of broader concerns about environmental security. The concept of "environmental security" has from the beginning been dominated by concern about environmentally induced conflict. However, it cannot be said with confidence that environmental change is an important contributor to violent conflict (Barnett 2001b; Gleditsch 2001; Levy 1995; Matthew, Gaulin, and Mcdonald 2003). The causes of violent conflict, particularly post–Cold War civil conflicts, are frequently complex and somewhat uncertain. Judgments about the effect of climate change on violent conflict must contend not merely with this uncertainty about conflict causation, but also with uncertainty about the way climate, ecological, and social systems will interact in the future such that violent conflict is more likely than would otherwise be the case. Because these things are unknowable, predictions of climate-induced conflict are untenable (Barnett 2003).

So, the argument that climate change is a security issue cannot be based on the notion that climate change will contribute to conflict. However, a number of researchers have argued that climate change is a security issue for certain communities, cultures, and countries (Barnett 2003; Edwards 1999; R. E. Kasperson and J. X. Kasperson 2001; Page 2000; Stripple 2002; Swart 1996). There are some particular climate risks that clearly constitute security issues, such as the loss of territory and sovereignty of atoll countries (Barnett and Adger 2003), collapse of the thermohaline circulation (Hulme 2003), or melting of the West Antarctic Ice Sheet (Vaughan and Spouge 2002).

Climate Insecurity and Justice: An Initial Consideration

This issue of climate insecurity becomes an issue of justice when one considers the causes of climate change and the determinants of vulnerability. Vulnerability to climate change is a matter of both biophysical risk and social vulnerability (Cutter 1996). Biophysical risk is in part a matter of chance—for example, that an individual is born in urban Europe as opposed to rural Eritrea—but also of class—for example, low-income urban residents tend to live in the most hazardous locations (Blaikie et al. 1994). Social vulnerability is in part a function of the availability of and access to human and social, economic and natural capital: the better the access, the more able the individual or group to manage and recover from an event (Adger 1999; Adger and Kelly 1999).

So the most climate insecure people will not be those who have the highest biophysical risks—if this were the case Japan would be as vulnerable as Papua New Guinea, and Las Vegas as vulnerable as Asmera. The most climate insecure people will be those who are highly exposed to biophysical risk and have little capacity to manage and recover from damaging climate events. Most of these people will live on the periphery of economic and political power. These may include farmers in Sub-Saharan African economies impoverished by colonization and structurally adjusted by "globalization"; coffee growers in the New Guinea highlands affected by declining terms of trade; landowners in the Solomon Islands dealing with environmental and social disruption due to forestry; remote indigenous communities in Australia and Canada dealing with the cultural legacy of colonization and political marginalization; and single mothers in Bangladesh farming small plots of flood-prone land. These people are among the least responsible for greenhouse gas emissions, but are among the most insecure to the effects of emissions. Climate change creates insecurity through the "double vulnerability" that arises when poverty is compounded by climate change (Barnett 2001b; O'Brien and Leichenko 2000). This is a justice issue because those that are least responsible for climate change are the most vulnerable to its effects.

Violent Conflict and Climate Vulnerability

Perhaps more than any other groups, societies in or recovering from conflict are vulnerable to climate change. There is much to be said about environment and development in societies experiencing and recovering from conflict; this discussion offers only a cursory introduction.

For the period 1946–2001 there were 225 armed conflicts, of which approximately 75 percent occurred within states (10 percent of these with direct participation from external states) (Gleditsch et al. 2002). Over the period 1989–2000 there were a total of 111 violent conflicts in 74 different locations (Wallensteen and Sollenberg 2001). The vast majority of these occurred within rather than between states. Since 1989, conflict has been increasingly restricted to developing countries (Gleditsch et al. 2002; Wallensteen and Sollenberg 2001). Some of these post Cold War conflicts, such as in Afghanistan, Sri Lanka, Algeria, Angola, Sierra Leone, Sudan, and Colombia, have been particularly protracted and intense, resulting in over a thousand battle deaths in most years. The five deadliest conflicts in the 1990s occurred in Rwanda (up to 1 million deaths), Angola (up to 500,000 deaths), Somalia (up to 300,000 deaths), Bosnia (up to 250,000 deaths), and Liberia (up to 250,000 deaths) (Murray et al. 2002, 347). About 90 percent of deaths in armed conflicts are civilian, and there are at least two and up to 13 people injured for every person killed (Murray et al. 2002). In 2002, there were 42 ongoing, predominantly violent conflicts that involved 31 countries (HIIK 2002). Of these, 16 were in Africa and 13 in Asia.

It is difficult to define *post-conflict*. There are uncertainties to do with timing because the formal cessation of hostilities does not necessarily mean that violent conflict is over; consider Iraq after formal hostilities ended on April 15, 2003, or that the annual number of violent deaths in El Salvador increased after the cessation of war (Pearce 1998). Further, there is no clear time beyond which a country ceases to be post-conflict; consider, for example, if Vietnam's development is now unaffected by the debilitating effects of the Indochina wars, or the Solomon Islands by the Second World War. The World Bank (1999a) avoids these problems by identifying post-conflict societies in terms of key factors, including an unstable security environment, significant disruption to the economy, full or partial collapse of the state, diminished civil society capacity, and widespread destruction of infrastructure.

For the purposes of clarity, table 6.1 identifies thirty-seven countries that are post-conflict, based on the surveys of the literature and identified post-conflict projects implemented by multilateral development agencies such as the World Bank, the International Monetary Fund, and regional development banks. This list is, of course, contestable. That many of these are still experiencing significant violence is testimony to the difficulties of identifying the end of hostilities, although for the purposes of this chapter the distinction between conflict and post-conflict is not overly important.

In the following discussion, *country* is taken to mean *society*, as it is the national level that is most discussed in the literature, and for which data is most available. However, it is well understood that vulnerability to climate change is a socially and spatially variable phenomenon, which, when coupled with the realization that within conflict situations there are clear winners and losers, means that national-level aggregate discussions such as these are imprecise. So, although a total of some 1.4 billion people live in the countries in table 6.1, not all these people are adversely affected by conflict.

Violent Conflict and Climate Insecurity

Table 6.1 offers some insights into the insecurity of post-conflict societies. The Human Development Index (HDI) is a composite measure based on life expectancy at birth, educational attainment (measured by adult literacy and enrolment in education), and real GDP per capita. It can be used as a crude proxy for social vulnerability to climate change because it captures some of the income, education, and health determinants of adaptive capacity. A low HDI on the scale of 0 to 1 suggests low adaptive capacity. By this measure, many post-conflict countries have high social vulnerability to climate change. Table 6.1 reflects the analysis of Project Ploughshares (2002) that half of the states in the

Table 6.1
Population, human development, and climate change in postconflict countries

Country	Population millions (2001)	Human development Index (HDI)	HDI Rank (of 176)	National communication to UNFCCC
Sierra Leone	4.6	0.275	175	No
Liberia	3.4	N/A	174(2001)*	No
Somalia	9.9	N/A	172(1996)+	No
Burundi	6.4	0.337	171	2001
Mozambique	18.2	0.356	170	No
Ethiopia	67.3	0.359	169	2001
Central African Repub	3.8	0.363	168	2003
D R Congo	49.8	0.363	167	2000
Guinea-Bissau	1.4	0.373	166	No
Chad	8.1	0.376	165	2001
Angola	12.8	0.377	164	No
Afghanistan#	23.9	N/A	N/A	No
East Timor±	0.8	0.421(1999)	159(est)	No
Rwanda	8.1	0.422	158	No
Eritrea	3.8	0.446	155	2002
Haiti	8.1	0.467	150	2002
Uganda	24.2	0.489	147	2002
Nepal	24.1	0.499	143	No
Republic of Congo	3.5	0.502	140	No
Sudan	32.2	0.503	138	2003
Burma	48.2	0.549	131	No
Cambodia	13.5	0.556	130	2002
Solomon Islands	0.5	0.632	123	No
Nicaragua	5.2	0.643	121	2001
Guatemala	11.7	0.652	119	2002
Honduras	6.6	0.667	115	2000
Algeria	30.7	0.704	107	2001
Iraq#	25.2	N/A	N/A	No
El Salvador	6.3	0.719	105	2000
Sri Lanka	18.8	0.730	99	2000
Palestine Territories	3.3	0.731	98	Israel (2000)
Azerbaijan	8.2	0.744	89	2000
Georgia	5.2	0.746	88	1999
Peru	26.4	0.752	82	2001
Bosnia-Herzegovina	4.1	0.777	66	No
Colombia	42.8	0.779	64	2001
Croatia	4.4	0.818	47	2002

Source: + Hassan 1998; UNDP 2003; *UNDP 2002b; ± UNDP 2002c; UNPD 2002a.
approximate location in country.

bottom third of the HDI ranking had experienced conflict since 1992, and that of Stewart and Fitzgerald (2001), who show that of the ten countries with lowest HDI's, eight have experienced recent conflict. Twenty-five countries in table 6.1 are in the bottom third of the HDI ranking.

As well as having high social vulnerability relative to most countries, many of the countries in table 6.1 must also contend with very high biophysical risk. It is notable, for example, that ten already experience water availability that the UNDP describes as being either "catastrophically" or "very" low (UNEP 2002b).

The ability of a society to meet food needs is indicative of its vulnerability to climate change. Violent conflict is strongly associated with malnutrition, high levels of which render a society vulnerable to famines triggered by climatic extremes. The majority of countries in table 6.1 have experienced famine or near-famine conditions in the past ten years, with the most protracted and recurrent food crises in flood- or drought-prone countries such as Eritrea, Ethiopia, Somalia, and Sudan. As of May 2003, the World Food Programme (2003) had identified significant food shortfalls in twenty of these post-conflict countries: Afghanistan, Algeria, Angola, Burundi, Central African Republic, Chad, Democratic Republic of the Congo, Eritrea, Ethiopia, Guinea-Bissau, Haiti, Iraq, Liberia, Mozambique, Nepal, Rwanda, Sierra Leone, Somalia, Sudan, and Uganda.

That post-conflict countries are highly prone to food shortfalls is testimony to the destructive effects of conflict on the ability of social-ecological systems to meet people's basic needs. This chapter now examines the adverse effects of violent conflict on the three determinants of adaptive capacity—the availability of and access to natural, economic, and human and social capital.

Violent Conflict and the Environment

Although there is a need for more research on the environmental effects of war (Brklacich et al. 2004), it is evident from a number of studies that violent conflict affects abundance and access to natural capital (Westing 1980, 1997). In many cases, spending on fighting is sustained by resource extraction without conversion of the returns to productive economic capital (Brzoska 1999). Preparing for war also often denies the use of land for productive purposes (Barnett 2001b).

In some cases resources are the main source of conflict. This is true of timber in Cambodia and Burma, gems in Afghanistan, and diamonds in Sierra Leone (Collier 2000; Le Billon 2001). Renner (2002) estimates that access to resources was the primary motivation to 25 percent of violent conflicts in 2001. In these conflicts, control and rapid exploitation of resources is of paramount concern and environmental impacts are not considered; logging in Burma, diamond mining in Angola, gemstone mining in Cambodia, and oil extraction in Sudan, for example, generate more environmental damage than would otherwise be the case in peaceful and legitimate resource extraction operations.

Violent conflict almost always involves denial of strategic space to opponents, sometimes with associated environmental impacts. The use of defoliants in Indochina, burning oil wells in Kuwait, the crop destruction in Eritrea, and draining marshes in southeastern Iraq are all examples of techniques used to deprive combatants of space and time to impede effectiveness (Westing 1980). Landmines are the ubiquitous means for denial with the most devastating long-term implications for access to natural capital. There are over 100 million landmines lying in 90 countries, denying access to land for productive purposes (Faulkner and Pettiford 1998; ICBL 2002). It costs between US $300 and $1,000 to clear a single mine (HRW 1993). Countries particularly affected include Angola, Afghanistan, Cambodia, and Iraq. So in these and other ways violent conflict has a major negative effect on many societies' and individuals' entitlements to natural resources, and this is a key factor in vulnerability to climate change.

Violent Conflict and the Economy

As well as having adverse effects on the abundance of and access to natural capital, conflict affects the amount and distribution of economic capital, at least in those places where conflict is conducted. Spending on weapons has opportunity costs for spending on social and environmental activities that can promote sustainability (Adeola 1996). Conflict is detrimental to foreign investment and aid, and what aid is received is directed into short-term crisis response rather than longer term development. Conflict disrupts domestic markets and in most cases export income from formal trade falls (Stewart, Huang, and Wang 2001). It depletes and damages the labor force, creates a massive health burden, and destroys productive assets such as factories and communications and energy infrastructure (Stewart and Fitzgerald 2001). Conflict is frequently associated with increased foreign debt (usually incurred for weapons purchases), capital flight, and increased income inequality (Stewart, Huang, and Wang 2001). Conflict reduces food production (Messer, Cohen, and Marchione 2001) and usually causes a reduction GDP per capita growth rate (Stewart, Huang, and Wang 2001). For example, the World Bank (2003a) finds that in El Salvador, income per capita would have been almost twice as high in 2000 had the conflict there been avoided. Conflict also creates poverty (Goodhand 2003), and poverty is a key determinant of vulnerability to climate change.

Violent Conflict and Society

Violent conflict also damages human and social capital. Labor is the principal capital asset of households in developing countries. The death of some 15 million people due to conflict in these countries between 1950 and 1990 is a huge loss for household and aggregate production (Stewart and Fitzgerald 2001). In many wars, a major objective is to remove local inhabitants from desired territory—including sites of resource extraction—by killing, starvation, and terror campaigns involving rape and amputation. Due to physical and mental trauma, those that are not killed have significantly reduced productive capacity. Importantly in terms of climate hazards, displacement, trauma, and the denial of access to resources means that many people in post-conflict societies are highly vulnerable to external shocks (Schafer 2002).

Conflict also creates refugees and internally displaced people. There were 19.8 million people of concern to the United Nations High Commission on Refugees (UNHCR) at the start of 2002, including 12 million official refugees (UNHCR 2002). The largest refugee populations are from war-torn countries, including Afghanistan, Angola, Burundi, the Democratic Republic of the Congo, Iraq, Somalia, and Sudan. The Global IDP Project (2003) estimates that throughout the world, 25 million people have been internally displaced by conflict.

These are people who have not crossed national borders and so do not qualify as "refugees." There are 13 million IDPs in Africa alone, with eight million in Angola and Sudan. Refugees and IDPs are extremely vulnerable to multiple sources of insecurity such as food shortages and disease, and are arguably the most vulnerable people to climate extremes.

Conflict is also highly damaging to social capital because it disrupts market exchanges, frequently involves social predation along vertical (class) or horizontal (ethnicity) lines (Goodhand and Hulme 1999), and breaks apart communities and families through displacement. Few institutions remain unaffected by violent conflict, and post-conflict societies are characterized by a lack of confidence between political and economic actors and weak or nonexistent judicial, financial, fiscal, administrative, and regulatory institutions (World Bank 1999b). Many are in situations of chronic political instability, with large extra-legal economies (Schafer 2002).

Conflict frequently weakens trust in the state, and post-conflict governments often lack legitimacy due to a lack of experience, low capacity, community expectations that are not easily satisfied, and nascent structures for communication of and community participation in decision making. Judicial systems and the rule of law are similarly transitional and ineffective, which, coupled with the need for restorative justice and reconciliation, creates a deficiency in conflict resolution capacity at precisely the time when it is most needed.

These environmental, economic, and social effects of violent conflict are important determinants of vulnerability to climate change. Violent conflict restricts people's access to human and social, economic and natural capital, which are necessary to adapt to climate change. Although more research is necessary to investigate the links between violent conflict and adaptive capacity, from the preceding discussion one can be reasonably conclude that violent conflict has negative effects on all the broad determinants of adaptive capacity identified by the Intergovernmental Panel on Climate Change (Smit and Pilfosova 2001). For example, violent conflict reduces the amount of economic resources available to individuals and states to pay for adaptation responses; suppresses the extent of technological development and diffusion needed to select the most appropriate adaptation responses; suppresses educational attainment and restricts the policy learning necessary for understanding the nature of climate changes, to devise appropriate responses, and successfully to implement those responses; damages the infrastructure needed to deliver resources and information throughout a society; and weakens institutions and social cohesion, and undermines the possibility of collective responses to changes. Indeed, it is reasonable to suggest that no other process can rival violent conflict for its ability to render a population vulnerable to climate change.

Conflict, Climate Insecurity, and Justice

The contributors to this volume have all argued implicitly or explicitly that the political-economy processes that create vulnerability are most often in some way unjust. This is particularly true in the case of violent conflict. Whereas largely economic processes such as unequal trading relationships, structural adjustment programs, and class structures are all forms of structural violence where the effects of actions may be unintentional and unobserved by the actor, with most forms of violent conflict actions are deliberate, somatic, and the effects are generally obvious to the perpetrator (after Galtung 1969). In violent conflict, people deliberately seek to kill or maim each other, with the specific intention of creating "winners" and "losers." Rarely, if ever, is violence "just," even if it is increasingly difficult to distinguish between civilians and combatants in many of the so-called new wars (Duffield 2001; Kaldor 1999).

However, attributing blame for violent conflicts is not easy because understanding of the causes of violence is imperfect. Nevertheless, many wealthy (and high greenhouse gas emitting) countries share some responsibility for violent conflicts because the roots of many conflicts lie in disruptions caused by colonization and antecedent wars. Many recent conflicts are to some extent continuations of Cold War conflicts where there was significant (if not always overt) involvement and arms transfers from super powers and regional powers. Examples include conflicts in Afghanistan, Angola, Chad, Democratic Republic of the Congo, El Salvador, Ethiopia, Iraq, Somalia, and Sudan. It has also been argued that through domestic reforms and the creation of "shadow economies," the trade-liberalizing, state-minimizing development programs advocated by the Bretton Woods institutions have created and sustained conflicts in places that were already to some extent vulnerable (Chossudovsky 1998; Duffield 2001; Fitzgerald 2001). Developed countries and their multinational companies are also beneficiaries of the "conflict trade" that is an essential part of the political economy of many conflicts (Cooper 2002). This includes trade in weapons, which are an important factor in the initiation, intensity, and duration of violent conflicts.

So many of the least vulnerable, most wealthy, largest emissions-producing societies are partly responsible for creating the structural conditions that produce and sustain many of the most extreme episodes of violence, which in turn structure insecurity to climate risks. The case of East Timor is an example of the compounded injustices associated with violence and climate insecurity. East Timor is one of the world's least developed countries. In 2001, GDP per capita was estimated to be US $478, infant mortality was 80 deaths per 1,000 live births, 420 women died for every 100,00 live births, and 45 percent of children under five years old were underweight (UNDP 2002c). This low level of development is a result of Portuguese colonization, severe fighting during the Second World War, and Indonesian colonial rule.

Indonesia's invasion of East Timor in 1975 would have failed but for U.S. supplies of OV10 Bronco jets, napalm, and M16 rifles to Indonesia (Jardine 1995; Kohen and Taylor 1979). It resulted in the death of 60,000 Timorese in the first two months, and the loss of up to 200,000 people due to death and emigration between 1973 and 1975 (Chomsky 1995). Still more violence and economic damage was caused during a period of violent retribution perpetrated by the Indonesian military and militia groups after a UN-sponsored referendum on August 30, 1999, in which the people of East Timor voted for independence from Indonesia. During the following weeks, a quarter of the population was forcibly deported into the Indonesian territory of West Timor (UNDP 2002c). This violence caused GDP to fall by 25–30 percent in 1999 (Hill 2001). As a result of this violent history, 97 percent of people in East Timor have experienced at least one traumatic event in their lives (Modvig et al. 2000).

East Timor is an agrarian society, with agriculture accounting for 85 percent of employment, 40 percent of GDP, and 90 percent of foreign exchange (East Timor Planning Commission 2002). Some 75 percent of the population lives in rural areas and the majority of people are engaged in subsistence production (UNDP 2002c). Yet ecological services have been severely affected by Indonesian colonization, including significant amounts of deforestation and defoliation under Indonesian rule (using U.S.-supplied weapons) (Bouma and Kobryn 2004). A heavy dependence on subsistence production, poverty, and environmental degradation make many people in East Timor highly vulnerable to drought. For example, the FAO (2003b) estimated that 150,000 people would require food assistance between October 2003 and March 2004. The bulk of East Timor's present and future social vulnerability to climate change can be attributed to colonization, war, and occupation. Climate insecurity is the latest manifestation of deeper and more brutal injustices.

Implications for Climate Policy

The particular vulnerability of post-conflict countries to climate change presents two challenges to climate policy. First, it is doubtful that climate change will ever have the same magnitude of impact on societies that war has and is likely to have. As a policy and justice problem, climate change is not the highest priority for post-conflict countries. They must contend with more immediate and pressing problems such as displaced persons, physical and mental trauma, and the availability of weapons.

Climate change activities may, of course, have some additional benefits in countries where there are severe biophysical risks. For example, in East Timor, soil erosion, deforestation, uncertainty about the extent and location of water resources, lack of water resource infrastructure, lack of advanced agricultural technologies, and a lack of climate records and monitoring, among many other things, render much of the population vulnerable to El Niño–induced dry periods. If climate funding mechanisms can help implement disaster management and early warning systems, reforestation, soil conservation, water resource infrastructure, food security measures, and the development of meteorological services, then the UNFCCC may contribute to immediate development problems in East Timor in a substantial way (Barnett, Dessai, and Jones 2003; Wasson 2001). Indeed, such activities, if implemented carefully, may contribute to peace building. The UNEP (2003) has made a similar argument about the benefits of the UNFCCC to Afghanistan.

So, the mitigation and adaptation activities under the UNFCCC need to be streamlined into sustainable development planning for post-conflict countries to be able to participate in and benefit from them. It is only through addressing immediate problems and the short-term returns from doing so that climate change policy and research can assist post-conflict countries. A procedurally just UNFCCC would make it worthwhile for these countries to commit scarce human resources to climate negotiations by providing a reasonable expectation that they will receive assistance for sustainable development. At present, the pool of potential funding is low, uncertainty about success is high, and the time and capacity requirements to participate in the convention and apply for funding are considerable.

The second challenge the case of post-conflict countries presents to climate policy stems from the ethical dissonance between the equitable solutions to climate change and the deeper substantive justice problems associated with violence and climate insecurity. Most of the literature on climate change policy is concerned with the fair distribution of costs within and between generations, taking into account both the costs of impacts and the costs of measures to reduce emissions (see Arler 2001; Azar 2000; Müller 2001; Toth 1999; Wiegandt 2001). Thus, climate policy is for the most part seeking equity—the fair distribution of costs and benefits among interdependent parties (after Paterson 2001). Justice, I propose, has a deeper meaning in that it intuitively refers to two additional issues: the risk that something unique and irreplacable may be lost—for example loss of life, loss of places, and loss of species (see Schneider, Kuntz-Duriseti, and Azar 2000); and the way past injustices structure vulnerability to climate change. This more substantive notion of distributive justice is in sharp contrast, and is far more than, the value of equity as it is commonly understood (as fair distribution). So, following this distinction, even if the UNFCCC resulted in an equitable distribution of the costs of reducing emissions, this might be far from a just solution. A truly just solution would be based on a broader spatial, temporal, and ethical analysis of the political and economic relationships among societies.

Conclusion

Examination of the relationships among insecurity, violence, climate change, and justice shows the extent to which climate change is a cross-cutting and complex problem. It also highlights the way the boundaries between the remits of various international environmental and development institutions, and between these and other international institutions such as the UN Security Council, are constructed and policed so that the artifice of policy impedes action on the real and complex problems that structure insecurity.

At best, the climate change regime can assist in remedying the effects of climate insecurity, whereas addressing the deeper political economies that produce insecurity is a far larger task. It would require arresting the processes of exchange—of raw materials, of labor, of knowledge, of weapons—that enrich and empower some and impoverish and disempower others. In short, addressing the political economy of insecurity would require a whole range of activities that are not merely about the environment, nor even just about "development," but are, more broadly, about peace and justice.

7

Adaptation: Who Pays Whom?

Paul Baer

The problem of adaptation to climate change is complex and multifaceted. However, I argue that there are two simple questions at its core: what actions should be taken to prevent or reduce harm to be caused by anthropogenic climate change, and who should carry the costs of those actions? In this chapter, I focus on the latter question, concerning *liability* for the funding of adaptation. I argue that obligations for funding adaptation are based on ethical principles governing just relationships between individuals in a "life-support commons," which are essentially the same as the norms of justice governing other forms of harm. Simply, it is wrong to harm others by abusing a commons, and if one does, one owes compensation.

In this view, ethics and justice address the rights and responsibilities of individuals; obligations between countries are derivative, based on the aggregate characteristics of their populations, and pragmatic, given the existing state system. Furthermore, liability can be disaggregated in other ways. As I argue, it is equally important that the distribution of liability can be differentiated between classes within nations. A stylized quantitative exercise applying these principles of justice to the adaptation problem in the final part of this chapter suggests net liability from the North to the South, but also net liability for adaptation from wealthy classes in the South.

Adaptation in the Negotiations

The United Nations Framework Convention on Climate Change (UNFCCC) gives limited attention to adaptation to climate change.[1]

Only in the last few years, with the creation of the Least Developed Countries (LDC) Fund and the Special Climate Change Fund (SCCF) under the UNFCCC, and the creation of an Adaptation Fund under the Kyoto Protocol, and the support for National Adaptation Plans of Action (NAPAs) have delegates and advocates begun to focus seriously on the problems of adaptation and adaptation funding.

Given the disproportionate share of emissions from the industrialized countries of the North and that the developing countries of the South are more vulnerable to climate impacts,[2] plausible interpretations of "common but differentiated responsibilities"[3] imply that the North should shoulder the major part of the costs of adaptation. Funding by industrialized nations for the Special Climate Change Fund and the LDC Fund, whose mandates include adaptation-related activities, establishes the validity of this argument. However, contributions to those funds are voluntary and small and not tied to responsibility.

To the extent that these arrangements are precedents for adaptation funding, they partially address the problem of common but differentiated responsibility; all the donors to the SCCF and LDC fund are wealthy countries with significant responsibility. However, the funds' voluntary nature allows other countries with equal or greater wealth or responsibility to avoid paying for adaptation. Moreover, the Adaptation Fund applies only to Kyoto parties, letting the UNFCCC parties that have not ratified Kyoto off the hook.

It seems likely that Northern governments are resistant to explicit claims for "polluter pays" liability for adaptation investments because there is a clear link between current responsibility for adaptation and eventual liability for compensation for actual climate damages. Northern governments might reasonably fear that acknowledging such claims would obligate Northern countries to the largest share of a potentially enormous financial liability.

Direct "polluter pays" liability has been avoided so far by emphasizing ability to pay rather than responsibility for climate change, while continuing to give rhetorical support to the importance of responsibility. The strong correlation between responsibility and capacity has allowed this compromise to justify an initial round of adaptation-related funding. However, reliance on capacity as the basis for sharing burdens implies that the magnitude of funding is determined by capacity limits or, in the end, on the limit on willingness to pay. When legitimate claims for adaptation funding or for residual impacts of climate change exceed the magnitude of about US $1 billion per year currently on the table,[4] the questions of ethical and legal liability will come to the forefront. My goal in this chapter is to contribute to this emerging discussion by framing the problem as one of liability for harm in a commons, and showing that there are established principles in ethics and law that should guide the development of the relevant rules and institutions.

The Climate System as a Life-Support Commons

References to "the global commons" and "the atmospheric commons" are fairly frequent in contemporary discourses on global change.[5] Those who use the terms tend to have fairly strong normative perspectives. Yet analyses of "commons problems" have developed a language that downplays normative judgment. In this literature, a unifying focus has been the concept of *externalities*, human actions that create nonpriced benefits or uncompensated harms to others than the actors themselves.

Externalities are related to other concepts such as "common goods," "public goods," or "collective action problems" (Cornes and Sandler 1996; Kaul, Grunberg, and Stern 1999; Oakerson 1992). The classic "commons," such as the village-controlled sheep-meadow made famous by Garret Hardin (1968), represents only one, albeit the best known, type of such goods. Analysis of "common-pool resources" has led to important distinctions between unregulated "open access" and regulated "common property" resources, and to extensive empirical and theoretical work concerning their governance (e.g., Burger et al. 2001, Ostrom 1990).

However, the problem of adaptation to (and compensation for) climate harm focuses not on sharing the sink capacity of the "atmospheric commons,"[6] but rather on the climate as a system whose modification brings harm through various pathways. Economists and others have generalized this type of common goods problem as "public bads," of which air and water pollution are examples. They belong to a broader category of "public goods," which are *non-rival*—their consumption by one party does not decrease the value to another party—and *nonexcludable*—it is difficult to prevent people from making use of them.[7] From this perspective, "climate stability" is a public good.[8]

Most public goods, such as street lights and national defense, are produced at a cost. The problem is the funding of optimal provision when there is an incentive to free ride. The problem with climate stability and clean air and water is different. These public goods exist prior to human intervention but can be degraded by human actions that cause physical harm to other people who depend on these goods in different ways. I suggest that the climate system, like clean air and water, should be considered a *life-support commons*.[9]

From an abstract perspective of individual (or corporate) incentives, life-support commons are similar to other public goods—an actor who pollutes a life-support commons can avoid costs while capturing private benefits unless a regulatory system exists to sanction "free riders." In economic terms, the problems are the same: balancing the sum of private benefits with the sum of social costs.[10] But the moral structure of the problem is different. In a life-support commons, the question of *the right not to be harmed* comes to the forefront. This moves us from economics and political science to ethics and law.

Ethics and Law in a Life-Support Commons

The ethical structure of the climate change problem is simple: deliberate acts that release greenhouse gases for one party's benefit harm others.[11] Limiting this harm by reducing greenhouse pollution—the primary objective of the UNFCCC—is one response. Another—my focus in this chapter—is establishing responsibility, and thus legal liability, for the harm caused by climate change.

That it is wrong to harm others (or risk harming them) for one's own gain is as close to a universal ethical principle as I am aware of. This principle can be justified in many ethical or moral frameworks, from divine revelation to deontological ethics to social contract theory.[12] It is an example of what some philosophers call common (or commonsense) morality (Beauchamp 2003; Portmore 2000) There is also a corollary principle, which is that if one does such harm to another, one owes compensation (Shue 1999).

Of course these principles are not absolute—in practice, there are many other relevant considerations, such as the relative size or importance of the benefit and harm, the cost or difficulty of preventing the harm, or the social relations between the parties. Laws and customs that govern particular people and activities represent the working out of these principles in the real world. One aspect of this dynamic is the creation of *rights*, which can include both the right to carry out an activity and the right to protection from harm from the actions of others. These rights are embodied in criminal law, which establishes penalties for violations of rights to protection from harm to person or property, and in common (civil) law, which allows injured parties to obtain compensation from the responsible parties.

The legal perspective is important because there are critical legal precedents that bear directly on the climate problem. In particular, western law has developed strategies for dealing with several aspects of the climate problem that are common to harms caused by many kinds of pollution. These include consideration of the separation in time and space of cause and effect, the scientific uncertainty of the causal chain, the collective nature of both the causal agents and the harmed parties, and perhaps most critically, the question of intent and the predictability of subsequent harm at the time that the actions were taken (Brennan 1993; Penalver 1998).

One important way in which modern law has dealt with harm caused by pollution of a life-support commons is through the creation of standards of acceptable risk. Environmental laws and regulations that have health-based standards (such as the requirement to protect the public health with an "adequate [or ample] margin of safety") are referred to as "rights-based" regulations (Powell 1999). Those that create a numerical standard for risk[13] create what I call a "statistical right" to protection from environmental harm, and violation of the standards can be subject to criminal penalties similar to other violations of rights to protection from harm to person or property.

Even where criminal sanctions are not in place, harm caused by pollution is subject to *tort law*—civil law allowing harmed parties to obtain compensation from the party causing the harm. Compensation can be *fault based* (based on the intent or the negligence of the party causing the harm) or it can be based on *strict liability*. The latter does not require finding fault—it simply requires that the product or process of a given enterprise be shown to have caused the harm in question. Case law and legal reasoning in the United States concerning environmental issues (so-called toxic torts) have evolved to address the issues of probabilistic and fractional causation. These cases are directly relevant to harms from climate change (Brennan 1993).

Fault-based liability has at least two justifications: a utilitarian basis related to social welfare gains from the deterrent effect, and a fairness basis in the "corrective justice" achieved by having the party causing the harm directly reimburse the victim (Perry 1992). Although these two conceptions have some different consequences (for example, punitive damages make sense only under a deterrence-based justification), they are not the main concern here. The important point is that several ethical principles that coexist in our society support liability for fault-based injuries. Such fault-based liability would clearly apply to damage caused by greenhouse pollution emitted since the time when the risks of anthropogenic climate change were widely recognized.

The moral logic of strict liability is less obvious. Why should I be responsible for harms I could not know I was causing, and thus could not have prevented? This is a common argument against liability for climate harm based on historical emissions. However, the argument *for* strict liability is also reasonable: if there are unexpected harms from some activities, should not the party that benefited from the actions bear their costs, rather than the victims (Keating 1997)? Strict liability has been upheld in a wide variety of tort cases (Brennan 1993) and has been codified in the U.S. Superfund legislation, which holds polluters liable for the cleanup costs of hazardous wastes even if the wastes were not known at the time to be harmful.[14]

The preceding discussion is meant to establish three main points: that the underlying structure of the climate change problem, that of regulating polluting behavior in a life-support commons, is well understood; that the ethical norms for behavior in such a commons are fairly clear; and that these ethical norms are well established in national contexts and codified in national law, in part through regulation that may involve creation of "statistical rights" and in part through tort law that includes both fault-based and strict liability. The question that arises is whether these ethical and legal principles should apply in a global life-support commons. My claim is that they should and that to some extent they do.[15]

International law reflects ethical norms for governing a life-support commons in its rhetoric (so-called soft law—see Dimento 2003). The Stockholm Declaration of 1972 declares in the famous Principle 21 (reaffirmed in Principle 2 of the Rio Declaration) that states have "the responsibility to ensure that activities within their jurisdiction or control do not cause damage to the environment of other States or of areas beyond the limits of national jurisdiction." The importance of liability is further recognized in Principle 22, which declares that "States shall cooperate to develop further the international law regarding liability and compensation for the victims of pollution and other environmental damage caused by activities within the jurisdiction or control of such States to areas beyond their jurisdiction" (UN Conference on the Human Environment 1972). The UNFCCC is itself an example of the recognition of the ethical principles governing a global life-support commons.

However, international law regarding compensation for pollution has not been implemented and the UNFCCC avoids establishing any legal liability for harm caused by anthropogenic climate change.[16] Given the ethical consensus in soft law, the reasonable conclusion is that the economic and political interests of polluters have so far outweighed ethical norms when it comes to the practical establishment of rights in a global commons. This chapter seeks to contribute to making those norms and rights legally enforceable.

Operationalizing Liability and Responsibility

Creating a framework for liability for climate damages and adaptation funding requires moving from the general discussion of ethical and legal principles to specific definitions and indices. I will first address the question of *legitimate claims* (the costs that must be paid), and then the question of *responsibility*.

Defining Legitimate Claims

What would constitute legitimate claims for payments for current and future climate harms? Costs associated with climate damages can be divided into at least two types: adaptation costs and residual damages (Tol and Verheyen 2004). Conceptually, residual damages are easier to identify, whereas in practice the difficulties of attributing particular climate damages (such as storm or drought damage) to anthropogenic climate change poses difficult problems. In comparison, it is conceptually difficult to identify what the appropriate level of investment in adaptation should be, but it is relatively straightforward to identify the investments that are actually made.[17]

There are few precedents for investments that protect from the effects of pollution. Some legal settlements have relocated communities when it has been impractical to clean up a toxic hazard.[18] But toxic pollution operates through biological mechanisms for which there is no obvious adaptation. Therefore, most legal settlements focus on cleanup, which is analogous to the mitigation of greenhouse gas emissions.[19]

Because climate change creates harm through macroscale physical impacts rather than through biological toxicity, there are many actions that can be taken to reduce the risks of harm associated with anthropogenic climate change.[20] It makes sense to undertake such actions in advance even when they are costly, rather than waiting for the harm and providing compensation—some of those entitled to and requiring compensation may be dead.

There are two different reasons for proactive adaptation. One is that there is a right to be protected from harm caused by others, which implies that all adaptation expenses required to reduce risk to an "acceptable" level (to provide a given "statistical right" to protection) are justified.[21] The other is a cost-effectiveness argument: it is often less expensive to invest proactively than to wait and compensate for the harm. This is the logic of insurance policies for buildings that require the installation of sprinkler systems.

Negotiating an acceptable definition of legitimate adaptation claims will be a difficult exercise, but it will no doubt draw upon both of these justifications for the level of funding. Similarly, it will be difficult to establish a mechanism that balances "polluter pays" responsibility for residual damages with the difficulty of attributing such damages to anthropogenic greenhouse gas emissions. For the purposes of this chapter, what matters is that there are ethical bases and legal precedents for negotiating some level of financial liability for the legitimate claims of potential and actual victims.

Defining Responsibility

Above I argued that causal and moral responsibility are both justifications for the "polluter pays" principle in a life-support commons. It is not a legally or philosophically complete argument, but I believe its conclusions are robust and that they provide the justification for further development of climate law that takes account of historical emissions.

There are many different ways historical emissions could be accounted for. These issues have been discussed in debates over using a responsibility index to allocate reduction targets,[22] rather than liability for adaptation or compensation.[23] First, how should we estimate *causal* responsibility? That is, what is the appropriate mapping between emissions and impacts? The causal chain is quite complex and suffused with uncertainties. Greenhouse gases cause increases in radiative forcing, the effects of which depend on the extent and duration of the gases' accumulation in the atmosphere. The remaining atmospheric stock from a country's emissions, which one can estimate using a carbon cycle model, is thus one plausible proxy for causal responsibility. Another possible proxy is the increase in global temperature from the time-integrated increase in radiative forcing.[24]

A second question is how to treat *moral* responsibility. Although I argued that ignorance of harmful effects does not eliminate ethical and legal liability, there is little doubt that it is a relevant factor in considering exactly how liability should be limited. In discussing responsibility for climate change, this has often meant choosing a cutoff date, prior to which emissions are not counted in a responsibility index. The year 1990 is often mentioned as a date beyond which knowledge of the harm from greenhouse gas emissions was no longer plausibly deniable (e.g., Tol and Verheyen 2004); selecting an earlier cutoff date can be thought of as making a compromise between strict and fault-based liability.

A third question is which gases and sources should be counted. This has practical aspects, such as the availability and reliability of data on the emissions of various greenhouse gases, as well as more subjective aspects, such as choices among methods for comparing various greenhouse gases.[25] How to count emissions from land use change also raises difficult questions—some countries deforested centuries ago and now have regrowing forests, whereas others are now extensively clearing land for agriculture, energy, and timber. Simple arguments that such emissions should or should not be counted are unlikely to be persuasive.

In addition to these questions, other issues such as the attribution of emissions to importers or exporters, changes in national borders over time, and the distinction between luxury and subsistence emissions, all bear on the question of an appropriate index of responsibility. But perhaps the greatest issue is the imperfect correlation between responsibility and capacity (ability to pay); that is to say, between historical emissions and current wealth. Some countries with high cumulative per capita emissions have remained (or become) relatively poor; some countries have become wealthy with relatively low emissions.

There are many ways one could modify an index of responsibility to account for capacity; for example, a "pure" index of responsibility (in which the emissions from all countries or regions are treated in the same fashion) could be scaled by a factor such as the percentage over or under the global mean per capita income (Hayes 1993; Smith, Swisher, and Ahuja 1993). In practice, developing an acceptable index of greenhouse liability from metrics of responsibility and capacity will not be easy. As with all such negotiations, countries will put forward formulas that favor their own interests, and find ways to justify them as fair. However, if there is to be anything approximating the necessary funding for adaptation and fair compensation for harm, such a formula will be necessary.

A Quantitative Model Using Real Data

In this section I develop a framework for calculating *net greenhouse liability* based on indicators for responsibility and legitimate claims. I present the framework at a general level, with an indication of its flexible application across different definitions of the indicators and for different groups. I then generate an example looking at net North-South liability (using the Annex I and non–Annex I definitions from the UNFCCC), at the net liability of different income groups in both North and South, and at selected regions and countries.

Estimation of legitimate claims for adaptation and residual impacts of a given community, class, or country is difficult. For the sake of my indicative calculation, I make the assumption that *claims are to a first order equal per capita*. This flies in the face of conventional wisdom that poor people and poor countries are more vulnerable to climate change than rich people or rich countries.[26] However, one could also argue that to the extent that property is also eligible for protection through adaptation (and for compensation if damaged), the greater amount of property at risk in rich countries would counterbalance the greater bodily risk of death and injury in poor countries.[27]

The point is that even if one makes a "conservative" assumption of equal per capita legitimate claims, the disparity in responsibility results—as the calculations below will demonstrate—in large net liability from wealthy to poor, whether at the country, regional, or class level. As the climate negotiators begin discussing how much should be spent on adaptation globally, this calculation can provide a method for estimating a reasonable lower bound for justified adaptation funding.

Definitions

As I argued in the previous section, responsibility for climate change is complex and controversial, and a wide variety of indicators of responsibility are defensible. For the reasons I outlined, I believe that cumulative emissions should form the indicator of responsibility. I use it for estimating liability in the following calculations, allowing various modifications in a sensitivity analysis.

Responsibility   The general framework allows the various indices to be calculated for arbitrary groups, whether they are countries, regions, or classes. For each group I define the responsibility r_i as the fraction of total responsibility, based on appropriately modified cumulative greenhouse gas emissions. For my reference case I use cumulative emissions of CO_2 since 1950 from fossil fuel combustion and cement manufacturing, with various modifications as a sensitivity analysis.

Legitimate Claims   For each of the selected groups, the total legitimate claims C are:

$$C = \Sigma c_i$$

where the claims c_i of each group would be identified by a common process or formula. As I suggested above, for this exercise I assume claims are equal per capita.

Net Liability   Where c_i is the monetary value of a group's legitimate claims, then the group's net liability L_i is simply equal to its responsibility-weighted share of the total claims minus the value of its own legitimate claims:

$$L_i = r_i \cdot C - c_i.$$

If we accept the premise of equal per capita claims, then a group's claim c_i is simply equal to its population share p_i times the total claims C. Thus the net liability L_i can be calculated as

$$L_i = r_i \cdot C - p_i \cdot C$$

or

$$L_i = (r_i - p_i) \cdot C.$$

A group is thus liable to pay compensation if its share of responsibility is greater than its share of population, or alternatively, if its per capita responsibility is greater than the global mean.

Results

With a given definition of responsibility, the fractions r_i and p_i are empirically determined, and a group's net liability as a share of total claims will be determined independently of the magnitude of total claims. To make a concrete calculation example, I use data from the World Resource Institute's Climate Analysis Indicators Tool (CAIT).[28] Table 7.1 shows results of this calculation of net liability for Annex I and non–Annex I countries. The first row shows cumulative CO_2 emis-

Table 7.1
Net liability of Annex I and non-Annex I regions for cumulative CO_2 emissions from fossil fuel energy and cement manufacture since 1950.

	Annex I	Non–Annex I
Cumulative emissions (GtC from energy and industry, 1950–2000)	154	56
Fraction of responsibility r_j	0.72	0.28
Population 2000 (billions)	1.17	4.73
Fraction of population p_j	0.20	0.80
Net liability as a fraction of vulnerability $(r_j - p_j)$	0.53	−0.53
Net liability based on total adaptation claims of $50 billion/yr ($billion/year)	26	−26
Net per capita liability ($/yr)	22.5	−5.6

Note: See text for discussion of row entries.

sions since 1950 from fossil energy and cement manufacture. The second row translates this into the fraction of responsibility. The third row gives the population in 2000, and the fourth row the fraction of total population. The fifth row calculates net liability as defined above by subtracting the fraction of claims (by assumption the same as the population fraction) from the responsibility fraction.

The aggregated net liability, together with actual population, gives the per capita share of net liability. However, because this would be a small and hard to interpret number, I have used an arbitrary estimate of total claims of $50 billion per year for an interpretation of both aggregate and per capita net liability.[29] Table 7.1 shows that Annex I countries have a net liability equal to 53 percent of total claims, which would translate into $26 billion dollars per year; the non–Annex I countries would be owed those amounts. In per capita terms, it would come to about $22 owed per Northerner (resident of an Annex I country), and about $6 owed to each Southerner (resident of a non–Annex I country).

The difference between the $26 billion in net flows and the $50 billion in total claims constitutes "internal" funding of adaptation—money owed from Northerners to Northerners and from Southerners to Southerners. I take up this issue again below. However, first I want to show the results of a sensitivity analysis based on alternative definitions of responsibility.

Sensitivity to Alternative Responsibility Indices

Table 7.2 shows net liability for Annex I and non–Annex I countries, the United States, the European Union,[30] China, and India, based on five other possible responsibility indices. In addition to cumulative CO_2 from fossil energy[31] (the reference case in table 7.1), table 7.2 shows net liability calculated on the basis of (1) cumulative CO_2 emissions since 1850 for fossil CO_2; (2) cumulative fossil CO_2 emissions since 1990; (3) cumulative CO_2 emissions from all sources (including land use) since 1950; (4) contribution to atmospheric CO_2 stocks from fossil CO_2 emissions since 1950 (which takes account of absorption by sinks), and (5) temperature change from fossil CO_2 emissions since 1950. Calculations for remaining carbon stocks and temperature change come from WRI's CAIT spreadsheets and use algorithms described in the CAIT documentation.

The figures in table 7.2 are net liability as defined above, that is, net of equal per capita claims; adding back the population fraction (shown in the first row of table 7.2) to each of the values in the subsequent rows gives the value of the responsibility index itself (share of global emissions on the specified basis). Although two significant figures and no range of uncertainty are presented, the combination of data uncertainty and (in the last two cases) model uncertainty should make it clear that these numbers have wide confidence intervals.

The resulting pattern is unsurprising given the global distribution of emissions over time. Extending responsibility back in time shifts the burden to the North, whereas shifting it closer to the present shifts the burden to the South. Including additional sources of CO_2 such as land use changes shifts the burden to the South, as does accounting for sinks. Values based on cumulative temperature change are similar to values based on cumulative emissions for the period from 1950.

This is by no means an exhaustive list of the permutations of even the selected factors, to say nothing of accounting for non–CO_2 gases, or for more subjective definitions of responsibility such as subsistence vs. luxury emissions.[32] The maximum and minimum values shown at

Table 7.2
Sensitivity of net liability to alternative definitions of responsibility index for aggregate emissions

Definition of Responsibility	Net liability as a percentage of total global claims					
	Annex I	Non-Annex I	U.S.	EU-15	China	India
Population Fraction 2000 (percent)	19	78	5	6	21	17
Cumulative CO_2 from Energy, 1950–2000 (%)	52	-52	22	12	-12	-14
Cumulative CO_2 from Energy, 1850–2000 (%)	57	-56	25	17	-14	-15
Cumulative CO_2 from Energy, 1990–2000 (%)	42	-41	19	8	-7	-13
CO_2 from all sources incl. land use, 1950–2000 (%)	32	-31	12	7	-11	-15
Change in Concentrations, CO_2 from Energy 1950–2000 (%)	50	-50	21	11	-11	-14
Change in Temperature, CO_2 from Energy 1950–2000 (%)	53	-53	22	12	-12	-15
MAX	57%	-31%	25%	17%	-7%	-13%
MIN	32%	-56%	12%	7%	-14%	-15%

the bottom of table 7.2 vary by about a factor of two for all selected regions and countries except India, but importantly the sign is the same for all formulations of net liability. Thus the direction of financial flows is not sensitive to the definition of responsibility.

Disaggregation by Class

I suggested above that the underlying principles of responsibility that are relevant for greenhouse liability are not based on nations except as a matter of pragmatism. The same distributional principles that apply between nations should apply within nations, with increased liability for those who are more responsible.

Information on the distribution of emissions within countries is fairly scarce. Furthermore, when accounting for historical responsibility, problems of aggregation will become even more difficult at the subnational scale. However, as there is a strong correlation between income and emissions, and between present income and past income, for the sake of illustration, I use current income distribution as a proxy for historical emissions.[33]

Information on income inequality is reported on a national basis. Income distribution by quintile is available for 116 countries,[34] including all but the smallest Annex I countries and most of the large non–Annex I countries. To estimate the income by quintile for the Annex I and non–Annex I regions, I take the median value for each grouping (which vary only slightly from the non-population-weighted mean) of the countries for which data was available. In addition, to estimate the relative responsibility of the highest income groups in each region or nation, I also estimate the income fraction of the highest decile, with a simple assumption that the highest decile receives two-thirds of the income of the highest quintile. The results, based on the reference case of cumulative fossil fuel and industrial CO_2 emissions since 1950 (presented in table 7.1), appear in tables 7.3, 7.4, and 7.5.

Table 7.3 shows the income distribution data itself, including the estimated aggregated values for Annex I and non–Annex I groups and for all the top deciles. Table 7.4 shows the net liability for each income group in each country or region, assuming equal per capita claims, and

Table 7.3
Percentage of total income for five regions or nations by quintile and for top decile

Region or country	Quintile 1 percent	Quintile 2 percent	Quintile 3 percent	Quintile 4 percent	Quintile 5 percent	Top decile percent
Annex I	7.9	13.1	17.3	22.6	38.9	25.9
Non–Annex I	5.6	10.1	14.8	21.3	48.0	32.0
United States	5.2	10.5	15.6	22.4	46.4	30.9
China	5.9	10.2	15.1	22.2	46.6	31.1
India	8.1	11.6	15.0	19.3	46.1	30.7

Table 7.4
Net liability as a percentage of total global claims, by income quintile, or decile, based on cumulative fossil CO_2 emissions since 1950 and the assumption that emissions responsibility is proportional to current income

Region or country	Quintile 1 percent	Quintile 2 percent	Quintile 3 percent	Quintile 4 percent	Quintile 5 percent	Top decile percent
Annex I	2	6	9	12	24	17
Non–Annex I	−14	−13	−12	−10	−3	1
United States	0	2	3	5	11	8
China	−4	−3	−3	−2	0	1
India	−3	−3	−3	−3	−2	−1

the reference-case responsibility index. Table 7.5 shows for each income group the dollar liability per capita associated with $50 billion in total claims, as in the earlier reference example. Again the two significant figure percentages (and the to-the-dime calculation of monetary liability) hide large uncertainties from many sources.

Tables 7.3–7.5 show that, given the definition of responsibility, the highest decile in the South has a small positive net liability, and that the poorest quintile in the North has very low liability. In the United States, liability increases more rapidly with income than in Annex I overall. The top quintile in China has small positive liability, whereas in India, even the top decile has negative liability.

Table 7.5
Dollar value of net liability per capita, based on $50 billion in total claims, by income quintile or decile

Region or country	Quintile 1 US$	Quintile 2 US$	Quintile 3 US$	Quintile 4 US$	Quintile 5 US$	Top decile US$
Annex I	3.8	11.8	18.1	26.1	50.8	70.5
Non–Annex I	−7.4	−6.8	−6.2	−5.3	−1.6	0.6
United States	3.9	16.2	28.1	43.9	99.6	135.6
China	−7.1	−6.4	−5.5	−4.2	0.1	2.9
India	−7.7	−7.5	−7.4	−7.1	−5.6	−4.7

Interpretation and Caveats

As I noted above, these calculations are sensitive to a large number of subjective assumptions, and should be taken as strictly indicative. Although this paper does not present a more comprehensive sensitivity analysis, the model calculations provide a framework for one. The general patterns of net liability remain fairly robust, whatever the assumptions.

It should be clear from the presented examples that although one can specify assumptions to allow arbitrary precision in calculation, it would be a mistake to seek a single "correct" formula and attempt to parameterize it precisely. Rather, the framework allows comparison of liability "scenarios." The previous discussions concerning ethics and law provide arguments why some scenarios may be normatively preferable to others, arguments that are only meaningful in the context of the real world of international politics.

Conclusion

The arguments and calculations in this chapter raise more questions than they answer. Yet in the face of the inadequate measures that have been undertaken to date, they support international legal liability for adaptation to climate change and compensation for climate harm. The basis for legitimate claims for adaptation funding, and for the establishment of liability tied to responsibility for emissions, is shown to lie in ethical and legal norms of behavior in a life-support commons. These principles underlie domestic pollution regulation and environmental tort law, and have been endorsed rhetorically in international law. It is now time to implement them globally.

On the basis of an assumption that the legitimate claims for adaptation funding are distributed globally on an equal per capita basis—a conservative assumption compared to usual conclusions that developing countries are more vulnerable and will require greater investment to adapt—net North-to-South liability is shown to lie in the range of 30–60 percent of total claims. A reference case using cumulative emissions from fossil and industrial CO_2 limited to the period 1950–present shows the net liability of the North to be equal to 53 percent of legitimate adaptation needs. Using a reasonable value of $50 billion in annual claims, this is a debt of about $22 per year for each Northerner and a credit of about $6 per year for each Southerner.

However, this liability is unequally divided between classes in the North and South. In the reference case, using the first-order approximation that emissions are proportional to income, the wealthiest decile in the North has 17 percent of net liability, compared to 2 percent for the lowest quintile in the North, whereas in the South, the top decile has a small positive liability (1 percent of total claims) in spite of the South's net negative liability, whereas the poorest quintile has a credit equal to 17 percent of total claims.

As noted throughout this chapter, these numbers are based on plausible but nonetheless controversial assumptions, and given the uncertainty in the data, should not be considered to be "precise" even for those assumptions. They are offered here as a contribution to efforts to conceptualize, and eventually negotiate, an adequate and equitable adaptation and compensation regime, in which "polluter pays" becomes more than an empty promise.

Acknowledgments

I gratefully acknowledge the contributions of Neil Adger, Tom Athanasiou, Steve Gardiner, Barbara Haya, Richard Howarth, Saleemul Huq,

M. J. Mace, Richard Norgaard, Jouni Paavola, Richard Plevin, Steve Schneider, Roda Verheyen, two anonymous reviewers, and the participants in the Justice in Adaptation to Climate Change conference at the University of East Anglia and the Stanford Environmental Forum where I presented earlier versions of this chapter. All remaining errors of fact and value are my own.

Notes

1. Article 4, Paragraphs 1(b), 1(e), 3, 4, and 8 address adaptation and funding for adaptation. See chapter 3 for details.

2. Annex I countries have a fifth of global population but contribute up to three-quarters of anthropogenic greenhouse forcings, depending on how responsibility is apportioned. The IPCC acknowledges disproportionate vulnerability of the South due to dependence on agriculture and lack of resources for adaptation (IPCC 2001b).

3. The "common but differentiated responsibilities" is the most frequently cited phrase because it appears in UNFCCC Article 3 on Principles. It also appears in Article 4 on Commitments in the context of measures including support for adaptation.

4. At COP6-bis in Bonn in 2001, the EU, Canada, Iceland, New Zealand, Norway, and Switzerland pledged to contribute €450 million annually by 2005 to the voluntary funds. With total CDM revenue running well under US $1 billion (den Elzen and de Moor 2002), the 2 percent surcharge for the Adaptation Fund will not add much to this.

5. Four books published since 1990 have been titled "The Global Commons."

6. The "atmospheric commons" is shorthand for the system of atmospheric, oceanic, and terrestrial sinks, which remove or store greenhouse gases. I have analyzed equitable sharing of global greenhouse gas sinks in detail in Baer 2002. See also Baer et al. 2000 and Athanasiou and Baer 2002.

7. "Public goods" are at times divided up further into "pure," "impure," "club goods," and "joint products." See Cornes and Sandler 1996.

8. "Climate stability" is a relative term in this context, meaning stability of the means and variability within historical experience.

9. I believe that this is an original formulation, although this concept is implicit in the literature, and at least one author has referred specifically to "common pool life support functions" (Rees 2002, 39).

10. Cornes and Sandler (1996) use the framework to analyze problems from military security to agricultural research to climate change.

11. I emphasize only that the polluting activities were deliberate, not that pollution itself was deliberate or that the harm they cause was understood at the time.

12. This principle does not hold in utilitarianism, which would permit harming others for personal benefit as long as the benefits outweigh the harms. The use of utilitarianism to justify cost-benefit analysis of problems such as climate change is one reason many people reject it.

13. For example, section 112 of 1990's Clean Air Act amendments, which regulates hazardous air pollutants (HAPs), authorizes the U.S. Environmental Protection Agency to delete a category of stationary sources of HAPs if the risk of premature mortality to the most exposed individual is less than one in one million (Powell 1999).

14. Superfund legislation is known as CERCLA, the Comprehensive Environmental Response, Compensation and Liability Act of 1980. See Revesz and Stewart 1995 or Stern-Switzer and Bulan 2002.

15. *Prima facie*, the rightness or wrongness of imposing harm on another person should not depend on their geographical location or political community. More robust philosophical arguments for the extension of ethical obligations to people in other countries have a long history; see, for example, Shue 1996 and Singer 2002.

16. Tol and Verheyen (2004) discuss the responsibility of states for pollution under international law, noting that in the UNFCCC negotiations the industrialized nations resisted state responsibility for climate change impacts. They also note that the small island states issued a declaration that signing the treaty did not renounce their rights under international law concerning state responsibility.

17. This is also a problem of "additionality" or "incremental costs"—separating the costs of an investment into the parts that are necessary specifically to reduce the harm from anthropogenic climate change, and the parts that are primarily motivated by other factors.

18. Love Canal is the most famous case. See Fletcher 2002.

19. There are *behavioral* adaptations to toxic pollution—such as not eating contaminated fish—that parallel behavioral adaptations to climate change. There has been little discussion of the costs of such actions.

20. As noted in the IPCC's Third Assessment Report, "There are many arbitrary lists of possible adaptation measures, initiatives or strategies that have a potential to moderate impacts." (Smit and Pilifosova 2001). See Fankhauser 1996, and others.

21. A combination of global mitigation investment and local adaptation investment is needed to reduce risk to acceptable level. That is to say, needed adaptation funding depends on the extent of mitigation.

22. An early contribution to this discussion is Hayes and Smith 1993. Following Brazil's pre-Kyoto proposal that burden sharing among Annex I countries be based on historical contribution to temperature (UNFCCC 1997), several analyses have assessed its ethical justification (Neumayer 2000) and technical difficulties (den Elzen and Schaeffer 2002). The World Resources Institute has produced a typology of responsibility indicators (Baumert and Markoff 2003).

23. Tol and Verheyen 2004 is an exception.

24. This underlies the Brazilian Proposal on historical responsibility.

25. The IPCC has established a method for comparing greenhouse gases on the basis of "Global Warming Potentials" (IPCC 1996). It has spawned a literature of critiques, defenses, and alternatives. See, e.g., Shackley and Wynne 1997, and Fuglestvedt et al. 2003.

26. The IPCC's Third Assessment Report notes that "the effects of climate change are expected to be greatest in developing countries in terms of loss of life and relative effects on investment and the economy" (IPCC 2001b, 8). Estimates such as that of Tol (2002) show net positive GDP impacts in developed countries compared to net negative impacts for most developing countries at 1°C of warming.

27. Putting the property of the wealthy in opposition to the lives of the poor is deeply problematic. However, although protecting lives and health should be the priority in adaptation, property deserves protection as well. In poor countries, an equal per capita share of the money to be used for adaptation will go primarily to reducing bodily risks, with sufficient funds to remain for protecting a greater proportion of property in poor countries than will be protected in rich countries.

28. WRI's Climate Analysis Indicators Tool is based on data from the Carbon Dioxide Information and Analysis Center, the Energy Information Administration of the U.S. Department of Energy, and the World Bank, and is available at <http://cait.wri.org>.

29. The US $50 billion per year figure is arbitrary but not unreasonable. Approximately 200 GtC of carbon were emitted globally from fossil fuel combustion between 1950 and 2000. Suppose we were to retroactively tax these emissions for the marginal damages they will cause—the classic Pigovian justification for pollution taxes. Estimates for this "social cost of carbon" vary, but Pearce (2003) argues that the "base-case" estimate is in the range of US $4–9 per ton of carbon (tC). This would value the damages from the historical emissions at US $800–1800 billion dollars. If this were to be paid off over 20 years (during which time another 200 GtC may have been emitted), it would amount to US $40–90 billion dollars per year. Note that Pearce's estimates were a response to a paper prepared for the British government (Clarkson and Deyes 2002), whose best-guess estimate was much higher: £70 tC (about US $130 tC by today's exchange rates), which would value the cumulative emissions since 1950 at over US $26 trillion.

30. Based on the 15 nations of the "old" EU.

31. CO_2 from cement manufacturing is included in "fossil energy."

32. See Agarwal and Narain 1991 and Agarwal, Narain, Sharma 1999 for luxury versus subsistence emissions, accounting for fair use of global oceanic sinks, and other issues, which are framed in the context of the allocation of emissions rights but are highly relevant to this discussion.

33. I realize this is a problematic assumption. Additional data concerning the distribution of current and historical emissions within countries would be desirable.

34. Income distribution data comes from the World Bank, but was accessed through the World Resource Institute's online interface, available at <http://earthtrends.wri.org>.

8

A Welfare Theoretic Analysis of Climate Change Inequities

Neil A. Leary

The consequences of climate change can be modified by mitigation and adaptation. Mitigation involves action to slow or constrain climate change, whereas adaptation aims to realize gains from opportunities or to reduce the damages that result from climate change. The analysis of these responses has largely focused on efficiency and cost effectiveness objectives. The message of this book is that justice goals also need to be given attention when deciding on responses to climate change. In this chapter I expand economic analysis to incorporate equity elements and exemplify the equity outcomes of climate change in the United States.

The tools of economics are widely recognized as relevant to questions about the efficiency and cost-effectiveness of policy choices. But they are less widely recognized as being relevant to questions about justice. In this chapter, I argue that welfare economics provides a useful framework for analyzing justice issues. For example, a welfare economic framework can be applied to investigate the distribution of climate change impacts and the impacts of climate change responses, and to evaluate tradeoffs between efficiency and equity objectives.

These questions form only a subset of the justice issues outlined in chapter 1 and elsewhere in this volume. The focus here is on the distribution of outcomes of action rather than on the procedural justice of who makes and implements policy decisions (see chapter 1 and Banuri et al. 1996, 85). Welfare economics reduces the consequences of climate change and climate change responses to a single metric of social welfare change using a social welfare function. This includes normative judgments about equity that can and should be made explicitly in the analysis, for example, on the basis of utilitarian, Rawlsian, and other approaches to social justice. The results of such analysis about efficiency and equity consequences form a useful input to policy evaluation and decisions. But it should be considered along with other information within a broader context of justice analysis such as that advocated by Paavola and Adger (2002).

This chapter provides an overview of the measurement of social welfare change from changes in individual welfare and explains how equity issues arising from climate change and climate change policy can be treated within the welfare theoretic framework. Mathematical notation is used to give precision to the arguments, but the key ideas are also explained in nonmathematical terms. Use of the social welfare framework to estimate welfare and equity changes is illustrated by application to the United States. The application demonstrates how social welfare changes can be decomposed into efficiency and equity effects. The results suggest that the impacts of climate change fall disproportionately on households of lower than average wealth and that in the United States, the estimated equity effects of climate change are of comparable magnitude as the efficiency effects.

Consumer Behavior and Individual Welfare

Welfare economists seek to measure the change in social welfare that would follow from public choices. The purpose is to rank choices according to whether they would yield outcomes that are more or less preferred by society in comparison with each other. The starting point for measuring changes in social welfare is individual welfare, which is measured by using the metric of money. The basis for monetary valuation is voluntary exchange: what amount of goods and services would the individual willingly forego to attain the benefits from a public policy? The amount of money that this bundle of goods and services would command in the market is taken as a monetary equivalent of the individual's welfare gain.

So far as possible, economists derive measures of individual welfare from constructions of individual preferences that are inferred from observed behavior. If an individual is observed to choose a bundle of goods and services, that person reveals that the chosen bundle is preferred to, or at least not preferred less than, all other bundles that feasibly could have been chosen. With this and other axioms of individual behavior, it is possible to represent individual preferences by a utility function.[1]

An individual's preferences and observed choices are presumed to correspond to what is best for the individual's well-being. This is the principle of consumer sovereignty. The utility function ranks different bundles of commodities according to the individual's preferences and also yields a scalar measure of individual welfare.

In studies of consumer behavior, the utility function is usually defined over a domain of marketed goods and services. For this reason, some have criticized utility as too narrowly focused to be a useful concept of individual welfare. However, the set of commodities over which the utility function is defined can include a much broader set of variables that are important to individual welfare than just marketed goods and services.

Private nonmarket goods such as leisure time and health status, for example, have all been included as arguments in the utility function. Public goods from which the individual derives benefits such as air quality, water quality, public safety, and aesthetic characteristics of the landscape have also been included. Even intangible characteristics of a state of the world that may not be used directly by the individual but for which he or she may have preferences, such as survival of endangered species, have been included. Thus the utility function is a representation of individual welfare that can encompass far more than just the material well-being provided by consuming marketed goods and services.

Armed with this concept, and observational and survey data, the researcher can empirically estimate demand functions from which to recover utility functions that are consistent with the empirical data and the preferences that are represented by the data. The utility functions can then be used to investigate the effects on the welfare of individuals of changes in prices of market goods and services, quantities of nonmarket goods and services, and incomes.[2]

In measuring welfare changes associated with climate change, individuals are assumed to have preferences over a vector of market goods and services, x, and a vector of nonmarket goods and services, z, that include private goods such as individual health status as well as public goods such as environmental quality. The quantities of market and nonmarket goods and services consumed by individual i, x_i and z_i, vary for different states of the world. States of the world are differentiated according to the climate, ϕ^j, and adaptation policy, α^k.

For simplicity, I consider only two climate states and two adaptation policy states. The present climate is denoted ϕ^0 and an altered climate is denoted ϕ', whereas the present and new adaptation policy cases are denoted α^0 and α' respectively. The utility function of individual i can be represented as

$$u_i(x_i, z_i) = u_i(x_i(\phi^j, \alpha^k), z_i(\phi^j, \alpha^k)). \tag{8.1}$$

The utility function reduces the benefits derived by the individual from bundles of the myriad market and nonmarket goods and services to a scalar measure for each bundle. The scalar measure gives an ordinal ranking of bundles that is consistent with individual preferences. Transformations of the utility function that change the scalar but preserve the preference ordering are permissible.

For convenience it is common to transform the utility function into one that measures utility in monetary units. This is done by using the expenditure function, evaluated at initial prices of x and quantities of z, which serves as a money measure of individual welfare. This is represented by

$$w_i(\phi^j, \alpha^k) = e_i(p^0, z_i^0, u_i(\phi^j, \alpha^k)) \tag{8.2}$$

where w_i is the welfare of individual i measured in money, p^0 is a vector of prices of x in the initial state, z_i^0 is a vector of initial state quantities of z consumed by individual i, $u_i(\phi^j, \alpha^k)$ is the utility level attained by the individual in state (ϕ^j, α^k), and e_i, the expenditure function of individual i, is the minimum expenditure necessary to attain $u_i(\phi^j, \alpha^k)$.[3] In this construction, climate and adaptation policy affect individual welfare through their effects on the prices of x and quantities of z.

Changes in individual welfare from climate change and climate change adaptation can be evaluated using the expenditure function in (8.2) as Leary (1999) described. Consider, for example, a change in the climate from ϕ^0 to ϕ' without any change in adaptation policy.[4] The change in climate would bring changes in prices, for example, the price of food, and in quantities of nonmarket goods, for example, the risk of injury from extreme weather. The utility levels attainable by individual i in the initial and changed climates are given by $u_i(\phi^0, \alpha^0)$ to $u_i(\phi', \alpha^0)$, respectively.

A monetary measure of the welfare change is the maximum payment that the individual would be willing to make to prevent a change in climate that would change utility from $u_i(\phi^0, \alpha^0)$ to $u_i(\phi', \alpha^0)$. This change in the welfare of individual i can be derived by use of the expenditure function to compare the minimum expenditures that would be necessary to attain these two different utility levels, evaluated at the original prices and quantities of z:[5]

$$w_i(\phi', \alpha^0) - w_i(\phi^0, \alpha^0) = e_i(p^0, z_i^0, u_i(\phi', \alpha^0)) - e_i(p^0, z_i^0, u_i(\phi^0, \alpha^0)).$$
(8.3)

Similarly, individual welfare changes for a change in adaptation policy from α^0 to α' in the new climate and for the total combined effect of a change in climate and change in policy are given by, respectively,

$$w_i(\phi', \alpha') - w_i(\phi', \alpha^0) = e_i(p^0, z_i^0, u_i(\phi', \alpha')) - e_i(p^0, z_i^0, u_i(\phi', \alpha^0)),$$
(8.4)

and

$$w_i(\phi', \alpha') - w_i(\phi^0, \alpha^0) = e_i(p^0, z_i^0, u_i(\phi', \alpha')) - e_i(p^0, z_i^0, u_i(\phi^0, \alpha^0)).$$
(8.5)

These welfare changes represent the harm or benefit done to the individual by changes in climate or in the adaptation policy. They are measured in monetary terms by calculating the payment to or from the individual that would enable the individual to attain an equivalent level of welfare as could be attained without the change in climate or policy. Whether the changes are positive or negative can vary across individuals and will depend upon how the changes affect the individual's costs of attaining different utility levels. These will depend, in turn, on the particular circumstances and preferences of the individual.

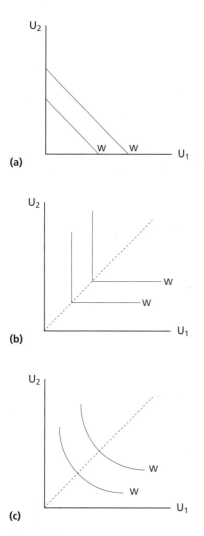

Figure 8.1
Indifference curves of three alternative social welfare functions. The indifference curves depict the trade-offs between the welfare levels of two individuals that would be deemed acceptable for social welfare functions that incorporate three different principles of equity. Panel (*a*) corresponds to a utilitarian social welfare function, panel (*b*) to a Rawlsian social welfare function, and panel (*c*) to a social welfare function that is intermediate between the utilitarian and Rawlsian in its regard for equity.

welfare among individuals, the closer would the indifference curves approach the right-angle indifference curves represented in the middle panel (figure 8.1b). Conversely, the less sensitive social preferences are to equity, the flatter would be the indifference curves and they would approach those corresponding to the utilitarian social welfare function.

But under what conditions is it possible to represent a social preference ordering by a social welfare function such as equation (8.6)? The minimum assumptions that are required to apply consumer demand theory imply utility that is ordinal and noncomparable across individuals. As Arrow (1963) famously demonstrated, if individual utility is ordinal and noncomparable, then it is impossible to derive a rule for establishing a social preference ordering from individual utility functions, or a social welfare functional, that is not dictatorial.

This is Arrow's "Impossibility Theorem." In this case we are restricted to the Pareto principle for comparing different states of the world and it is not valid to construct social indifference curves such as those figure 8.1 depicts. So the assumptions that are sufficient for consumer demand theory are not sufficient for social choice theory.

This dilemma led Sen (1977) and others to explore other assumptions about measurability and comparability of individual utility and their implications for social choice. Roberts (1980) shows that if utility is cardinal and fully comparable across individuals, then social welfare functions can be derived that are nondictatorial and satisfy other desired properties.[6] The form of social welfare functionals derivable from these assumptions is

$$W[u(x, z)] = F\{\overline{W}(x, z) + g[u(x, z) - \overline{W}(x, z) \, \iota], x, z\}, \qquad (8.7)$$

where $\overline{W}(x, z) = \Sigma a_k u_k(x, z)$, summed over $k = 1$ through n individuals, is a weighted average of individual welfare, $u(x, z)$ is a vector of individual welfare functions, and $g(x, z)$ is a linear homogenous function of deviations of individual levels from average welfare.

This class of social welfare functions is capable of expressing a variety of ethical judgments.[7] Imposing additional restrictions on the range of possible ethical judgments is required to derive and operationalize a specific social welfare function with which to measure social welfare change. For example, Jorgenson and Slesnick (1983, 281–289) rule out direct dependence of F on the social state and impose notions of horizontal and vertical equity and a constant degree of inequality aversion.

Their horizontal equity requirement is a weak form of anonymity that requires that households with identical preferences (i.e., identical characteristics) be treated identically. Thus, for example, households with an equal number of members and in the same wealth class are assigned equal weights in the social welfare function. Vertical equity requires that the weights be greater for households of lesser wealth than for households of greater wealth. This means that social welfare is higher for distributions of total expenditure that are more equal.

The social welfare function that Jorgenson and Slesnick derive from these and other assumptions[8] is

$$W[u(x,z)] = \ln \bar{V} - \gamma \left\{ \left(\sum a_k(p, A_k) \left| \ln V_k - \ln \bar{V} \right|^{-\rho} \right) \middle/ \sum a_k(p, A_k) \right\}^{-1/\rho}, \quad (8.8)$$

where V_k is the translog indirect utility function for individual k, $\ln \bar{V} = \Sigma a_k(p, A_k) \ln V_k / \Sigma a_k(p, A_k)$ is a weighted average of measures of individual welfare, a_k is the number of household equivalent members of household k, which is a function of prices and characteristics of household k, A_k, and ρ and γ are parameters.

The point to take from the above is that social welfare can be derived as a weighted average of individual welfares less a penalty for deviations of individual welfares from the average. Equity considerations are incorporated in the weights assigned to different categories of households and by the size of the penalty for deviations from equality in the distribution of welfare. The penalty is determined by two parameters, ρ and γ, in the form of the social welfare function presented in equation 8.8.

The parameter ρ, which ranges from negative unity to negative infinity, determines the curvature of the indifference curves of the social welfare function and is called the degree of inequality aversion. For ρ equal to negative infinity, the second term of equation 8.8 vanishes and the social welfare function reduces to the utilitarian case in which social welfare is equal to average welfare. In the applications reported in the section below, ρ is taken to be negative unity to give the greatest possible weight to equity considerations. The parameter γ is assigned the maximum value that is consistent with the Pareto principle to give maximum weight to the penalty for inequality.

Analogous to the case of individual welfare, the social welfare function can be transformed to one that measures social welfare in monetary units. This is accomplished by means of the social expenditure function introduced by Pollak (1981). The social expenditure function is the minimum total social expenditure necessary to attain a given level of social welfare and is a function of prices, z and W. In an initial state (ϕ^0, α^0), social welfare is $W(\phi^0, \alpha^0)$ and the corresponding money metric social welfare is

$$M^0 = M(\phi^0, \alpha^0) = M(p^0, z^0, W(\phi^0, \alpha^0)). \tag{8.9}$$

This money measure of social welfare can be decomposed into money measures of efficiency and equity following Jorgenson (1985). Efficiency is measured with reference to the maximum level of social welfare that can be attained through redistributions of aggregate expenditure. This potential social welfare, denoted W^*, will correspond to an equal distribution of welfare among individuals. This does not correspond to an equal distribution of wealth among individuals as individuals with the same allocation of wealth can nonetheless have different levels of welfare.

The money measure of efficiency is given by

$$M^*(\phi^0, \alpha^0) = M(p^0, z^0, W^*(\phi^0, \alpha^0)). \tag{8.10}$$

The corresponding money measure of equity is the difference between the money measure of actual social welfare and the money measure of potential social welfare:

$$M^e(\phi^0, \alpha^0) = M^0 - M^* = M(p^0, z^0, W(\phi^0, \alpha^0)) - M(p^0, z^0, W^*(\phi^0, \alpha^0)). \tag{8.11}$$

M^e will equal zero for perfect equality in the distribution of individual welfare and will be less than zero for unequal distributions. From equation (8.11) it can be seen that actual money welfare is equal to the sum of money measures of potential welfare and equity:

$$M^0 = M^* + M^e = M(p^0, z^0, W^*(\phi^0, \alpha^0)) + [M(p^0, z^0, W(\phi^0, \alpha^0)) - M(p^0, z^0, W^*(\phi^0, \alpha^0))]. \tag{8.12}$$

Using this framework, money measures of social welfare change can be calculated and decomposed into efficiency and equity changes.[9] If the climate and policy states change from (ϕ^0, α^0) to (ϕ', α'), the total welfare change is given by

$$M(\phi', \alpha') - M(\phi^0, \alpha^0) = M(p^0, z^0, W(\phi', \alpha')) - M(p^0, z^0, W(\phi^0, \alpha^0)).$$

(8.13)

The change in social welfare is decomposed into efficiency and equity changes as follows:

$$M(\phi', \alpha') - M(\phi^0, \alpha^0) = [M^*(\phi', \alpha') - M^*(\phi^0, \alpha^0)] + [M^e(\phi', \alpha') - M^e(\phi^0, \alpha^0)],$$

(8.14)

where the first bracketed term is the efficiency change and the second is the equity change.

To summarize, the changes in climate and adaptation policy act on social welfare through their effects on individual welfare levels that result from changes in the prices of market goods and services x and quantities of nonmarket goods and services z. The social welfare change is measured in money by use of the social expenditure function, evaluated at the initial prices of x and quantities of z.

The change has two components. The first, a measure of efficiency, is the change in the maximum potential social welfare that could be achieved if welfare were equally distributed in both the initial and new states. If the combined effects of changes in climate and adaptation policy raise the level of individual welfare that could be achieved if welfare were equally distributed, then the efficiency change is positive. Conversely, if the individual welfare that would be attained with equally distributed welfare decreases, the efficiency change is negative.

The second component is a measure of equity. If the effects of climate and policy changes are distributed so as to lessen deviations of individual welfare levels from the average, then the gap between actual and potential social welfare is diminished and the equity change is a positive contribution to social welfare. But if deviations from average welfare increase, then the gap increases and the equity change is a drag on social welfare.

Note that the measure of efficiency change from this decomposition of social welfare change generally does not correspond to a simple sum of individual welfare changes, which is often characterized as a measure of efficiency change. In the modern welfare framework, efficiency changes are made by comparing points of maximum potential social welfare in which welfare is distributed equally among individuals. In contrast, standard net-benefit calculations compare points using the actual distributions of individual welfare. This would correspond to maximum social welfare only if welfare is distributed equally, or if the utilitarian social welfare function is accepted as the true social welfare function.

The important implication here is that a net-benefit calculation as the sum of individual welfare changes would not correspond to a measure of efficiency change that is consistent with welfare theory. Hence, measures of efficiency change cannot, as is often assumed, be separated from ethical judgments about the distribution of welfare and wealth.

An Application to Climate Change Impacts and Adaptation in the United States

Modern welfare economics can be applied at scales ranging from individual project analysis to national, multinational, and global scale analyses. To illustrate the approach, I present estimates of household and social welfare impacts of climate change and climate change adaptation in the United States. Applications of similar welfare theoretic approaches to global scale climate change damages from national and regional scale estimates appear in Tol et al. 2004, and Fankhauser, Tol, and Pearce 1997.

The application uses a modeling framework developed by Jorgenson, Wilcoxen, and Slesnick that links a computable general equilibrium (CGE) model of the U.S. economy with a model of household and social welfare.[10] The impacts of climate change on selected economic sectors and activities are introduced to the CGE model to simulate their joint effects on prices and quantities of commodities and on other economic variables. Money measures of the resulting household welfare changes are calculated for different classes of households using equation 8.5 and an empirically estimated household expenditure function. Social welfare changes are calculated by means of the social welfare function (equation 8.8) and a corresponding social expenditure function.

Changes in selected market sector costs due to climate change and adaptation responses are projected over the period 1990–2080 by means of highly simplified impact functions that model cost changes as nonlinear functions of global mean temperature change, atmospheric concentration of carbon dioxide, and global mean sea level rise. Impact functions are constructed for changes in production costs in commercial agriculture, forestry, and fisheries, capital requirements for protecting coasts and air quality and repairing storm damages, and household costs for space heating and cooling. The impact functions for agriculture, forestry, and fishery costs incorporate autonomous adaptations. The changes in capital requirements assume adaptation policies to protect developed parts of the U.S. coast from sea level rise and to impose more stringent controls on emissions of tropospheric ozone precursors so as to comply with existing air quality standards.

Impact functions are constructed to replicate the range of impact estimates found in the literature up to 1995, when the welfare analysis was conducted. More recent estimates of impacts have tended to indicate less severe negative impacts and more beneficial impacts, but the range of potential impacts is not much changed.[11] Estimates of costs range widely from net benefits to net costs for agriculture and forestry for a given scenario. To reflect the range of estimates and the underlying uncertainty, three different parameterizations of the impact functions are developed to correspond to three different levels of vulnerability: low, medium, and high.

Transient scenarios of changes in carbon dioxide concentration, global mean temperature change, and global mean sea level are taken from simple climate model projections (IPCC 1992). The analysis uses two emission scenarios (known as IS92a and IS92e) and three different estimates of the equilibrium warming that would result from a doubling of the carbon dioxide concentration from pre-industrial level: these are 1.5°C, 2.5°C, and 4.5°C.

Different assumptions about emissions, doubling temperature, and degree of vulnerability are combined to construct a total of eight scenarios of climate change impacts plus a base case scenario. These assumptions account for some of the key uncertainties but do not provide a complete exploration of them. The constructed scenarios yield a range of average global temperature increase of 1.35–4.5°C and global mean sea level rise of 27–90 cm by 2080. The temperature increases correspond closely with the most recent estimates of the IPCC, approximately 1.3°C–4.7°C by 2080, but extend beyond the range of the most recent estimates of sea level rise, approximately 7–65 cm by 2080 (IPCC 2001, 14).

Impacts for the different sectors and activities are projected for the eight scenarios using the impact functions and are input to the CGE model. The CGE model simulates market interactions among households, domestic producers, government, and the rest of the world and solves for market clearing prices and quantities of labor, capital, and 35 goods and services for each year of the simulations. Simulations with the CGE model provide projections of changes in aggregate consumption, investment, and national income.

The simulations also yield corresponding estimates of changes in household welfare by household type and changes in social welfare of the United States. The latter are decomposed into efficiency and equity changes. We present a brief overview of the results here; Leary (1995) presents a more detailed description of the analysis and results.

Figure 8.2 displays the changes in real national income simulated by the CGE model for the eight scenarios relative to a base case simulation. The simulated changes in income generally rise through time in absolute terms and as a percentage of base case income. By 2080, the final year of the analysis, the changes in national income due to climate change and adaptation policies range from a loss of 2 percent to a gain of 1.2 percent.

Associated with the market changes simulated by the CGE model are changes in the cost of living and household income that bring changes in household welfare. Estimates for a reference household range from a present value welfare loss of US$12,300 (for the case of IS92e emissions, 4.5°C doubling temperature, and high vulnerability), to a welfare gain

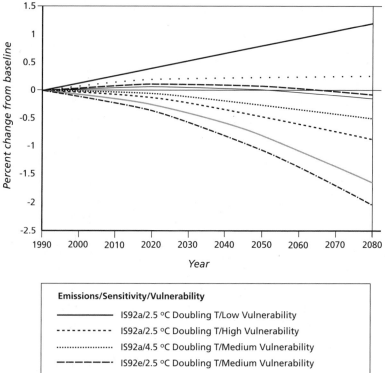

Figure 8.2
Estimated changes in real national income projected for the United States under eight scenarios of climate change and adaptation, 1990 to 2080. *Source*: Leary 1995.

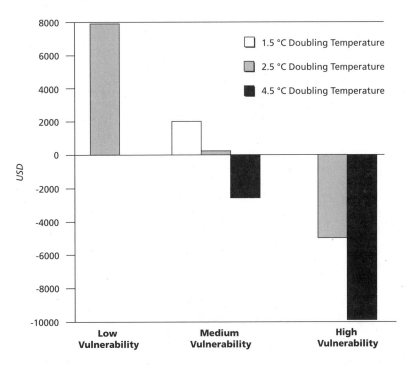

Figure 8.3
Estimated welfare changes for reference households due to climate change and adaptation, 1990 USD, present value. Results for scenarios based upon the IS92a projection of greenhouse gas emissions are displayed in the figure. Scenarios based upon the IS92e projection, not displayed, show a similar pattern of welfare changes. *Source*: Leary 1995.

of $7,900 (for the case of IS92a emissions, 2.5°C doubling temperature, and low vulnerability).[12]

Figure 8.3 displays the welfare changes for a reference household for the six scenarios that are driven by the IS92a projection of emissions. The results span a range of several thousand dollar increases and decreases in household welfare changes, taking into account a number of possible adaptations.

Household welfare changes are estimated to be neutral to beneficial for a doubling temperature of 2.5°C or less if vulnerability is low or medium. Household welfare changes are adverse for more severe impacts of climate change—those represented by high sensitivity and vulnerability (i.e., 4.5°C doubling temperature or high vulnerability). The pattern of welfare changes follows that of the estimated effects on national income: household welfare increases for scenarios with increases in national income due to climate change and decreases for scenarios with decreases in national income.

Under scenarios for which the welfare consequences of climate change are adverse, the measures of household welfare change represent the maximum amount that the reference household would be willing to pay in the present to avoid the future consequences of climate change. Alternatively, for scenarios that result in beneficial effects for households, the estimated welfare changes represent the minimum payment to the household that would make it as well off as the simulated effects of climate change on marketed economic activity. The estimated welfare changes are mostly less than 1 percent of household lifetime wealth. But in absolute terms they suggest that households might be willing to pay significant sums to avoid the effects of climate change if they were known to be adverse. Clearly this has significant policy implications.

The changes in household welfare vary with the level of wealth of the household. Households of greater wealth are projected to experience larger absolute changes in welfare than are households of lesser wealth. However, the estimated changes are larger percentages of household wealth for poorer households than for wealthier households. For example, for the scenario that combines IS92a emissions, a doubling temperature of 2.5°C, and a high degree of vulnerability (i.e., a plausible "medium" scenario), welfare losses are 0.4 percent and 0.55 percent of household wealth for households with wealth equal to double and half the U.S. average, respectively.

Thus, if climate change generally has negative impacts on household welfare, the estimated effects are distributed regressively. Conversely, if climate change raises household welfare, the estimated effects are distributed progressively. A prime reason for this result is that the largest effect of climate change on household welfare in this analysis is transmitted through changes in the cost of food. Because households of lower wealth typically spend a larger share of their budgets on food than do wealthier households, an increase or decrease in food cost would impact poorer households disproportionately.

Table 8.1
Estimates of aggregate measures of welfare charges, decomposed by efficiency and equity, for the United States under eight climate change scenarios

Scenario	Emission projection	Doubling temperature	Vulnerability to climate change	Efficiency change (billions 1990 USD)	Equity change (billions 1990 USD)	Social welfare change (billions 1990 USD)
1	IS92a	2.5°C	Low	360	125	485
2	IS92a	2.5°C	Medium	30	−10	20
3	IS92a	2.5°C	High	−220	−95	−315
4	IS92a	1.5°C	Medium	85	40	125
5	IS92a	4.5°C	Medium	−65	−85	−150
6	IS92a	4.5°C	High	−410	−190	−600
7	IS92e	2.5°C	Medium	50	0	50
8	IS92e	4.5°C	High	−505	−240	−745

Source: Leary 1995.

The estimated changes in household welfare are aggregated into a measure of social welfare change by means of a social welfare function of the form in equation 8.8. Table 8.1 presents results. Estimates of social welfare change range from a loss of US$745 billion for scenario 8 to a welfare gain of $485 billion for scenario 1.

The estimated social welfare changes are decomposed into an efficiency change and an equity change, following equation 8.14. The estimated money measures of equity change range from 25 percent to almost 60 percent of the total change in social welfare. In most cases, the efficiency and equity effects move social welfare in the same direction.

In four of the scenarios, both the efficiency change and equity change are negative. In these cases, the negative welfare effects of climate change are distributed so as to exacerbate inequality in the distribution of welfare across U.S. households, adding the loss of social welfare from the efficiency effect. In two other scenarios, both the efficiency and equity changes are positive. In these cases, benefits from climate change are estimated to increase equality and thereby add to the gain in social welfare. In the two remaining scenarios, the equity change is roughly neutral (table 8.1).

The primary determinant in this analysis of whether climate change would result in a net gain or loss in household and social welfare in the United States is the effect on agriculture. Studies suggest that climate change could have either beneficial or harmful effects for U.S. agriculture, depending on the interplay between carbon dioxide, temperature and precipitation effects on crop yields, the temperature and precipitation changes projected, and the extent and effectiveness of adaptation measures assumed to take place.

The impact functions used in the analysis were constructed to be consistent with results in the published literature up to the mid 1990s. More recent analyses have tended to more often point in the direction of beneficial impacts for agriculture in the United States than harmful impacts (see, for example, National Assessment Synthesis Team 2001). An updating of the impact functions to reflect the more recent results would give greater weight to the potential for beneficial outcomes. But even incorporating more positive impacts on agriculture, simulations would still yield a range that would span from benefits to losses of similar magnitudes as obtained with the estimates used in this study.

The estimated welfare effects of climate change summarized here integrate an extensive but far from exhaustive set of potential impacts. Nonmarket impacts such as changes in human health and the health of ecosystems are not included, nor are market impacts of changes in water supply, quality, and transportation; recreation and tourism opportunities; and construction costs. The costs of adjustments of moving labor and capital from sectors and regions that are negatively affected to those that are beneficially or less negatively affected are also omitted.

Regional differences in impacts are not accounted for and it is likely that the impacts will differ markedly across regions of the United States. The simplistic impact functions used to introduce impacts into the CGE model treat impacts of gradual changes in average climate conditions that are assumed to be predicted with perfect foresight and do not address changes in variability nor discontinuous changes that are imperfectly foreseen. How these omissions and limitations would affect the estimates of welfare changes is a matter for further research. For these reasons the results should be viewed as illustrative of the approach and not as comprehensive estimates of the welfare effects of climate change in the United States.

Conclusion

To apply the welfare theoretic framework to the analysis of welfare changes and their equity components requires first that individual welfare be measurable and second that welfare be comparable across individuals such that individual welfare can be "added up" to arrive at a measure of well-being of the society. But there is no universal agreement on how to measure and compare individual welfare nor on the rules for adding up. In the context of climate change, Arrow et al. (1996, 65) conclude that there is no global welfare function that can generate complete and consistent valuations of the outcomes of climate change and climate change policies. The implication is that it is not possible objectively to identify a globally optimum climate change policy and that a global social welfare function cannot provide a decision rule for climate policy.

Still, social welfare functions can be constructed that have heuristic value for structuring information about the potential consequences of different choices for the well-being of society at large. Impacts on households are translated into monetary terms and can be aggregated into measures of social welfare change for a variety of ethical judgments concerning equity. The measures of social welfare change can be decomposed into efficiency and equity effects, and the illustration from the United States demonstrates that the equity effect can be substantial relative to the efficiency effect.

It is critical to note that different assumptions and different ethical judgments can be made that would alter welfare measurements. For example, Fankhauser et al. (1997) recalculate global damages of climate change from regional estimates under different assumptions about the form of a global social welfare function and values of parameters that represent alternative ethical judgments about aversion to inequality.

They find that estimates of global welfare changes can vary by as much as a factor of ten depending upon these assumptions.

When comparing different adaptation or mitigation policies, varying assumptions and ethical judgments could result in changes in the social preference rankings of different policies. But this is true of other measures of social well-being, such as the Human Development Index, and other measures of inequality, such as the Gini coefficient. By contrast, welfare theoretic measures can helpfully make the assumptions and ethical judgments explicit. Further, the measures are based upon observational evidence of human choices. Although the welfare approach cannot support a simple decision rule for climate policy, it can provide information about efficiency and equity consequences and trade-offs that can be considered along with other information in a pluralistic framework for justice analysis, argued throughout this book to be critical for reconciling consequentialist with other elements of fairness.

Acknowledgments

The analysis of social welfare impacts of climate change in the United States was conducted in collaboration with Dale Jorgenson, Richard Goettle, Daniel Gaynor, Daniel Slesnick, and Peter Wilcoxen. The chapter benefited substantially from discussion of an earlier manuscript that was presented at the Justice in Adaptation to Climate Change seminar held at the Zuckerman Institute for Connective Environmental Research in September 2003. I thank the participants for their comments, most particularly Samuel Fankhauser, Joanne Linerooth-Bayer, Jouni Paavola, and Neil Adger. I also thank two anonymous reviewers for their recommendations for improving the chapter.

Notes

1. If an individual's preferences are reflexive, complete, consistent, and continuous, then it is possible to represent them by a utility function. See Deaton and Muelbauer 1980, 25–30, for a discussion of choice axioms of consumer behavior and their implications for the existence and properties of utility functions.

2. Although the utility function can be defined over a set of commodities that extends beyond market goods and services, observational data of individuals'

choices with respect to nonmarket factors and the constraints on these choices is sometimes lacking and this impedes empirical applications. Still, there are a variety of innovative approaches for estimating demands for nonmarket goods and services and using these to estimate welfare changes.

3. See Deaton and Muelbauer 1980, 37, 179–181, for derivation of the individual expenditure function from the model of consumer behavior and for the use of the expenditure function as a money metric measure of individual welfare.

4. This does not mean that no adaptations to the change in climate are made, only that there is no change in public policy with regard to adaptation. Individuals adapt as best they can to the change in climate given the opportunities and constraints within the existing policy. The climate state may or may not reflect mitigation policies, depending upon the context. To simplify the discussion, climate and mitigation policy are taken here to be exogenous.

5. This does not mean that climate change is assumed to leave prices of x and quantities of z unchanged. To the contrary, it is these changes that result in a change in welfare. But to make valid comparisons of individual welfare change from one state of the world to another, it is necessary that a common set of reference prices p and quantities z be used in evaluating the expenditure function for each state of the world. Different reference p and z can be used, and different reference points give rise to different measures of welfare change. Throughout this analysis, the prices and quantities corresponding to the initial state of the world, $p°$ and $z°$, are used as the reference for welfare comparisons. The monetary measure of welfare change that is generated by this approach is the payment by, or to, the individual that would leave the individual as well off without the change in world state as he or she would be if the change did occur. This is the equivalent variation measure of welfare change.

6. Other properties of the social welfare function that are required include unrestricted domain, independence of irrelevant alternatives, positive association, and nonimposition. Jorgenson and Slesnick (1983, 274–289) present a summary of axiomatic approaches to social welfare functions.

7. Unlike the Bergson-Samuelson social welfare function in equation 8.6, the more general function represented by equation 8.7 is not welfarist in that W is not only a function of the distribution of individual welfares. F and the weights a_k are direct functions of the social state. This allows for social welfare to be a function of relative levels of individual welfare and not just absolute levels. It also permits incorporation of procedural equity.

8. They assume that the individual utility function takes the form of the log of the translog indirect utility function use it as a cardinal measure of individual welfare that is fully comparable.

9. Jorgenson (1990) uses this framework to estimate changes in living standards in the United States and to decompose changes in living standards into changes in efficiency and equity. He estimates that in 1947 social welfare per capita of US$2,175 (1982 dollars) was 42 percent less than the potential level

due to unequal distribution. Over the period 1947–1985, social welfare per capita grew by an estimated 2.9 percent per year. Growth in potential welfare, or efficiency, accounted for growth in per capita social welfare of 2.5 percent per year. The rest of the estimated growth in social welfare resulted from growth in the equity term as individual welfare became more equitably distributed.

10. The Jorgenson-Wilcoxen-Slesnick modeling framework, and its application to the analysis of welfare change due to environmental regulation, energy price shocks, carbon taxes, and economic growth, are described in Wilcoxen 1988, Jorgenson and Wilcoxen 1990, Jorgenson, Slesnick, and Wilcoxen 1992, and Jorgenson 1990. The analysis of welfare change from climate change impacts summarized here is described in detail in Leary 1995. Contributors to the analysis of climate change impacts in the United States include Dale Jorgenson, Richard Goettle, Daniel Gaynor, Daniel Slesnick, Peter Wilcoxen, and Neil Leary.

11. There is an extensive literature on the impacts of climate change on the United States that is summarized in the U.S. national assessment of climate change impacts (National Assessment Synthesis Team 2001).

12. There are 16,000 different household types in the Jorgenson, Wilcoxen, and Slesnick modeling framework. An urban household located in the Northeastern United States with four members, headed by a white male aged 35 to 44 years, and having a level of wealth equal to the average of all households is used as the reference household in the JWS framework.

III

Fairness in Adaptation Responses

Equity in National Adaptation Programs of Action (NAPAs): The Case of Bangladesh

Saleemul Huq and Mizan R. Khan

The impact of climate change is likely to have the greatest impact in the 49 least developed countries (LDCs) because of the overwhelming dependence of their economies on climate sensitive resources, as well as because of their low adaptive capacity. This profile further challenges planning for sustainable development and the realization the Millennium Development Goals (MDGs) within these regions of the world. In response to the dilemmas, the UN Framework Convention on Climate Change (UNFCCC) has approved and funded the preparation of National Adaptation Programs of Action (NAPAs) by the LDCs. For their preparation, the seventh Conference of Parties in 2001 adopted a set of guidelines, containing the activities and criteria for selection of urgent and immediate measures for enhancing the adaptive capacity of the countries. At present, many LDCs are at the initial stage of preparing their NAPAs.

The question of equity is of utmost importance in this preparation stage, so that the needs and concerns of the most vulnerable sections of the population are reflected from the beginning. The NAPA guidelines contain provisions for ensuring local equity in the NAPA process. However, like other countries, the LDCs are characterized by structural inequities within which vulnerabilities to natural disasters, for example, are socially determined and constructed.

In this chapter we examine the NAPA process in Bangladesh and the role of equity and justice in procedural terms. We argue that if *procedural* justice, meaning fairness of the *process* used to prioritize the activities, can be ensured in the NAPA process, considerations of equity in outcome can be addressed. This requires a bottom-up approach to each step of the NAPA, so that the immediate needs and concerns of the most affected communities are included in the list of projects for funding under NAPA.

This chapter, therefore, raises several key issues in these contexts. How can the NAPA process factor in equity considerations? How can the COP-approved NAPA guidelines treat equity? How can the resulting planning strategies adequately address equity in implementation? Our analysis in this chapter is based on both secondary and primary sources. There is sparse documentary evidence or experience at this stage in implementing planning for adaptation. We examine the NAPA guidelines, the NAPA proposal submitted to GEF by the government of Bangladesh, and related government policy and planning documents. The content analysis of these data reviews how procedural justice, participatory planning, and adaptation to climate change has been framed within Bangladesh.

The chapter first reviews the differential vulnerabilities of groups of population to the impacts of climate change. It then explains diverse elements of equity considerations relevant in the NAPA process. The third section analyzes the NAPA guidelines documents, showing how procedures of equity are addressed in specific planning guidance. The final section presents thoughts on ensuring application of those equity provisions in the NAPA process.

Differential Vulnerabilities in Bangladesh

According to the Third Assessment Report of the IPCC (2001c), agriculture, water, coastal zones and marine ecosystems, human settlements, human health, energy, and industry face the greatest risk from climate change on a global basis. A 45 cm sea level rise (SLR) would inundate 10.9 percent of Bangladesh's land area, exposing 5.5 million people in coastal areas to danger and harm (IPCC 2001b). Bangladesh is therefore recognized one of the most vulnerable countries to the impacts of climate change (Huq 2001). Geographic, socioeconomic, and demographic features of Bangladesh contribute to the profile of vulnerability to present day natural disasters, including those events that are driven by climate.

Bangladesh is located at the confluence of the three mighty river systems of the world: the Ganges, Brahmaputra, and Meghna. The region covers an area of 141 million ha (of which 13 million ha lies in Bangladesh) and has a population of 600 million. Over 90 percent of Bangladesh's streamflow originates outside the country and empties into the Bay of Bengal (Ahmad et al. 1994). Bangladesh is the lowest riparian state and bears the brunt of flooding in the region. In addition, dry season flow in the Ganges has decreased substantially due to increasing withdrawal upstream over recent decades.

Only 20 percent of Bangladesh's territory lies above two meters of mean sea level and there is around 700 km of vulnerable coastline. This geographical predicament is accompanied by high population density of around 800 per sq km, as high as in many primarily urban city-states such as Singapore or Hong Kong. The agricultural sector of Bangladesh contributes about 23 percent of GDP, and the majority of the population is reliant on agriculture.

A number of climate related events have taken place in the country in the past fifty years. Between 1960 and 2002, Bangladesh experienced over 40 cyclones with up to half a million human casualties per event. The country also experienced seven major floods between 1974 and 1998. In 1998, flooding inundated two-thirds of Bangladesh for two months, causing the death of 1,000 people and affecting 40 million people. These dangerous climate events have had severe economic consequences as well. Bangladesh lost US $5 billion in economic revenue, or 10 percent of its gross domestic product, due to the 1991 cyclone and 1998 flood.

Table 9.1 summarizes the projected impacts of climate variability and climate change on sections of Bangladesh's economy and society. About 55 percent of the population of Bangladesh faces the risk of inundation. Historically, water shortage has not been a problem in Bangladesh, but because of withdrawal of Ganges water upstream by India, the northwestern part of the country is facing increasing risk of drought. The greatest threats from climate change impacts are the recurring floods, cyclones, and the predicted sea level rise. Agriculture, coastal areas, fisheries, and forestry would be greatly impacted from the predicted climate change. Several national and international studies on the impacts

Table 9.1
Sectoral impacts of climate variability and change in Bangladesh

Sectors	Impacts
Population at risk	Poverty will increase; low agricultural outputs due to drought, salinity and flooding will limit livelihood options. Up to 55 percent of the population is already affected by inundations, water-borne diseases such as diarrhea and cholera would exacerbate. About 8.5 million people live in drought-prone areas, mainly in the northwest.
Infrastructure	One-meter sea level rise will cost over $5 billion or 10 percent of GDP. Affected infrastructure includes water systems, housing and settlements, transport networks, utilities, and industry.
Agriculture and food security	About 17 percent decline in rice production and a 61 percent decline in wheat production projected. Agriculture employs about 30 percent of the population and contributes 23 percent of GDP.
Coastal zone	Vulnerability acute due to combined effects of saltwater intrusion, drainage congestion, extreme weather events, subsidence, and changes in upstream river discharge.
Fisheries	Fisheries contribute 5.5 percent of GDP and 80 percent of animal protein intake of diet. Sea level rise and intrusion of saline water into rivers and other water bodies in the coastal region would cause fish habitats to decline.
Forestry and biodiversity	Sundarbans, the world's largest mangrove forest, is potentially threatened due to a combination of high evapotranspiration and low flow in winter resulting in increasing soil salinity. High scenario sea level rise would eradicate the whole area while increasing floods would affect forestry production.

Source: Huq, et al. 2003; World Bank 2003b.

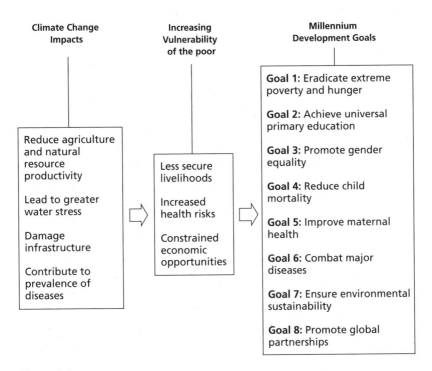

Figure 9.1
Climate change impacts and increasing vulnerability threaten the achievement of the Millennium Development Goals.

of climate change indicate no significant positive impacts on the economy of Bangladesh (Islam 2001).

Inequity in the distribution of resources is prevalent within agriculture and resource dependent societies. It is well known that vulnerability is a function of the impacts of climate change and the level of generic adaptive capacity as well as capacity within communities (IPCC 2001b). Figure 9.1 attempts to represent the impacts of climate change on the poor and the consequent impacts on achieving the Millennium Development Goals (MDGs) adopted at the Millennium Summit in 2001 and endorsed at Johannesburg in 2002. It is evident that climate change impacts potentially reduce productivity of agriculture and natural resources, creates greater water stress, damages infrastructure, and increases the prevalence of disease (table 9.1). These sectoral impacts will be more evident at a disaggregated level and affect the livelihood options available for the poor. They make livelihoods more insecure and increase health risks for the poor, who are often not covered by any health services. They also constrain economic opportunities because of the economy-wide effects. These impacts, in turn, will adversely affect the achievement of the MDGs, both directly on the goals of eradicating extreme poverty and hunger, combating HIV/AIDS, reducing child mortality, improving maternal health, malaria and other diseases, ensuring environmental sustainability, and the development of global partnerships for development.

Climate change also affects Millennium Development Goals such as universal primary education, as well as promotion of gender equality and empowering women (AfDB et al. 2003). Thus, the impacts of climate change are likely to undermine efforts aimed at achieving sustainable development. Combating climate change and adapting to its impacts are, we would argue, preconditions to progress toward sustainable development. At the same time, equitable economic development will enable nations to withstand the effects of climate change. One of the principles of the UNFCCC states:

The Parties have a right to, and should, promote sustainable development. Policies and measures to protect the climate system against human-induced change should be appropriate for the specific conditions of each Party and should be integrated with national development programs, taking into account that economic development is essential for adopting measures to address climate change (UNFCCC 1992, article 3.4).

Adaptive capacity is a function of several factors, such as levels of income, knowledge and skills, technology, access to information, equity in resource distribution, and access to opportunities (IPCC 2001b). In all these counts, the poor and the marginalized have low adaptive capacity in most of the LDCs; poverty is both a condition as well as the effect of low adaptive capacity. Poverty, particularly in its extreme forms, persists due to the prevailing structural factors within these societies and hence represents a vicious cycle.

In Bangladesh, almost two-thirds of the labor force—about 38 million people—is engaged in agriculture, and this is the sector likely to be hit hardest by the impacts of climate change, particularly in the coastal zone of Bangladesh (table 9.1). The extent of vulnerability to

Table 9.2
Social characteristics of Bangladesh and its coastal districts

Parameters	Bangladesh	Coastal districts
Land area (sq. km)	147,570	42,154
Administrative districts	64	16
Population (1998) in million	126.2	31.8
Poverty level (percent of pop)		
Poverty Line I	−47.8	−52.8
Poverty Line II	−28.3	−26.0
Household size	5.6	6.7
Farming households (percent)	66.2	70.0
Landlessness (up to 0.5 acre)	18 percent of rural households	40.0 percent

Source: Government of Bangladesh Bureau of Statistics 2001.

livelihoods is somewhat hidden if one looks at the aggregate impacts on economic sectors, as table 9.1 shows. It is more appropriate to gauge vulnerabilities and multiple stresses from the perspective of climate change impacts on the existing livelihood options of the poor at a disaggregated level.

Table 9.2 shows that there are more people under a basic needs poverty line I (absolute poor, with daily average intake of 2,150 calories) in the coastal zone than in the country as a whole. But the share of people under poverty line II (hardcore poor, with daily average intake below 1,850 calories) is slightly smaller in the coastal areas. This might be explained by the income of some coastal fishermen and women. In nominal terms, such incomes may be high. Shrimp export is the second highest foreign currency earner, after the garments sector. But farm sizes are larger in the coastal areas, and the consequent landlessness is a higher 40 percent, coupled with lack of basic services such as health and electricity. The poor and the marginalized live in the most risk-prone and hazardous zone. As new islands are formed along the coastlines, poor farmers rush to settle there despite their vulnerability to storms and flooding.

From table 9.1 it is evident that a number of livelihood systems would be vulnerable to the impacts of climate change in varying degrees. The farmers, fishers, shrimp producers and fry collectors, fuel wood gatherers, salt producers, and honey collectors are likely to be most affected groups, facing multiple stresses. Despite the fact that the marine fishing community comprises more than 5 percent of total households, their socioeconomic status remains at the lower rung of the society. These politically marginalized groups have the least capacity to influence national decision making.

In a survey within thirteen communities in six coastal districts (Bagerhat, Gopalganj, Jessore, Khulna, Narail, and Satkhira), the respondents identified eleven types of impacts related directly or indirectly to climate variability and change or other natural causes. Communities identified storm surge and tidal flooding as the highest cause of vulnerability (79 percent), followed by salinity (63 percent), drought (58 percent), windstorm (58 percent), water and insect-borne disease (58 percent), heavy rains (47 percent), loss of biodiversity (47 percent), river erosion (42 percent), and cyclone (42 percent) (CARE Bangladesh 2002). Household well-being indicators most affected by these impacts are income, food, housing, education, and health. Income and food availability are severely affected by flood, drought, and salinity. Health is severely affected by flood, salinity, water, and insect-borne diseases.

Conceptualizing Equity in Planning for Adaptation

The evidence from Bangladesh and other regions of the world suggest that the impacts of climate change on the livelihood systems make the poor more vulnerable (see also chapter 4, by Dow and colleagues, chapter 10, by Paavola, and chapter 11, by Thomas and Twyman). From an equity and human security point of view, the distribution of vulnerability is an unfair burden borne by those who are least able to adapt. But the vulnerability of the poor has also been demonstrated to be critical from a purely instrumental perspective. The Brundtland Commission, for example, viewed economic growth as the only feasible weapon in the fight against poverty, for "those who are poor and hungry will often destroy their immediate environment in order to survive" (World Commission on Environment and Development 1987, 52–54). So the satisfaction of basic needs of the poor, they argue, should be assigned utmost priority in achieving sustainable development. The WCED report singled out poverty as the root cause of environmental degradation in the developing world. Poverty is therefore both a condition and an effect of low adaptive capacity in the LDCs. However, vulnerability is a socially determined phenomenon, because of inequitable distribution of resources and low capacity of the poor to adapt (Pelling 1999; Adger 1999; and chapter 5, by Leichenko and O'Brien). These perspectives on the relationship between vulnerability and equity suggest some key principles under which the NAPA preparation process can consider equity.

First, a livelihood, rather than a sectoral, vulnerability approach would present a more realistic picture from the human security point of view. The NAPA guidelines set the level or degree of adverse effects of climate change and reduction of poverty as two of the four broad sets of criteria for prioritizing activities for developing the adaptation program. So the extent of vulnerability of the poor will be more clear and manifest if the planning process focuses attention more on the loss of existing livelihoods of the local communities, rather than just looking at the effects on individual sectors of the economy.

Second, a focus on immediate and near-term impacts of climate variability, rather than long-term climate change, prioritizes the most vulnerable. The rationale here is immediate and today's needs concern the poor more than long-term issues. Adaptation planning is a continuous process, and if poor and resource dependent sections of society can adapt to the impacts of climate variability today, they would be better equipped to face any eventuality under the longer-term climate change.

Third, planning should ensure that indigenous knowledge of the most vulnerable communities are given due recognition during NAPA preparation. All local experience and culturally specific knowledge within LDCs, whether categorized as indigenous or not (Agrawal 1995), is a critical resource. Respecting traditional and indigenous knowledge requires a more bottom-up approach to knowledge generation than the traditional top-down approach adopted in previous climate change impact assessments (fig. 9.2). Spatially specific vulnerabilities are manifest within communities and households. Hence, adaptation planning

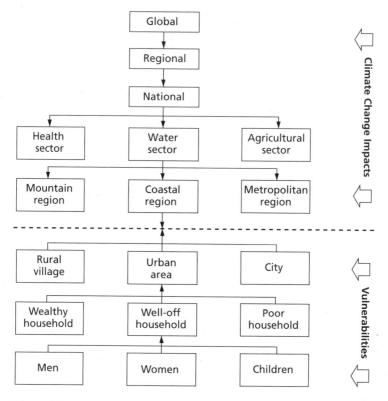

Figure 9.2
Harmonizing bottom-up and top-down information and knowledge in assessing climate impacts, vulnerabilities, and adaptation to climate change. *Source*: Adapted from Huq and Reid 2003.

needs to be based on the knowledge and information at this ground level. However, as the impacts are manifest beyond the community level, top-down information needs to undergo verification on the ground.

Fourth, planning should ensure *procedural* fairness in the NAPA preparation process. Procedural justice is concerned with the fairness of the *process* used to arrive at a decision (Korsgaard, Schweiger, and Sopinza 1995; Alexander and Ruderman 1987). Procedures in this context are fair when they vest process control or voice in those who are affected by some event. So the best mechanism to ensure procedural justice is participatory planning and designing of projects and programs.

Many researchers argue for looking into the modes and levels or stages of participation of the communities in designing and decision making over projects or programs (Midgley et al. 1986; Uphoff 1982; Pretty 1995). Midgley and colleagues (1986), for example, explain four types of state responses to participation: 1) the antiparticipatory mode, 2) the manipulative mode, 3) the incremental mode, and 4) the participatory mode. Participatory planning is ultimately built over time on incremental steps and policy changes toward a real participatory regime. By contrast, Pretty (1995) explains the different stages of community participation in project planning and implementation. Interactive and spontaneous participation or self-mobilization are the most fair and ultimate goals of much participatory planning. Therefore, the unrestricted opportunity to express one's point of view and to participate at all levels of decision making and project planning enhances procedural justice. Some of the characteristics of a process that is procedurally just are that it should be unbiased, be representative of participants and stakeholders, be concerned with needs and well being of the stakeholder, and be flexible and ethical. Ensuring procedural justice in the NAPA preparation process is likely to ensure distributive justice through its implementation phase, because fair process will ensure that the NAPA projects reflect concerns and needs of the vulnerable poor.

Whose Knowledge Counts?

The majority of existing assessments of climate change impacts and vulnerabilities have relied on top-down methodologies promoted, for example, by the IPCC. Many countries use such methods in preparing their impact and vulnerability assessments for Initial National Communications for the UNFCCC. In LDCs, the assessments relied on inputs from international and national experts and the results were provided to the international negotiations and national policymakers. Populations affected and the indigenous knowledge played an insignificant role in these assessments (Huq and Reid 2003).

In the next generation of adaptation assessments and policies such as the NAPAs, it will be essential to give greater recognition to the existing indigenous knowledge and experience of the vulnerable communities. Given the constraints and the often ineffective role of external assistance populations, LDCs effectively need to rely on their existing resilience and coping capacity to present climate variability in order to enhance their adaptive capacity to a future climate change. Recognition of this reality will entail a more bottom-up approach and methodology giving due value to the knowledge and experiences of the vulnerable communities themselves in preparing the NAPAs, rather than the traditional top-down approach followed in the past (fig. 9.2). In doing so, not only will the NAPAs be better able to help the vulnerable communities adapt to climate change, by making recommendations that are grounded in their own reality, but also enhance the importance and esteem of the communities by giving value to their own indigenous knowledge and experience.

Equity Considerations in the NAPA Guidelines

This section examines the NAPA guidelines approved by COP7 in Marrakech in 2001 in the light of the issues raised above. The guidelines are the only direct instruction of the government implementing this process and therefore set the tone for the whole planning process for adaptation in the most vulnerable nations. They are too important to be taken as given. Section D of the guidelines contains the guiding elements for preparation of NAPAs with elements of the document explicitly promoting equity. These elements include a participatory process involving stakeholders, particularly local communities, considerations of sustainable development, and considerations of gender equity.

The section within the guidelines detailing the NAPA preparation process gives specific instructions on the procedures and process:

The setting up of a national NAPA team . . . composed of a lead agency and representatives of stakeholders including government agencies and civil society. This group would be constituted using an open and flexible process that will be inclusive and transparent. (Decision 28/CP.7, Para 8a: NAPA Guidelines Annex)

To conduct a participatory assessment of vulnerability to current climate variability and extreme weather events, and to assess where climate change is causing increases in associated risks. (Decision 28/CP.7, Para 8bii: NAPA Guidelines Annex)

Organize a national and/or subnational consultative process to solicit inputs and proposal ideas in order to help develop a short list of potential NAPA acti vities. . . . This process will allow adequate dialogue between the national team and the public with time allowed for public comment and revisions. (Decision 28/CP.7 Para 8ci: NAPA Guidelines Annex)

The criteria for selecting priority activities reflect recognition of differential vulnerability and hence flow on the equity in outcome of the planning process. The criteria for prioritizing adaptation activities suggest that these

will be applied to, *inter alia*:
a) Loss of life and livelihood; b) Human health; c) Food security and agriculture; d) Water availability, quality and accessibility; e) Biological diversity; f) Land-use management and forestry; g) Coastal zones, and associated loss of land. (Decision 28/CP.7 Para 16: NAPA Guidelines Annex)

It is evident from these extracts that the NAPA guidelines at least consider equity aimed at ensuring procedural and distributive justice in the NAPA process. The first guiding element is the participatory approach involving local communities so that needs and concerns of the impacted communities are reflected in the activities to be undertaken in the NAPAs. Vulnerability assessment within NAPAs should also be based on community participation, so that the process reflects indigenous knowledge and day-to-day experiences that the poor encounter from climate events. The national NAPA team is to include representatives of the civil society and it was emphasized that the selection process be transparent, so that dictated or guided selection does not take place. Through these inclusive and participatory exercises, grassroots inputs in the form of proposals for specific actions and investments are encouraged. The guidelines emphatically suggest that "the NAPA document will undergo public review and be revised accordingly" (Decision 28/CP.7: NAPA Guidelines Annex). This iterative process of soliciting community opinion and responses could potentially move toward procedural justice in the NAPA preparation phase.

In the same way, ensuring sustainable development means that needs of the poor are taken into consideration, without which sustainable development can in no way be ensured in the LDCs. Gender equality is a corollary of the participatory approach, in which the women, who are likely to be differentially burdened by the impacts of climate change, are included in the NAPA process. Women are responsible throughout rural developing societies for managing water, sanitation, agricultural production, and distribution, all of which are at risk from specific climate change impacts. Several authors have documented the vulnerabilities of women during and after natural disasters. Their input and concerns thus need to be fully incorporated into adaptation planning (Kumar-Range 2001; Masika 2002; Enarson 2002).

The NAPA process solicits ideas for new investments and projects. One of the prime criteria of prioritization is their contribution to poverty alleviation. The guidelines suggest that livelihood security of the poor, such as human health, agriculture and food security, water, land use, and forestry and coastal zones, should be priorities. These are the sectors, most vulnerable to the impacts of climate variability and climate change, which support the livelihoods of the poor. The guidelines emphasize that the focus of vulnerability assessment should be on impacts from current climate variability. The underlying assumption is that adequate adaptation by the poor to existing vulnerabilities would prepare them to adapt to future eventualities from long-term climate change.

Ensuring Equity in the NAPA Process

Equity implications of the NAPA guidelines will depend on the system of governance and the institutional culture and traditions in individual countries. The LDCs greatly differ in this respect. In many of the island LDCs, national scale public consultations are common practice among relatively nucleated populations. In some other LDCs, systems of governance are more centralized and bureaucratized. Still, in most of the LDCs, public consultation and review of important policy issues are becoming more common. If equity issues are to be internalized sequentially into every step of the NAPA preparation process it is crucial to define inclusion (composition of the group), the functioning of the participatory process and representation at different levels (Uphoff 1983). The well-established set of principles for accountability and fairness from decades of experience in participatory development apply to this situation.

The establishment the national NAPA team involves critical decisions. The composition of the team needs to be analyzed, whether it includes representatives of vulnerable communities such as farmers and fishermen. Are members from these groups representing their vocations, their localities, or some other social grouping? What was the process of selection? These issues would ensure equity in the NAPA team selection process. The second step is the participatory rapid assessment of vulnerabilities. How does this participatory process take place? What was the basis of rapid assessment—research studies, historical records, people's age-old experiences and knowledge, or a combination? Have the experiences of community adaptation to climate events been taken into consideration? Have indigenous knowledge and practices of coping mechanisms been analyzed?

A third set of questions relates to what kind of public participation takes place. What were the modalities of public consultation? Does the country have any tradition of community consultation? If not, how was it initiated? Was it a combined group across all strata of the society? If so, could the poor voice their concerns before the powerful elites? Is their thinking incorporated into the list of potential ideas for NAPA activities? The fourth set of issues asks if the set of criteria applied in an objective and unbiased manner? What weights are given to which criteria? Is poverty reduction as a criterion given the highest consideration? As poverty reduction is a complex phenomenon, the process needs to address whether the criteria has been viewed narrowly, in terms of some potential material or income gains, or whether it includes social empowerment and development of capabilities of the poor as well. Poverty reduction activities to enhance the adaptive capacity of the poor may not always pass the economic efficiency criteria. How are such cases resolved among the tradeoffs involved?

Finally, the NAPA process needs to consider how its documents have undergone public review for their validation. Have the comments from the community leaders been taken into consideration for revision of the program? Who among the community leaders participate in the final review? If these considerations are taken care of, the equity concerns through procedural justice are likely to be promoted in the entire NAPA process.

Preparation of NAPA in Bangladesh

Bangladesh received funding for preparation of a NAPA in mid 2003 and is among the forerunners within the LDC group in implementation. A national NAPA team was established under UNDP as the executive agency. The national team includes members of civil society, including one media representative, plus expert teams to include national climate scientists, forestry and biodiversity, water and agricultural scientists, and economists as well as research and policy analysts concerned with issues of vulnerability. It is clear, however, that no representatives from the most vulnerable groups or their professional associations have been included in the NAPA team. It needs to be seen how far the urban civil society members represent the concerns of the vulnerable groups.

For consultation at the subnational level, the country is divided into several ecological zones, so that concerns of each specific area with participation of all stakeholders are reflected in the NAPA proposals. Two national workshops are planned—one at the beginning and the other at the end. The final workshop validates the NAPA document and will include a representative subset of participants from the national and subnational level exercises.

Given concern over impacts of climate change on Bangladesh over the past decade, there are already a number of climate change studies, including studies focused on vulnerability by both Bangladeshi and overseas researchers, obviating the need for new data generation. Yet the NAPA process should explicitly focus on the vulnerabilities of livelihood support systems, with a perspective of human security against threats from climate-related events and hence much previous work may only be tangentially important. Human security is a serious question in Bangladesh, the most densely populated country in the world, apart from some city-states. For example, in Bangladesh, a one-meter sea level rise could put 15 million people at risk. (IPCC 2001b). This outnumbers the total population of the 43 AOSIS small island countries. Although the populations at risk in the low-lying delta areas are dense, they are increasingly stable in terms of both land tenure and demography. The overall population growth rate now in Bangladesh is one of the lowest in the developing world, presently standing at 1.4 percent due to family planning and a reduction in fertility rates to 3.4 in the past two decades (BCAS 1998).

The NAPA climate change process does not happen in isolation. Increasingly, developing countries are driven through external processes to produce plans and strategies, for example, to meet the Millennium Development Goals. The Interim Poverty Reduction Strategy Paper (IPSRP) of Bangladesh, for example, is presently in the process of fine-tuning. The IPRSP sets targets to some social indicators, such as halving poverty, and infant and maternal mortality by 2015, along the lines of MDGs. However, if the goal is to be achieved by the next decade, Bangladesh needs to sustain an increased GDP growth rate of 7 percent per year over the decade (Government of Bangladesh 2002). The IPRSP recognizes the link between environment and poverty: 80 percent of the total population depend on natural resources or on processing of natural resource based products. Isolated poverty alleviation strategies will therefore not be effective if these are not environmentally sound, participatory in nature, and focused on building local and national capacities. But the poverty strategy does not consider the risks associated with climate change-related natural disasters. The only environmental agenda within its medium term policy matrix is to "integrate environmental conservation into the national development strategy." But there appears to be little consideration of how this integration could take place in the poverty strategy. Therefore, the relationship between environment and other issues considered in poverty alleviation, such as education, health, and energy, should have been clearly stated. Inevitably, there are implicit trade-offs in the perceptions of policymakers between growth and long-term adaptation to climate change. This perception of trade-off, we argue, is unsupportable. What is needed is an integrated perspective of the linkage between environmental challenges, including climate change, agriculture, and natural resource management, and environmental capacity building.

Policy integration and the enormous risks associated with climate change impacts make NAPA a significant challenge to society. But on the positive side, Bangladesh has a growing culture of democratic practice and participatory planning process. Experience in countries such as

India has shown that countries with robust environmental practices are the ones with strongest democratic input from the base to the top as well as high degree of local self-governance. Multiparty democracy in Bangladesh has taken root and there are efforts to decentralize its governance process down the local level. The initiation of the National Environmental Management Action Plan (NEMAP), based on public participation, has been widely acclaimed by communities beyond Bangladesh. Its implementation through several programs is also based on a partnership among the government, private sector, nongovernmental, and donor communities. The nongovernmental and community based in Bangladesh have greatly contributed to empowerment at grassroots level. Bangladesh has a vibrant civil society and NGOs such as Grameen Bank and BRAC, the biggest of their kind in the world. The programs of micro-credit, pioneered by Grameen Bank, are spread all over Bangladesh and their beneficiaries now cover about 15 million borrowers, 90 percent of whom are women. Through a radical revolution in banking, the Grameen Bank has proved that poor people with no collateral are more creditworthy than the rich. The local elected councils have introduced a quota system for women's representation, aimed at their social and political empowerment. Several parliamentary acts against repression of women have been passed in recent years, with the aim of speedy dispensation of justice to the victims. BRAC, the biggest NGO in the world, covers 68 million people, over half of the country's total in its different development programs (BRAC Annual Report 2001). Several thousand medium- and small-NGOs are engaged in micro-finance and other development programs. The government has introduced tuition-free education up to higher secondary level for girls. This NGO involvement in poverty alleviation and empowerment has been acclaimed worldwide. These processes of community empowerment are expected to enhance the resilience and adaptive capacities of the poor. However, state response to participation is inevitably incremental, in the sense that the regime supports participation, but policies and guidelines for decentralization of decision making and authentic participation by the communities are vaguely formulated. So community participation in decision making and in direct resource is a potential but limited resource for dealing with the large scale adaptation challenges to well being facing Bangladesh in the next decades.

Conclusion

The preparation of NAPAs by the 49 least developed countries represents an opportunity for applying the principles of equity and justice in ensuring that the voices and priorities of the most vulnerable communities to climate change are incorporated into planning for critical futures. Specifically, future funding for implementing the NAPAs can ensure that the urgent and immediate needs of the poorest and most vulnerable are not neglected. Further, we would argue that an equity-focused NAPA and its effective implementation will complement the realization of the Millennium Development Goals.

Application of provisions contained in the NAPA guidelines focused on procedures during its preparation will depend, among others, on the system of governance and the institutional culture and traditions in individual countries. The LDCs greatly differ in this respect. In some LDCs, systems of governance are more centralized and bureaucratized, whereas in others, there are more open and participatory structures. The NAPA process follows the trend in externally driven development planning, and in most of the LDCs public consultation and review of important policy issues are becoming part of life. These evolving participatory structures need to become the focus of procedural justice in the NAPA preparation process. To this end, great care must be taken to see that equity considerations are internalized sequentially into the steps of the NAPA process.

In this chapter, we have raised a number of questions by which to gauge the level of participatory process and ultimately the level of procedural justice. As most of the NAPAs are in the preparatory stage in the LDCs, including in forerunners such as Bangladesh, experience on procedural equity is sparse.

We strongly believe in a process-oriented idea of fairness in climate adaptation. If procedural justice can be ensured in the preparation phase, distributive justice is likely to follow during the implementation phase. To ensure that this happens, nongovernment and community-based organizations and civil society representatives of the most impacted livelihood groups, as with all developing planning processes, are crucial to the sustainability and success of anticipating and planning for the inevitable and unjust burden of risk facing the developing world.

10

Justice in Adaptation to Climate Change in Tanzania

Jouni Paavola

While negotiations on the mitigation of climate change and adaptation to it take place at the international political arenas, individuals and households will bear the brunt of climate change impacts at the local level. This is also where many adaptive responses to current climate variability and future climatic conditions take place. Yet the national level also merits attention. National institutions form an important nexus in multilevel governance of adaptation to climate change. All national governments will be engaged in adaptation planning and some of them are already preparing their National Adaptation Plans of Action (NAPAs) under the United Nations Framework Convention for Climate Change (UNFCCC). National policies, plans, and projects are important because they constitute the conditions within which households, firms, and other organizations adapt, as discussed in chapter 1. Therefore, all national policies, plans, and projects (or their absence) have important justice implications.

This chapter examines predicted climate change impacts and current and probable future vulnerabilities in mainland Tanzania[1] to shed light on the justice dilemmas confronting national adaptation planning and decisions on adaptation measures. This is a timely exercise as Tanzania completed its initial communication under the UNFCCC (URT 2003) and NAPA process is ongoing. Likely incidence of climate change impacts and the distribution of current and future vulnerabilities are important for planning and decisions regarding adaptation because they will influence how procedural justice can be achieved. That is, procedures for adaptation planning and decisions need to acknowledge background inequalities that influence to what degree different groups can participate and to ensure that their views and interests are acknowledged.

Tanzania is predicted to experience significant changes in climate (see Hulme et al. 2001), and multiple stressors make Tanzanians vulnerable to predicted climate change impacts. Average income levels in the country are among the lowest in the world and livelihoods depend on risky primary production. Lack of human capital and lack of access to technological alternatives accentuate vulnerability. Finally, the state lacks capacity and suffers from corruption. A case study focusing on the country thus sheds light on the challenges of just and effective adaptation to climate change in the developing world more broadly.

This chapter shares the view that distributive and procedural justice are both important in environmental decisions and governance (Paavola and Adger 2002). Distributive justice encompasses the distribution of pecuniary costs and benefits and the incidence of nonmonetary burdens and advantages. Equality is a useful starting point when examining distributive justice, but other principles such as need, capacity, and contribution may also need to be accommodated (see Shrader-Frechette 2002). Vulnerability has an important role in justice analysis because of its close linkages with need and capacity. The emphasis in this chapter is on distributive justice in the incidence of climate change impacts and distribution of vulnerability that present challenges in achieving both procedural and distributive justice in national adaptation planning and decisions.

The chapter suggests that predicted climate change impacts on food production, forests, water resources, human settlements, and human health will disproportionately burden the rural poor, who are already the most vulnerable group in Tanzania. Women, children, and pastoralists with their insecure entitlements to environmental resources are also among the most vulnerable groups. National adaptation planning and decisions need to make a particular effort to recognize and involve these groups. National adaptation plans and measures also have to address issues that are of particular significance for these groups. Complex interactions between climate change impacts on one hand and between sources of vulnerability on the other hand mean that vulnerability reduction requires several complementary responses. First, it requires effective governance of environmental resources such as forests and water. Forests, for example, provide essential ecosystem services, are an important source of rural livelihoods and cash income, and form a safety net during periods of extreme environmental stress. Second, institutional reforms and investments in infrastructure are needed to improve access to markets and to expand the range of income-generating activities available in the rural areas. Third, maintenance and enhancement of human capital requires public programs and spending on health, education, and social welfare.

In what follows, the next section discusses the assessment of justice implications of climate change impacts. The following sections review climate change and impact predictions for Tanzania and examine vulnerabilities in the country. The chapter concludes by discussing the justice implications of predicted climate change impacts in the light of current and future vulnerabilities, their implications for national adaptation planning and decision making, and ways to alter them.

Justice, Climate Change Impacts, and Vulnerability

Adaptation to climate change presents several difficult justice dilemmas to the international community (see Paavola and Adger 2006). Is there a right to be free from dangerous climate change? What is the responsibility of those who have caused climate change for its impacts? Developing countries are going to suffer disproportionately from climate change impacts, but they have contributed little to the problem. Their capacity to adapt is also much more limited than that of developed countries. Does this create a duty to assist developing countries to adapt and, if so, to what extent? A duty to assist would open up further justice dilemmas. How should assistance be distributed between developing countries and adaptive measures? How and by whom should decisions on these issues be made?

The UNFCCC affirms the duty to assist and identifies vulnerability as a key criterion for the distribution of assistance, but it has left open its extent (see chapter 3, by Mace). Decisions of the Parties to Convention have established the National Adaptation Plans of Action (NAPAs) as the process for generating national adaptation priorities. The guidelines for the preparation of NAPAs require multidisciplinarity and public consultation from the NAPA process. But this leaves open the question of what kind of challenges the NAPA process has to respond to and what kind of adaptation measures ought to be prioritized in the light of incidence of predicted climate change impacts, distribution of vulnerabilities, and background inequalities. This chapter seeks to shed some light on these issues.

This book as a whole argues that justice needs to be understood broadly so as to encompass both distributive and procedural justice (see chapter 1). Distributive justice encompasses the incidence of beneficial and adverse effects, both pecuniary and nonpecuniary, of both climate change and adaptation responses. Procedural justice in turn relates to who makes decisions regarding adaptive responses and how, and it encompasses issues such as recognition, participation, and distribution of power (Fraser 2001; Lind and Tyler 1988).

Distributive and procedural justice can be based on different foundations. Cosmopolitan theories argue that justice is universal and communitarian theories that it is specific to communities (Attfield 1999). Some approaches suggest that justice can be achieved by distributing one overarching good such as utility fairly, whereas other approaches insist that different goods occupy different spheres and justice needs to be achieved in each of them in their own terms. There are good reasons to believe that several complementary solutions need to be used to resolve justice dilemmas related to adaptation to climate change (Paavola and Adger 2002, 2006). Yet equality is the best starting point for analysis: if there are reasons for deviating from equality, they should be made explicit and justified (Barry 1999; Shrader-Frechette 2002). Possible justifications for departures from equality include need, capability, and desert, for example (Barry 1999).

Need and capability are related to vulnerability, one of the core concepts of research on adaptation to climate change. Adaptation research frequently defines vulnerability as a function of exposure, sensitivity, and adaptive capacity (Adger 2003a; Smit and Pilifosova 2003; Yohe and Tol 2002). For justice analysis, the key element of this definition is the sensitivity of vulnerable groups to climate change impacts that can be used to justify favoring them in adaptation planning and decisions. The definition also emphasizes that vulnerable groups have capacity to cope with environmental stress (Adger 2003a; chapter 11, by Thomas and Twyman).

The natural disaster literature also offers a useful definition of vulnerability. Wisner et al. (2004) define vulnerability as "the characteristics of a person or group and their situation that influence their capacity to anticipate, cope with, resist and recover from the impact of a natural hazard" (Wisner et al. 2004, 11). This definition regards vulnerability as the absence of adaptive capacity. The natural disaster literature definition draws attention to multiple factors such as assets, sources of livelihood, class, race, ethnicity, gender, and poverty, which are likely to demarcate vulnerable groups. This view of vulnerability informs my analysis below.

The starting point in this chapter is that climate change impacts cannot easily be boxed and that they interact in complex ways. Similarly, social vulnerability is manifested in and influenced by a variety of socioeconomic factors that cannot be easily captured by any one variable or indicator. This complexity makes it difficult to choose and design adaptation measures that would generate sought-after outcomes. The key sources of vulnerability analyzed in the chapter reflect those examined by the IPCC (2001b, 895–899) and include:

1. *Physical and intangible human capital* consists, for example, of longevity, health, nutritional status, literacy, education, skills, and information, and their lack is a source of vulnerability because it has an adverse effect on incomes, human development, and the capacity to act to alter these outcomes.

2. *Technological alternatives* such as transport and telecommunication networks, public utilities, and agricultural inputs may not be available, which reduces incomes and constrains both livelihood diversification and specialization. It can also form an impediment for human development.

3. *Levels of income* may not buffer sufficiently against environmental stress and *sources of income* such as agriculture may be risky—dependence on them is thus a source of vulnerability.

4. *Inequality of incomes and human development* are sources of vulnerability as they create deprived and vulnerable groups and reduce social cohesion and capacity to act collectively.

5. *Social capital* enhances the capacity to act collectively and *the quality of institutions* contributes to economic growth and delivery of public services. Their lack is an obstacle for broadening the set of adaptation alternative for agents and for improving their incomes and human development outcomes.

The checklist describes vulnerability as a set of static independent descriptors, but vulnerability also has a dynamic side to it (Leichenko and O'Brien 2002). Static and dynamic descriptors of vulnerability help to identify and characterize vulnerable groups, but they are not necessarily root causes of vulnerability—factors that constitute that state and dispose certain individuals and groups as vulnerable (see Adger and Kelly 1999). Stressors also interact either by dampening or magnifying each others' impact. For example, Leichenko and O'Brien (2000, 228) examine how climate change and economic globalization may create "double losers" such as the continent of Africa (see chapter 5, by Leichenko and O'Brien, and chapter 11, by Thomas and Twyman).

Current Climate Variability, Predicted Climate Changes, and Impacts

Tanzania already experiences significant climate variability. Households and communities have adapted to it in various ways, which will also be important for adaptation to climate change because it will manifest in the country mainly as increased climate variability. Current climate variability involves recurring droughts, which rural farming communities cope with by modifying their livelihood practices in several ways (Paavola 2004). Many farming communities cultivate maize, rice, and cassava and rear chickens and goats for their subsistence. Cattle play a central role in parts of the country. A traditional strategy for coping with climate variability in farming includes crop switching. Farmers plant rice or maize in years with adequate rains and switch to millet or complement other crops with cassava in dry years. Another way to cope is to extend cultivations in dry years. The use of forest resources for generating cash income by producing and selling timber, charcoal, or bricks also increases during droughts. Other coping strategies include sending children to cities to work for upkeep and cash income. Pastoralists cope with droughts by selling cattle and dividing up households and herds to subgroups that relocate in search of water and grazing.

Current livelihoods and coping measures also have interactions and environmental impacts. Expansion of cultivations and the use of forests as safety nets can result in deforestation, which causes soil erosion, alters water flows, and threatens livelihoods. Reduced water retention means that river basins can flood after rains more frequently. This causes property damage in human settlements and increases the incidence of waterborne diseases such as gastroenteritis, typhoid, and cholera. Between rains, the availability of water is likely to decrease. Relocation of pastoralists breaks up families in addition to herds, and can increase the incidence of HIV/AIDS. Relocation can also result in conflicts between farmers and pastoralists over water use and damage done to cultivations by cattle. Droughts have also increased migration to cities where the newcomers have a difficulty in supporting themselves and contribute to homelessness, drug abuse, and crime.

Climate change will increase climate variability and put current coping measures under stress. Tanzania is projected to warm by 2–4°C by 2100, somewhat less than northwestern and southern Africa. Inner highlands are predicted to warm more than coastal areas and cold and dry seasons will warm more than warm and wet seasons. Rainfall is predicted to decrease by about 0–20 percent in the inner parts of the country, with dry seasons becoming longer and drier. In contrast, rainfall may increase by 30–50 percent in the northeast, southeast, and the Lake Victoria basin (Hulme et al. 2001; IPCC 2001b; Mwandosya, Nyenzi, and Luhanga 1998, 1–24).

The impacts of these climate changes have been discussed at length in the IPCC reports and in national vulnerability and impact studies (IPPC 2001b; Mwandosya, Nyenzi, Luhanga 1998), and here it suffices to summarize their main findings. Tanzania will experience climate change as increased climate variability (Clark, Webster, and Cole 2003; IPCC 2001b). Predicted changes in mean temperature, rainfall patterns, and rainfall variability are likely to prolong dry seasons and to increase

Table 10.1
Summary of predicted climate change impacts on Tanzania

Climate impacts	Current situation	Future situation
Food production	Climate variability has a significant impact on food production and security	Staple crop yields will decrease and food production risks increase
Forests and land cover	Substantial stocks of forest resources, but land use changes and harvesting levels cause deforestation	Land cover changes, fires and coping with droughts accelerate deforestation
Water resources	Periodic droughts and flooding	Periodic droughts and flooding become more frequent Deforestation increases seasonal flooding and water scarcity
Human settlements	Low-lying settlements affected by floods	Floods will cause property damage more frequently
Human health	Water and insect-borne diseases cause significant mortality and morbidity	The spread and incidence of water and insectborne diseases increases

the severity of periodic droughts. This will be pronounced in the interior part of the country. The northeast, southeast, and the Lake Victoria basin will be less exposed to droughts, but they are likely to experience more frequent and severe flooding. The predicted sea level rise of 0.1–0.9 metres will aggravate flooding in the coastal areas.

Predicted climate changes (see table 10.1) will significantly impact food production. Warming will shorten the growing season and, together with reduced rainfall, reduce water availability. Warming will also increase crop losses due to weeds, diseases, and pests. Regional predictions suggest that Tanzania may loose 10 percent of its grain production by 2080 (Parry et al. 1999; Downing 2002b). Maize, a staple crop grown by half of Tanzanians and providing a third of their daily calorie intake, is likely to be hit hard. Average maize yield is predicted to decrease by 33 percent by 2075 if CO_2 concentrations double and temperature increases 2–4 degrees. Yields may decrease by 80 percent in the central Tabora-Dodoma region (Mwandosya, Nyenzi, and Luhanga 1998, 181). There is considerable uncertainty regarding the yields of cash crops such as coffee, cotton, and tea. Increasing frequency and severity of water stress will also adversely affect livestock rearing, particularly cattle.

Land cover is also predicted to change as a result of climate changes and increased frequency and intensity of fires. Grassland savannah and dryland forest are predicted to become more common. This can have significant adverse consequences for rural livelihoods. Forests and woodlands are an important source of fuel in Tanzania, where biomass accounts for 90 percent of total energy use. Moreover, sale of timber and charcoal offers income that is particularly important during droughts. Forests also provide poles and timber for construction, fodder for livestock, as well as fruits, medicinal plants, gums, resins, and meat. Studies indicate that forest products may contribute a half of total income for some households (Meshack 2003).

Tanzania's water resources will experience varied climate change impacts. Some watercourses such as the Rufiji will have slightly increased water flows, but the Ruvu supplying Dar es Salaam and the Pangani supplying Tanga will have reduced water flows. Whereas the annual flow changes are only about 5 to 10 percent, predicted minimum flows in the dry season are less than half of the present ones in Ruvu and Pangani, and predicted peak flow in rainy season about twice the present one for the Rufiji (Mwandosya, Nyenzi, Luhanga 1998, 34–50). Increased water flows contribute to floods that adversely affect human settlements and health. Reductions in water flow will impact the use of water for power generation, irrigation, and public water supply. Increased evaporation and reduced rainfall may also affect the recharge of groundwater and its use.

Human settlements will be affected by flooding and the scarcity and low quality of water. Floods will become more frequent, especially in the coastal region. This will likely result in the destruction of infrastructure and property in the floodplains, which in the cities are populated by the poor and marginalized households. Floods will also affect public health as they will flood pit latrines and pollute both wells and surface waters with human wastes. Droughts will impact all settlements, requiring more time for water collection and resulting in reduced water use and impaired hygiene (see Johnstone et al. 2002). Impaired hygiene will have adverse health effects (Cairncross 2003), whereas increased use of time for water collection reduces income-earning and other opportunities.

Human health will be affected by climate change because the increased frequency of droughts and flooding increases the incidence of water-borne diseases such as typhoid and cholera. Flooding and increased rainfall are also likely to increase the incidence of insectborne diseases such as malaria, schistosomiasis, and trypanosomiasis and to expand their range (IPCC 2001; McMichael et al. 1996; Patz et al. 2002; Rogers and Randolph 2000).

Tanzania will face many other climate change impacts as well, but the ones on agriculture, forests, water resources, human settlements, and human health are the most threatening for the majority of Tanzanians. These climate impacts interact in complex ways. Decreasing agricultural yields may result in expansion of cultivations by reducing fallow periods and by clearing forest. Coping by appropriating forest products for cash income and subsistence needs may also result in deforestation. Deforestation and other land cover changes may alter water retention, evaporation, ground water recharge, and run-off in watersheds. The results can include increased peak flows, reduced average flows, and seasonal loss of water flows. More frequent flooding will impact settlements and health, and the greater scarcity of water will impact farming, cattle, and human health. There are also intimate connections among nutrition, health, and income-earning capacity. In general, malnutrition and food shortages increase morbidity and mortality related to infectious diseases and reduce the ability to generate income and to provide for subsistence needs (Fogel 1986, 1994; Szreter 1997).

Vulnerability and Its Multiple Sources in Tanzania

Lack of human capital and access to technologies, low levels and unequal distribution of income and well-being, and lack of social capital and

Table 10.2
Summary of current and future vulnerabilities of Tanzania to climate change

Vulnerabilities	Current	Future
Human capital	Health and educational outcomes are poor and deteriorating. Rural outcomes are worse than urban ones	Future deterioration in health and educational outcomes is possible and urban-rural divide is likely to persist
Access to technologies	Weak communications, transport and utility infrastructure	Infrastructure will improve and provide better access especially in urban areas
Income levels and risks	Subsistence agriculture the most important and environmentally risky source of livelihoods and income	Subsistence farming remains important but is increasingly complemented with market participation and its risks
Inequality	Urban-rural divide important manifestation of inequality both in terms of income and human development	Inequality is likely to increase both in terms of incomes and human development
Social capital and the quality of institutions	Capacity for collective action present but institutions lack quality and the state suffers from lack of capacity	Considerable uncertainty regarding the stability and strength of civil society as well as state capacity

state capacity are key sources of vulnerability in Tanzania (see table 10.2). Lack of human capital prevents Tanzanians from improving their incomes. Their life expectancy at birth is only 46.5 years, in part because adults die prematurely of HIV/AIDS, malaria, tuberculosis, and diarrheal diseases (URT 1997; WHO 2002). Infant mortality rate is also over 100 per 1,000 live births and mortality of children under five is 164 per 1,000 live births. Half of the population is undernourished, and of children under five, 29 percent are underweight and 44 percent under height. Adult literacy rate is a comparatively high 75.1 percent (UNDP 2002a). Although nearly all children start primary education, only half of them complete it and completion rates are lower among the poor and in rural areas (World Bank 2002b, 99). Life expectancy, literacy, and school enrollment have decreased over the past decade and HIV/AIDS and fiscal constraints make it difficult to alter these trends in the near future.

Access to technologies is important for coping with environmental stress. For instance, seasonal weather forecasts are useful only if affected people have access to communication technologies. National radio stations provide the main media access in Tanzania and there are 278 radios per 1,000 people—over twice as many as in the neighboring countries (World Bank 2002b, 4). Private radio and TV stations provide additional access to media in urban areas. There are only three landline and five mobile phone connections per 1,000 people—the average in least developed countries (UNDP 2002a). Newspapers are distributed mainly in the urban areas. Radio will continue to provide the main access to media, but urban areas will enjoy a wider set of media such as the internet in the future.

Transport infrastructure influences access to markets, livelihood opportunities, and vulnerability to food, water, and fuel shortages. Tanzania's transport networks are sparse even by African standards (Platteau 2000, 35–36). The country has about 100 kilometers of classified roads per $1,000 km^2$ but only a small proportion of them are passable in all seasons and only 1 percent is paved.[2] There are two rail systems but less than 4 km of railroad per $1,000 km^2$ in the country.[3] Yet transport infrastructure has improved significantly over the last decade and is likely to continue improving.

Access to public utilities such as water, sewer, and electricity networks influences health outcomes and the availability of time and resources for income-generating activities. Official figures indicate that 90 percent of urban and 57 percent of rural Tanzanians have access to safe water and that 99 percent of urbanites and 86 percent of rural dwellers have access to adequate sanitation. Yet less than half of urban population and only 4 percent of rural population has access to piped water (Clarke and Wallsten 2002) and sewer systems exist only in 18 cities, where they serve about 17 percent of the population. Only 7 percent of urbanites have access to flush toilets or ventilated latrines, and less than 1 percent of rural population has access to anything other than the traditional pit latrine. Pit latrines pollute groundwater—often the most important source of drinking water—and can cause epidemics of cholera and typhoid when flooding occurs. Hand pumps do not guarantee safe supply of water during droughts and flooding and cause epidemics where groundwater is polluted by human wastes. About a quarter of the population of cities and 1 percent of rural population have access to electricity, but it is used mainly for illumination while less expensive charcoal is used for cooking. Charcoal is a renewable and affordable source of energy, but its widespread use is also associated with indoor air pollution, respiratory illnesses, and deforestation. A greater proportion of population may enjoy better access to utilities in the future as continuing urbanization will make service provision easier.

Low levels and risky sources of income add to vulnerability in Tanzania. The country had the second lowest per capita income of PPP US $523 of 173 countries in 2002 (UNDP 2002a). Real per capita income has not improved for fifteen years. Primary production generates half of GDP, whereas services account for about a third and manufacturing for less than 10 percent of the GDP. Tanzania exports 10 percent of its GDP, with export of coffee, cashew nuts, cotton, tea, tobacco, and sisal making over half of Tanzania's total exports in 1998 (World Bank 2002b, 269). Minerals are a growing export item that makes the country even more dependent on natural resource exports. Moreover, wildlife and other environmental resources attract a growing number of tourists. Unfavorable price trends have plagued Tanzania's export and remain a risk, unless the export portfolio becomes more diverse. However, the composition of Tanzania's GDP has been stable and it is unlikely to change rapidly in the future.

Tanzania is a relatively equalitarian least developed country—its Gini coefficient is 0.388, equal to that of United Kingdom (UNDP 2002a, 194–195). However, over half of the population is below the national poverty line and one out of five lives with less than PPP $1 a day (UNDP 2002a). In human development, the clearest divide prevails between urban and rural populations. Rural communities have lower developmental attainments because of their low incomes and lack of access to markets and public services. Under increasing fiscal pressures and market orientation inequality is likely to increase in the future both in terms of incomes and human development.

Social capital and quality of institutions influence the ability of communities and nations to cope with environmental stress collectively, and their lack is a source of vulnerability. Precolonial, colonial, and postindependence experiences have shattered traditional authority structures in Tanzania. For example, the country was subjected to villigization in the 1960s and 1970s to provide health care, education, water supply, and transport (Pinkney 1997, 2). The ruling political party Chama Cha Mapinduzi (CCM) intervened deeply into the new *ujamaa* villages to break up traditional authority structures and to create new ones. This created authority conflicts between party organization and public administration (Yeager 1989). There is heterogeneity in the country in ethnic, linguistic, religious, economic, and spatial terms, but it has not become divisive. Tanzanians have embraced their somewhat limited freedom of association by creating thousands of nongovernmental organizations (TANGO 2002). Most frequently, individuals belong to church organizations, burial societies, and farmers' groups (Narayan and Prichett 1997, 9). These organizations work reasonably according to their members and accommodate heterogeneity at the local level (Narayan and Prichett 1997, 11). Many villages also manage their resources collectively and have established a *sungusungu*, a neighborhood watch, to protect public safety and property (Tripp 1997).

African states—both political systems and public administration—are considered weak and sometimes the reason for underdevelopment (see Englebert 2000).[4] In Tanzania, political participation was first possible only through the ruling party CCM (Pinkney 1997). Although CCM controlled the media and its membership and privileges were misused, its rule was not based on violence. Its egalitarian ethos was based on more widely shared values and its leadership contributed to important developmental attainments (see Pinkney 1997, 87–88; Tripp 1997). CCM endorsed the transition to a multiparty system in 1992, which has helped to maintain relatively peaceful political life in the mainland. These political developments are reflected in the assessments of the Freedom House (Freedom House 2003).[5] Throughout the 1970s and the

1980s, Tanzania earned a score of six for both rights and civil liberties and was deemed "not free." The country has improved its scores for both rights and civil liberties to four during the 1990s and is now deemed "partially free." However, the opposition party Civic United Front (CUF) have suffered from violence and the Islamic Awareness Society has engaged in small-scale terror in Zanzibar.

Tanzania inherited a limited central public administration from the colonial era and established local governments in 1962 (Pinkney 1997). It also increased state control over the economy during the 1960s and the early 1970s. This gave public sector employees a powerful position. The Arusha Declaration of 1967 addressed this problem by adopting a leadership code of conduct that denied party and state leadership's engagement in economic activities. However, decreasing real earnings created incentives for earning side income and corruption. Close linkages between party organization and public administration also resulted in patronage and other misuses of political power. Public administration often lacks the capacity to carry out its tasks. For example, some local governments have failed to collect up to half of local poll taxes (Fjeldstad and Semboja 2001).[6] The perceived level of corruption is high. In 2002, Tanzania scored 2.7 in Transparency International's (2003) *Perceived Corruption Index*, where scores range from zero for highly corrupted to ten for free from corruption.[7] However, a World Bank survey found that the level and complexity of taxes, inadequate infrastructure, and export and import regulations were greater business obstacles than corruption (World Bank 2002b).[8] Ongoing reforms are addressing problems of public administration, but their impact is not yet clear. For example, public sector pay reforms have increased salaries, but they are still below the level deemed adequate for subsistence.

Predicted Climate Changes, Justice, and Adaptation

An urban-rural divide is the most important axis of inequality in Tanzania and other developing countries (for the original urban bias argument, see Lipton 1977). Aggravation of this inequality would be the most significant justice consequence of predicted climate change impacts. Climate change will adversely affect food production and energy and water supply, which are preconditions of well-being for rural households. Predicted climate changes will also have adverse consequences for their incomes. At the same time, rural populations are more vulnerable to climate change than the urban ones. Health status, nutritional status, and educational attainment are all lower in rural areas than in the cities. Rural inhabitants also lack access to technological alternatives, markets, and public services and have lower levels of income than urbanites. Finally, rural local governments have less capacity and resources than the urban ones.

The urban poor are another vulnerable group, but they face more specific environmental stresses than the rural people. The urban poor often settle on risky areas such as steep slopes or low lying valleys that are prone to landslides or flooding. In Dar es Salaam, two-thirds of the population (over two million people) live in flood-prone areas (UNEP 2002b, 241). Although the urban poor suffer from many of the same vulnerabilities as the rural people, such as poor health and education and low incomes, they have better access to casual employment, other sources of income, and public services. Their exposure can also often be reduced effectively by land use planning and infrastructure development.

Predicted climate change impacts also have other distributive consequences. Women's activities—tilling fields and collecting firewood and water—will be adversely affected by changing climate. More time will be needed for carrying out these activities and less will be left for other activities such as earning cash income. More market-oriented activities of male members of households will be less affected. Predicted climate change impacts could thus increase gender inequality. This is particularly so given the low participation of women in formal labor markets.

Predicted climate change impacts are also likely to increase the participation of children in economic and household production activities. There is evidence of this already having happened because of the past decade's economic hardships and the HIV/AIDS epidemic. Moreover, families are sending children to work in cities for maintenance and cash income to cope with the ongoing drought. Children who participate in economic and household production activities often have to drop out of school. Other predicted climate change impacts also influence children more negatively than adults. For example, nutritional deficiencies, illnesses, and lack of education in childhood have irreversible consequences that can burden affected individuals throughout their adulthood.

Pastoralists are another vulnerable group whose livelihoods are likely to be affected significantly by predicted climate changes. They are also vulnerable because of their poverty and because their entitlements to key environmental resources such as pastures and water are contested and uncertain. Pastoralists are already blamed for water scarcity in parts of the country and there have been violent conflicts between them and farmers (see Paavola 2004).

The NAPA process and future national adaptation planning and decision making would need to make a special effort to recognize and involve the above discussed and other particularly vulnerable groups. Ordinary consultation of the private sector, the NGOs, and various governmental organizations does not guarantee adequate involvement of the most vulnerable groups, even if consultations are taken out to the regions. Many vulnerable groups face the same kind of obstacles in effective participation in consultations as they face in access to markets and public services. In the post-NAPA future, a multitiered adaptation planning framework, where adaptation plans and priorities are generated in a bottom-up inclusive process, could offer a greater degree of participation for those who live in remote rural locations and who do not have resources to spend for voicing their concerns.

But procedural justice is not the only thing that matters: adaptation plans and measures also need to alleviate the vulnerability of the most vulnerable groups in order to be just. The best starting point for examining distributive aspects of national adaptation plans and measures is to ask what would be the implications of their absence. This would mean that households and organizations would have to adapt on their own. Although they can often adapt efficiently, they only do so given the resources in their command and in the face of alternatives that are given to them. That is, private adaptation takes place in a setting that allocates decision-making authority according to willingness and ability to pay—those who are able and willing to pay allocate resources to adaptation to benefit themselves. That is, private adaptive responses do not allocate resources so as to prioritize the improvement of most vulnerable people's situation. Democratic decisions on which public responses are based distribute decision-making power differently and generate different distributive outcomes. This is why public responses should complement private adaptation. Private adaptation solutions may appear attractive because of the weak capacity of public administration. However, exclusive reliance on private adaptation is problematic because of the above discussed reasons and because it diverts attention away from the importance of improving state capacity.

There is likely to be no magic bullet for adapting to climate change in Tanzania because climate change impacts and sources of vulnerability are linked together in complex ways. It is more likely that a set of complementary measures are needed for satisfactory and equitable adaptation. Effective environmental governance, strengthening of national markets, and enhancement of human capital are examples of measures that are needed for fair adaptation to changing climate in the country. As discussed below, these measures complement each other in important ways and cannot be considered substitutes.

Effective environmental governance should be a priority because rural (and to an extent urban) communities depend on environmental resources. Effective environmental governance could maintain stocks of resources such as forests that are needed to overcome periods of environmental stress. Because of the government's weak capacity to implement national policies, governance solutions have to include user participation. Tanzania's forest policy already delegates some management authority to local communities (Ylhäisi 2003) and the solution can be used in the management of water resources, coastal resources, and infrastructure (Dungumaru and Madulu 2003; Kironde and Yhdego 1997; Kyessi 2005; Maganga 2003). Decentralized environmental governance can build capacity and social capital at the local level for other undertakings. However, local collective entities do not necessarily have the authority, expertise, and resources of the central government and they do not have incentives to transfer lessons to others. Therefore, government, civil society organizations, intermediate levels of administration, and local communities are all needed in co-management.

Effective environmental governance insures against the worst outcomes but it should not remain the only public adaptation measure. Effective environmental governance can maintain stocks of environmental resources and facilitate their subsistence and other uses. However, a subsistence economy may not be diverse enough to cope with climate variability and risks. Moreover, it does not realize potential gains from specialization that is necessary for improved productivity. Effective environmental governance should therefore be complemented with strengthening of national markets and improving access to them. This requires infrastructure investments in communications and transport networks and institutional reforms that reduce corruption and improve the security of entitlements, enforcement of contracts, and availability of credit. Well-functioning national markets reduce vulnerability and assist in adaptation in several ways. Improved access to markets opens up a wider range of income-generating activities and facilitates specialization that increases productivity. It also helps to overcome local food shortages and local monopolies.

Strengthening of markets should not be pursued as an exclusive solution, however. Improved market access is likely to increase the pressure on natural resources as well as to increase inequality. Effective governance of environmental resources complements improved access to markets by maintaining safety nets that are particularly important for the poor. These safety nets will be needed as long as levels of income are low and sources of income are subject to considerable environmental risks. Strengthening of markets would also be an insufficient response in another sense. Poor nutrition and health outcomes and limited educational attainment are obstacles for the improvement of incomes and other developmental outcomes and thus for the reduction of vulnerabilities. Mortality and morbidity have exacted a heavy toll from the poor households in the past and the HIV/AIDS epidemic is shattering entire communities.

Improving health and physical well-being can have a high social return. Public services focused on maintaining and enhancing human capital could assist in fair adaptation. Local resources can often be mobilized for health promotion (Szreter and Woolcock 2004). Yet if literacy rates and educational enrolment continue to decrease, effectiveness of educational campaigns and health promotion may decrease. Thus a broad commitment to public programs and spending on health and education will be important, and it cannot be replaced by improved access to markets or improved incomes.

Finally, a distinction should be made between the state of vulnerability and the set of factors that constitute it. Modifying outcomes such as poor nutrition or lack of food security does not necessarily eliminate vulnerability. Reducing vulnerability demands changes in factors that lie behind poor nutrition or lack of food security. Food aid may alleviate hunger and guarantee survival but does not affect root causes of insecurity such as inequality or access to markets. This is why proactive measures are important. This does not mean that the treatment of symptoms of vulnerability is wrong: there are times when it is a question of life and death. Reactive measures are needed to share the burden of immediate stresses and hazards. But reducing immediate vulnerability is not enough. More fundamental changes in institutions are needed to bring about permanent reduction in vulnerabilities.

Conclusion

This chapter has examined the justice implications of predicted climate change impacts in the light of current and likely future vulnerabilities in Tanzania. Projected warming, altered rainfall patterns, and increased climate variability are likely to have their greatest impacts on food production, forests, water resources, human settlement, and health in Tanzania. The rural population, particularly women, children, and pastoralists, is likely to suffer more from the predicted climate change impacts than urban population. Rural communities are also already vulnerable to environmental stress.

The NAPA process and the future national solutions for adaptation planning would need to make a special effort to involve and facilitate the participation of these groups. Their interests will also demand certain features from just national adaptation measures. Effective governance of environmental resources, improvement of functioning of and access to markets, and public services maintaining and enhancing human capital would benefit the most vulnerable groups and together be robust enough to address the linkages between climate change impacts and sources of vulnerability. Public adaptation measures have to harness the potential contribution of local communities and users, but they also have to include an element of state-building and enhancement of state capacity in order to be sustainable.

Acknowledgments

This chapter is based on a work undertaken as part of the Strategic Assessment of Equity and Justice in Adaptation to Climate Change undertaken by FIELD, IIED, CSERGE, and the Tyndall Centre. It is also a part of Programme on Environmental Decision Making at CSERGE supported by the UK Economic and Social Research Council. I thank Neil Adger, Suraje Dessai, Paula Saukko, and two anonymous reviewers for their helpful comments and suggestions. Any shortcomings remain my own responsibility.

Notes

1. This geographical focus on continental Tanzania is warranted because Zanzibar faces climate change impacts more akin to those facing other small island states than those facing the mainland.

2. Densely populated western European countries have 1,500–2,500 km of roads per 1,000 km². Less densely populated developed countries have 200–700 km of roads per 1,000 km².

3. Sparsely populated developed countries typically have 15–30 km and densely populated developed countries 30–100 km of railroad per 1,000 km².

4. A state is weak when it lacks the capacity to (1) make decisions unconstrained by special interests, (2) take decisions on the basis of comprehensive information and by involving the relevant government organizations, and (3) ensure that its decisions are complied with (see Polidano 2000, 809–810).

5. Freedom House ranks political rights and civil liberties with scores ranging from 1 to 7. "Free" countries have a score of less than 2.5 for rights and

liberties. Partially free countries have scores between 3.0 and 5.5. Countries are not free if their scores are higher than 5.5.

6. Tax evasion has its roots in poverty and mistrust of local governments that have misused public funds in the past.

7. Tanzania shared its score with Côte D'Ivoire, Honduras, India, Russia, and Zimbabwe, whereas Uganda, Kenya, and Zambia had worse scores.

8. For comparison, in Uganda and Kenya, corruption was deemed to be the second most important business obstacle (World Bank 2002b, 132).

11

Adaptation and Equity in Resource Dependent Societies

David S. G. Thomas and Chasca Twyman

This chapter examines the implications of climate change for equity and justice in developing, natural resource dependent societies for two reasons. First, a considerable body of research suggests the poorest and most vulnerable (of which natural resource–dependent groups in the developing world are an example) disproportionately experience the negative effects of environmental changes. Second, international conventions and other programs have increasingly recognized the need to engage resource users to achieve their desired aims, as part of more holistic approaches to sustainable development. These two issues encapsulate, therefore, issues of distributive and procedural justice in both vulnerability and in adaptation responses, particularly when framed within the efforts of the UNFCCC.

The climate change literature is replete with the received wisdom that developing countries are more vulnerable to the effects of climate change than those that are more economically developed (Beg et al. 2002; Burton 1996; Smit and Pilifisova 2001), because of the low capacity to adapt of the developing nations. Following distinctions made thoughout this book, justice can be considered to have *distributive* and *procedural* elements, where the former relates to the distribution of benefits and adverse affects of climate change across society, and the latter to how and by whom decisions on adaptive responses are made. In many respects equity issues relating to outcomes are most acute in natural resource dependent communities in the developing world because of the multitude of primary and secondary impacts that filter down through natural and social systems (Adger et al. 2003b). As elaborated earlier in this book, adaptation to climate change therefore potentially creates significant dilemmas of justice to the international community in this North-South context.

The predominant focus of the UNFCCC on national and larger scales potentially leaves a vacuum at subnational levels with regard to the equitable nature of the impacts of adaptive strategies to climatic change. This is significant, because climate change has the potential, indeed likelihood, of impacting on and disrupting the development process. Kates (2000) and others even suggest that adaptation processes and strategies are likely not simply to disrupt development, but to enhance inequalities in well being, by creating winners and losers (see chapter 5, by Leichenko and O'Brien).

In this chapter we explore these issues through several themes. First, we consider the fundamental question of whether there is a reason to be concerned about equity and justice issues in climate change impacts and adaptations in the developing world. Second, we consider equity and justice within current natural resource use and access in the developing world, and to provide a baseline against which future adaptation issues can be set. Third, we explore the processes and structures through which responses to climate variability and change occur among natural resource dependent groups. Finally, we give consideration to the impacts of international conventions and agreements on local level resource use, through the processes of national actions and governance. Our examples are primarily drawn from the African context, which reflects both the identified susceptibility of that continent to climate change impacts (IPCC 1997) and our own direct research experiences and activities.

Equity in Vulnerability and Impact Assessment

Tropical and subtropical agricultural systems are, in the main, regarded in scientific assessments to be those most vulnerable to disruption by even minor temperature increases (e.g., Tol et al. 2000). Despite uncertainties in many scenarios regarding low-latitude precipitation changes, a common prediction is of high decadal temperature increases (0.2–1.7°C) (Hulme 1996; Ringius et al. 1996), and a likely increase in extreme drought and flood events (IPCC 1997). It is not surprising therefore that many general regional and national surveys in the developing world predict gloomy outcomes of climate change, with significant vulnerabilities identified, for example, for regions of west Africa (Denton, Sokona, and Thomas 2000), South Africa (Kikar 2000), and India (Kumar and Parikh 2001).

These surveys, projecting significant impacts and identifying vulnerabilities, are often conducted using national level data and formal institutional criteria. Yet there are an ever growing number of detailed local and regional studies that show considerable resourcefulness in the face of external change (Mortimore and Adams 2001; Scoones 2001; Reij and Waters-Bayer 2001). There is also some recognition of these local level differences in the climate change literature, but more as "complexities" in trying to achieve generalizations than as realities (see Smit and Pilifosova 2001, 898). These local pictures also raise issues of equity and justice within and between communities. For example, Pelling (1999) illustrates how responses to extreme weather events always benefit some groups through the creation of economic opportunities such as waste clearance, capturing of aid flows, and other sources.

High reliance on natural resources in the developing world is often portrayed as a significant dimension of perceived vulnerability to climate change impacts. In Africa it is commonly considered that agriculture is the primary rural activity, though agricultural productivity has been in decline in recent decades (World Bank 2000). IPCC (1997) used figures indicating a third of Africa's land area being used for agriculture, 30 percent of African GDP being derived from agricultural production, and 75 percent of the population living in rural areas and being engaged in agriculture as evidence of high vulnerability to climate change.

However, empirical studies suggest that only 20–40 percent of rural African income is currently derived directly from the land (Bryceson 2002), due to a process of "deagrarianization" attributed to long-term occupational adjustment and spatial relocation in rural areas (Bryceson 2002). There is also significant evidence indicating that African rural livelihoods are diversified (Dercon and Krishnan 1996) rather than overly focused on agricultural production, as suggested by the gross country level data used by the IPCC (1997) and others.

The concept of diversification embraces household and community livelihood structures that can include diversification *beyond* and *within* agriculture and natural resource use (Twyman, Sporton, and Thomas 2004). Diversification within natural resource use *may* support the notion of the vulnerability of current African livelihood patterns to climate change. However, the fact that diversification occurs *at all* is indicative of a level of responsiveness to external forcing factors that may be significant in terms of the capability to adapt. This is particularly so as there is evidence that livelihood changes can be triggered by or occur despite the effects of drought (Mortimore and Adams 2001) or changes in the natural resource base (Thomas and Twyman 2004).

A number of equity and justice issues are implicated in the discussion above. First, for individuals and communities reliant on natural resources, climate change represents hypothetical stresses in the context of other livelihood disturbing factors (see Dow and colleagues in chapter 4). Table 11.1 elaborates these factors and their interactions. Drought and flood have different impacts and temporal and sociopolitical scales to the stresses associated with conflict, HIV/AIDS and the vagaries of economic globalization. But this observation does not mean that adaptation issues can or should be ignored: climate change is happening. Second, despite the relatively low level of greenhouse gas emissions, many developing world governments have ratified the UNFCCC (Grubb and Depledge 2001), and will therefore respond to the obligations of the convention, including adaptation needs.

A third justice issue relates to policy processes and planning for climate change by governments. The socioeconomic vulnerability of the developing world demands that equity has to be included within all dimensions of the climate debate if it is to remain relevant to vulnerable groups and the governments of the countries within which they reside (e.g., Sokona and Denton 2001). Issues of equity require realism on the part of those assessing and developing adaptation strategies at national levels. They need, through open and inclusive processes (see Huq and Khan in chapter 9) to recognize climate as only one of many factors that disturb livelihood and that have differentiated outcomes.

Table 11.1
Examples of factors affecting developing world natural resource-dependant livelihoods

Factor	Impacting on	Short-term response	Long-term response	Risk factor
Droughts	Famine, plant resource base, livestock, moisture availability	Food aid, short term migration	Decrease sensitivity: drought resistant crops and animals, diverse livelihoods, migration	Spatially variable, high in subtropical Africa, southern Asia
Floods	Resource base, communications, life	Relief and aid, migration	Decrease sensitivity: Diverse livelihoods, resettlement	High in some catchments/countries
HIV/AIDS	Labor, household structure, poverty		Unknown, increased risk to other disturbing factors	Very high throughout developing world
War	Famine, displacement, (male) labor, poverty	Migration	Migration and displacement, declining rural production, increased vulnerability	High in some countries and regions
Land shortage	Food production for subsistence and markets	Migration, non-agricultural livelihoods, poverty	Formalized land redistribution, livelihood diversification	
Global market pressures	Crops and livestock, land tenure, wealth polarization, increasing risk in production	Adaptation to market pressures, lower returns on crops/livestock	Diverse livelihoods, move off land to give way to successful producers	High where policies/market economy favors capitalism

Equity and Justice in Current Natural Resource Access and Use: Lessons for Adaptation Strategies

There is growing evidence of the complexity of equity and social justice within current natural resource dependent systems. As we argued above, natural resource dependent societies already adapt livelihood strategies and activities to a wide variety of external factors. Further, there is a long legacy of inequitable access to, and control and use of, natural resources in the developing world (e.g., Berry 1989; Leach, Mearns, and Scoones 1999), especially in Africa. Therefore, contemporary understandings of adaptation to change (and the inherent equity and social justice dimensions) must be embedded within their historical contexts. This section explores equity and social justice in adaptation strategies of natural resource dependent societies through three contemporary examples from southern Africa. The examples draw lessons from policy interventions in resource management in farming areas of Botswana (Area 1) and water management (Area 2) and rangeland systems (Area 3) in Namibia, as figure 11.1 shows.

Distributive Justice in Botswana's Dryland Mixed-Farming Systems

Distributive justice refers to the distributional consequences of environmental decisions and actions. In southern Africa, research has shown that households and communities are recognizing new natural resource use and livelihood opportunities in response to a range of drivers (Thomas, Sporton, and Twyman 2002). These adaptations occur in the context of both formal and informal opportunities, and, whether or not government interventions exist, rural people have demonstrated their resourcefulness. However, some interventions, and some instances where interventions have not been taken, are contributing to an uneven distribution of impacts and growing polarization of well being.

Our own research on a rural livelihood support and diversification program known as the Financial Assistance Programme (FAP) in Botswana has shown that intervention-generated opportunities may not be taken up evenly at the subnational level. The FAP awarded grants of up to 90 percent of total cost to support new or expanding business

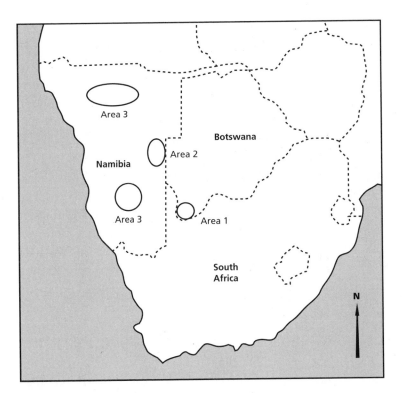

Figure 11.1
Three study sites on equity of outcomes and processes in resource management interventions in Botswana and Namibia. The research for the case study on distributive justice in Botswana's dryland mixed-farming systems was conducted in part of Kgalagadi District (Area 1 on map), and that for the case study of equity and empowerment in Namibia's communal rangelands in Omaheke District (Area 2 on map). The research for procedural justice and decentralization of rural water supply in Namibia was conducted in number of locations in the northern and central location of the country, within Area 3 on the map.

initiatives. Available in urban and rural areas, it was mainly seen as a way of supporting rural development. The FAP had the potential to generate livelihood diversification as it minimized the risks borne by individuals and could be applied flexibly in different urban and rural locations. Initiatives have included livestock purchases; agricultural developments such as market gardens and horticultural schemes; and other small enterprises, including brick making, bakeries, and transport services.

There have been notable discrepancies in the way FAP was implemented between districts in Botswana. In southeast Botswana, close to the market town of Lobatse, a range of individuals received FAP funding for a diversity of projects. However, in remote and arid southwest Botswana, many potential FAP benefits were not realized for two main reasons: very few non-smallstock-related schemes were supported and, significantly, the absence of financial infrastructure restricted the ability of individuals to make applications (Thomas, Sporton, and Twyman 2002).

A number of households in southwest Botswana applied to the FAP for schemes such as chicken breeding and small tourism initiatives, but only those relating to the dominant agricultural practice in the area, smallstock farming, received support. Consequently, individual attempts to diversity within and beyond agriculture were not supported. Frequently those who were better off were able to provide their 10 percent contribution to the total cost and thus benefit from the scheme. People repeatedly commented on the remoteness of the area relative to financial and other services, with two days' travel needed to visit a bank or the application office, meaning that any application required a considerable investment in time. The less well off often lacked the time and the means to travel in order to apply.

Formal attempts at progressive distribution of livelihood resources do not always have the intended outcomes. Some interventions are arguably even increasing, rather than reducing, vulnerability, particularly among poorer groups. Interventions for small stock livelihood support in southwest Botswana through the FAP, for example, were generally appropriate for natural resource based livelihoods. But the focus of the intervention had the unintended potential to increase vulnerability by restricting attempts at diversification by individual households.

Well-being differentials were also increasing as poorer farmers were excluded from access to the intervention due to too lengthy and complex an application procedure. These experiences contrasted with those of other areas where a wide variety of livelihoods were supported by the program. Interventions to promote resilience, well being, and adaptive capacity can therefore contribute to the widening of gaps in well being and to unsustainable natural resource use, as well as inhibiting local creativity and innovation in adaptation.

Procedural Justice and the Decentralization of Rural Water Supply in Namibia

Procedural justice is closely linked with notions of legitimacy. In particular, procedural justice is concerned with the absence of effects on others, or in the case of the presence of such impacts, informing the affected parties and obtaining their consent. However, when policies affect institutions that govern a key natural resource, especially at the local level, some fundamental questions relating to equity and justice need to be raised. For example, water resource management in rural dryland Africa is increasingly viewed as a local responsibility, rather than a state-centerd provision. This follows a global trend in community management of natural resources recognizing that local people may have a greater interest in the sustainable use of resources than more centralized government or private management institutions (Brosius, Tsing, and Zerner 1998). The decentralization of rural water supply in Namibia provides an interesting case.

The Directorate of Rural Water Supply is driving the decentralization process by handing over responsibility for water points to communities. Following the principle of cost recovery and financial sustainability through decentralization, the aim is for all rural water points in communal areas to be community managed by 2007. Under this policy, communities elect a water point committee to supervise the operation and maintenance of the water supply. Members of the committee are trained to manage the borehole pump, or pipeline-accessing tap. The committees must also embrace the issue of grazing management, because water and grazing for domestic stock are closely related.

In some cases, where wildlife and domestic stock compete for water resources, communities will also need to involve and collaborate with existing local institutions responsible for wildlife management. This may prove problematic because the emergence of community-based institutions for natural resource management is a relatively recent phenomenon in Namibia and members lack appropriate technical and organizational skills. It is intended that the water point committees will receive initial training from DRWS, but this will focus on water issues and may lack integration with other sector approaches. Once training is complete and committees are established, the government will lease the water point to the community.

Although on the one hand this can be seen as local level empowerment in decision making, it is also a cost recovery approach to rural water supply. The directorate is aware that this approach could cause marginalization at the local level but also admits that it will be difficult to identify in practice. Their approach maintains the principles of procedural justice at the core, and they have identified the need for additional extension officers to introduce this system to communities and "sensitize" them to the policy implementation process. For those communities that can be identified as "very poor," water points will continue to be subsidized by the government. However, the overall aim is that the "very poor" households in communities will be subsidized by the "rich." How this is to be achieved in practice is still unclear and the potential for exploitation and inequity remains.

Equity and Empowerment in Namibia's Communal Rangelands

Inclusive and democratic empowerment in resource management has been highlighted as a desirable development goal in itself (DFID 1997) and as an alternative route for development (Pieterse 1999). In practice, there are problematic assumptions in equating empowering structures with equitable processes. For whom is equity defined, and for what specific purposes? Is equity universally desirable (or possible), or will we always have "winners" and "losers"? Who defines the winners and losers and the parameters of equity? Overall, we need to question how closely equity and empowerment are linked.

Research in Namibia has examined empowerment and equity debates within the context of vulnerability, sustainability, and livelihoods in Okonyoka, a settlement of fewer than 150 people in Eastern Namibia's southern communal rangelands (Twyman et al. 2001). People here are adapting their livelihoods in response to NR variability and changes in social institutions and land use policies. Drought-coping strategies, rangeland privatization through fencing, and changes to social networks have had both positive and negative impacts on livelihoods. Of note is that Okonyoka is the first settlement in the area to erect a community fence, but surrounding settlements are likely to emulate this, given the positive environmental and societal results.

Such fences can, however, inhibit neighboring people's livelihoods, particularly the poor or socially excluded, and can change long-standing regional drought-coping strategies. Though Namibia's policy context is presently highly dynamic, such moves have the potential to radically change communal area landscapes. In a regional perspective, a community showing initiative, innovative thinking, and critical self-organization would be attractive for further government or NGO support. However, this case can be viewed positively or negatively, because there are both winners and losers. The selective use of procedural justice measures in this case by the people of Okonyoka (i.e., consulting with some but not all neighboring communities, especially those deemed "illegitimate") illustrates the problematic relationship between empowerment and equity.

These observations of community self-empowerment have marked implications for equity considerations and for those involved in the formalization of outcomes (Twyman et al. 2001). Equity impacts on both the self-empowering community and on marginalized neighboring groups need considering. Wider evidence to support this can be drawn from research in the Machakos District of Kenya (Tiffen, Mortimore, and Gichuki 1994; Morton 1999). Here changes in national policies allowed the reinstatement of "traditional" soil erosion strategies, facilitating a shift to more intensive market-oriented production. The reinstatement of traditional practices can be equated with self empowerment, and aggregate assessments of the outcomes in terms of productivity and wealth generation showed significant livelihood improvement (Tiffen, Mortimore, and Gichuki 1994). Morton (1999), however, identified losers as well as winners, with the marginalization of some households, leading to polarization of well-being, a potential outcome in the Okonyoka case above. Therefore, only with such multi-scale analysis of equity and empowerment can best-case scenarios be assessed and particular attention paid to supporting strategies that will enhance secure livelihoods and aid poverty reduction, in addition to enhancing our understanding of fairness.

Implications of Natural Resource Use Case Studies for Climate Change Adaptation

From the perspective of community level equity and justice in resource use and management, the cases above show clearly that community management is not the utopia widely suggested in current debate and practice. Procedural justice that empowers local actions needs to create "policy space" (cf. "head room" of Tompkins and Adger 2004) within which local actions can develop. Furthermore, even when this occurs, devolved decision making (an element of procedural justice) does not necessarily lead to distributive justice and equity in terms of resource access and actual local level decision making. As a result, winners and losers are produced at a range of scales, and equity may well be sidelined as an unobtainable ideal. So if climate change in developing countries impacts on the natural resource base, for example, by affecting species distributions, crop growing seasons, and water availability, the resource space for equity is likely to be reduced. Although resource shortages do not necessarily create conflict, they may well create different spaces in which it is more likely for winners and losers to polarize. The case of fencing in Namibian communal lands, with its drought dimension, is a prime example of this complexity. Furthermore, given the variability of institutions potentially adapting to climate change at a range of different scales, the explicit role of equity in outcome (whether intended, unintended, expected, or unexpected) needs to be a central concern.

Global to Local: Room for Maneuver in Responses to Climate Change

There is growing recognition that individuals and communities in the developing world can be highly resourceful in responding and adapting to external disturbances and change. Whether or not climate change at the local level is manifestly different in its impact on livelihood strategies from other agencies of disturbance and change, the ability to adapt and respond appears to be manifest in developing world communities if there is space or head room (Tompkins and Adger 2004) for adaptation to occur at multiple temporal and spatial scales. Space may be real tangible space, economic space, or policy space. For developing communities that depend on agriculture, climate change impacts may be regarded as reducing environmental opportunities (Tol et al. 2000), although many case studies indicate that adaptation within agriculture can be opportunistic and can have multiple facets that do not rely on the availability of physical space (Mortimore and Adams 2001; Tiffen, Mortimore, and Gichuki 1994). The ability to diversify beyond and within natural resource reliance clearly exists in the developing world, as witnessed by widely documented evidence of livelihood diversification. Economic space and capacity for diversification beyond and within natural resource use is also needed, as is policy space that allows local level innovations and responses to evolve. This is a major lesson from the case studies from southern Africa outlined in this chapter.

These observations would suggest that at the national and international levels, policy responses to climate change should be oriented toward creating or facilitating the emergence of this "room for manoeuver" (Clay and Schaffer 1984), thus enabling rather than inhibiting local and regional adaptation options. Clearly, international responses to climate change, including the mitigation process, must not compromise the development process if international justice is to be achieved (Kates 2000). Advocating a room for maneuver approach is not to suggest a lighter touch to climate change adaptation policy. Rather, it calls for recognition of the need to *create* space, and the right kind of space, and to *facilitate* appropriate, innovative, and creative adaptation, that retains principles of equity and social justice at its core.

Beg et al. (2002) indicate that there may be useful synergies between the UNFCCC and other international conventions such as the UN Convention to Combat Desertification (UNCCD) and the UN Convention on Biological Diversity in achieving successful regional and local outcomes that facilitate sustainable development. The Desertification Convention is worthy of consideration in the light of justice issues, because it places significant emphasis on local actions and empowerment for its success and stakeholder inputs were important at the negotiation stage (Corell 1999; Thomas 2003). A cornerstone of the Desertification Convention is the production of National Action Programs (NAPS) that have a considerable emphasis on bottom-up strategies of consultation, empowerment, and activity, and a placement of antidesertification strategies and activities within a framework of sustainable resource use and development. The issues of scaling from global to local in the UNCCD may be rather problematic (Scoones and Toulmin 1999), an issue that is equally pertinent to the UNFCCC. The actual engagement of local communities and bodies within UNCCD production in production of NAPs also appears to be highly variable, with empirical research indicating that consultation can be cursory and wider national policy frameworks prohibitive of effective integrated programs that genuinely facilitate local empowerment.

This process of facilitation is highly complex. The case of distributive justice in Botswana's dryland mixed-farming system illustrates how policies can potentially open up spaces for adaptation, in this case livelihood diversification. This was successful in southeast Botswana, but the narrow interpretation and application of the policy in southwest Botswana restricted the space available for diversification, and thus inhibited livelihood adaptation. Conversely, the lack of policy intervention in the case of equity and empowerment in Namibia's communal rangelands demonstrates that if no direction is provided, the principles of equity and procedural justice can be severely compromised at the local level in the name of empowerment. These two cases demonstrate the need for spaces of adaptation, but at the same time indicate that careful facilitation and guidance is needed if fair and just outcomes are to be achieved.

Empowerment is regarded as a key element of creating equity in decision making (World Bank 2000), and is seen as a central element of reducing vulnerability (Skoufias 2003; Tompkins and Adger 2004). However, it needs to be coupled with notions of procedural and distributive justice within *all* levels of decision making. It is not sufficient to regard the creation of space for empowerment at international and national levels as a successful and just achievement in dealing with climate change impacts, just as local empowerment is not a simple recipe for the generation of just and equitable outcomes at community and household levels. The issues of scale raised by adaptation to climate change themselves generate a range of complexities for the processes necessary to engender equity and justice. These include the relationships between the global processes of emission reduction strategies and international conventions and national responses and local outcomes. These scale dependent responses involve critical interactions between environments and abilities to respond and adapt; the effects of national decisions and policies on local opportunities and abilities; and the relationships between adaptive responses occurring at different levels.

Acknowledgments

The studies reported on in this chapter were funded as the PANRUSA and CINDE projects by the UK Department for International Development.

12

Extreme Weather and Burden Sharing in Hungary

Joanne Linnerooth-Bayer and Anna Vári

Weather-related disasters such as droughts, floods, windstorms, and avalanches have killed well over a million people in the past two decades, and the economic losses of natural disasters have increased ninefold from the 1960s to the 1990s (Munich Re 2003). Economic losses escalate because of changing land-use practices and concentration of capital in high-risk areas—this is why absolute losses are higher in the developed world. Yet in terms of GNP, poor countries and regions suffer disproportionately higher losses (Linnerooth-Bayer and Amendola 2000). Moreover, 90 percent of fatalities from natural disasters occur in developing countries.

Although there is only mixed evidence that climate change has contributed to escalating economic losses due to natural disasters to date (Miletti 1999), the Third Assessment Report of the Intergovernmental Panel on Climate Change (IPCC) predicts that over the next half century climate change will increase the intensity and frequency of extreme weather (IPCC 2001b). There is scientific agreement that even in the unlikely event that deep reductions in greenhouse gas emissions were embarked upon now, greenhouse gases already in the atmosphere would give rise to significant climate change impacts, as Schneider outlined in chapter 2. This adds to the urgency of helping vulnerable communities adapt to floods, storms, and other extreme weather.

Adaptation can take many forms including loss reduction measures such as reforestation and land use changes that mitigate the intensity of the hazard. Adaptation can also involve alleviating the consequences through flood prevention investments or relocation of the population to safer areas. In resource-constrained countries, however, households, farmers, businesses, and governments cannot undertake costly loss reduction measures, and many regions and countries will continue to suffer large stochastic losses from extreme weather and other natural disasters. For this reason, many developing countries are considering private and public insurance pools as one measure for reducing vulnerability to weather-related disasters.

Insurance pools for catastrophic losses require large capital reserves and a management infrastructure. This means that many private and public systems are neither affordable nor available for poor regions, which raises questions of how to construct a loss reduction and burden sharing regime that encompasses poor and vulnerable households and businesses. Who should absorb the risks and losses from rare but catastrophic extremes? To what extent should at-risk communities take responsibility for prevention measures and postevent losses? And to what extent should others obsorb these costs? How should democratic societies make these loss allocation decisions? What principles of fairness or justice guide these choices?

Several chapters in this book suggest that context-sensitive analyses of adaptation to specific climate-change impacts can yield an encompassing view of distributive and procedural justice. This chapter focuses on adaptation to floods and examines views of fairness in reducing and sharing economic risks and losses in the poor and highly exposed region of the Upper Tisza river in northeastern Hungary. We investigate how the economic losses from flooding in this region can be reduced by structural and nonstructural measures and how they can be shared or transferred through a national system that combines taxpayer support for relief and reconstruction with private insurance pools.

We report on a pilot project that examined local stakeholder views on distributive justice regarding the design of a national flood risk-management program and that used a participatory stakeholder process for generating consensus on a public-private insurance program. The purpose of the project was to test the feasibility and usefulness of a model-based participatory process for flood risk management. The project interviewed key stakeholders and administered a questionnaire to 400 respondents within and outside the Upper Tisza basin in northeast Hungary. The survey demonstrated that the public has varied and competing views on how to reduce and share the flood burden and, in contrast to traditional economic assumptions, these views did not always coincide with economic interests. Rather, the views appeared to be based on fundamental notions of "what is fair" in the light of attribution of responsibility for the losses and the vulnerability of the victims.

In addition to examining the principles and worldviews underlying the plural expressions of fairness among the active stakeholders and public, we also report from a test of a participatory process to reach a consensus on the form of a national insurance and compensation program. We conclude by discussing the relevance of this study for developing countries and particularly to the implementation of article 4.8 of the UN Framework Convention on Climate Change that calls for consideration of insurance. We indicate how the international community can support regional and national pooling arrangements, and examine an innovative system adopted for the purpose in Turkey.

Loss Reduction and Loss Pooling in Hungary

The Upper Tisza River basin in northeastern Hungary is one of the highest flood-risk areas in the country and one of the poorest regions in Europe. The mainly agricultural incomes struggle to support the local economy, particularly among the disadvantaged Roma (Gypsy) population (Horváth et al. 2001). The intensity and frequency of floods appear to be increasing (Pecher, Stoiko, and Kichura 1999). Since 1998, record-breaking water levels have occurred annually, but the extensive network of levees surrounding the river has prevented major losses until recently. In 2001, a major flood burst through the protective levees, causing extensive damage. Becuse flood waves up to eleven meters high, originating in upstream Ukraine, arrive in Hungary at very high speed, there is little time for warning or preparation.

The Hungarian government has invested huge sums in about 3,000 kilometers of levees along the Tisza River and continues to invest in maintaining and raising the embankments. In the event of a levee breach, Hungarian taxpayers finance the rebuilding of homes and provide direct financial assistance to victims in Tisza. After the 2001 flood, the government fully rebuilt, on raised concrete platforms, over 1,000 homes that had been washed away. This *loss-sharing* is a typical manifestation of social solidarity throughout the formerly socialist countries of Central Europe.

Vulnerability to flood events can also be reduced through *risk transfer,* which includes insurance, weather hedges, and other financial arrangements that are put into place before the disaster, usually at the expense of those at risk. Compared to insurance uptake in western countries, a surprisingly large number, about 40 percent, of the households in the Tisza region have purchased flood insurance policies, which are required for a home mortgage. These policies are affordable, and flood risks are considered insurable, because insurers offer only limited coverage mainly for breakage or over topping of the levees. According to Kunreuther and Roth (1998), a risk is insurable if it can be reliably estimated and if insurers are free to set premiums; however, premiums may be unaffordable in areas with frequently occurring disasters. In the Tisza area, premiums are kept affordable by another form of solidarity that is often overlooked. Because private insurers offer flat-rate rather than risk-based premiums, there are significant cross-subsidies from residents living in low-risk areas, for example in large cities like Budapest and Szeged, to people living in the Upper Tisza region and other high-risk areas. This diversification over low- and high-risk areas greatly increases the insurability of flood risks in high-risk areas.

With increasing flood losses, however, many Hungarians view current practices as unsustainable. Not only are insurers becoming more reluctant to offer low-rate insurance in repeatedly flooded areas, but Hungary's government can hardly afford to continue its expensive levee renewal program and generous reconstruction policies given new economic priorities on entry into the European Union in 2004. Moreover, generous government compensation will do little to discourage settlement in this area and to encourage the local governments and private sector to take measures for reducing the losses. Government officials, particularly those at the finance ministry, would welcome more private responsibility for reducing and insuring flood losses. Many Hungarians, however, regard the transfer of increased liability for flood losses to citizens in very poor areas, such as the Upper Tisza region, as unfair.

One of the more controversial issues in Hungary, common in many countries, is thus the respective roles of government and the private market in providing protection and postdisaster financial assistance to flood victims. This is an issue of fairness in reducing and sharing the burdens imposed by floods.

There is no single, universally valid set of fairness criteria that can inspire effective personal, institutional, or national commitments to a fair distribution of environmental risk burdens. Competing conceptions of what is good and bad, acceptable and unacceptable, characterize most policy debates. Elster (1992) argues that these competing conceptions of fairness are context dependent, so much so that it is difficult to generalize. In his words, "the study of local justice will never yield much by way of robust generalizations. . . . local justice is above all a very messy business. To a large extent it is made up of compromises, exceptions, and idiosyncratic features that can be understood only by reference to historical accidents" (Elster 1992, 15).

At the other extreme from Elster, Wilson (1992) argues that fairness is part of a universal moral sense that is neither environmentally determined nor culturally relative. Young (1994) takes a third view by noting that although generalizations are difficult, similar concepts do continue to reassert themselves. Douglas (1985) and other cultural theorists (Thompson, Ellis, and Wildavsky 1990) suggest how and why these reassertions take place. According to cultural theory, views of fairness are not ad hoc but reflect predictable cultural biases and worldviews. According to Rayner (1994), views of fairness cannot be separated from ideas about community and social organization, or the need to establish shared values for the conduct of community procedures and the distribution of rights, goods, and burdens. The central idea of cultural theory is that in order to maintain solidarity, different forms of social organization (cultural groupings) generate predictable arguments concerning fair process and outcome. These include procedures for allocating responsibility, for self-justification, or for calling others to account. The three active solidarities described by cultural theory are hierarchy, individualism, and egalitarianism. Hierarchies are characterized by positional authority, inequality, and procedural rationality, and they stand in sharp contrast to egalitarianism with its emphasis on equality and moral rightness. It further contrasts with individualism, which emphasizes personal initiatives and rights.

Risk Reduction and Loss Pooling for the Upper Tisza Region

Institutional Priorities

Cultural theory is helpful for interpreting competing stakeholder views on fairness with regard to reducing flood risks in the Tisza region and on instituting a national program for sharing the losses. Interviews were carried out with twenty-four stakeholders representing central, regional, and local governments, farmers and entrepreneurs, NGO activists and insurance companies (Vári, Linnerooth-Bayer, and Ferencz 2003). From these interviews, three flood policy strategies emerged that are roughly consistent with the cultural theory worldviews: state protection, individual responsibility, and holistic development of the region.

State Protection   One widespread view perceived state protection as the most appropriate institutional solution. Under this scenario the government would continue to absorb a large share of the costs of reducing flood risks and supporting reconstruction by its investments in levees, generous compensation of flood victims, and controlling development in the flood-risk areas by top-down zoning regulations. Justification for this strategy was based on claims that the government is responsible for protecting its citizens, and if it is negligent in providing this protection, it must be held accountable and absorb the losses. Critics saw this approach to increase the central government's budget deficit and, despite regulation, to encourage development in the flood-prone areas.

Individual Responsibility   An alternative strategy perceived by some stakeholders was to promote individual responsibility. Here, the government could withdraw resources from the area and rely on market forces to encourage individual responsibility for reducing losses and for insuring against them. The stakeholder discourse in Hungary does not widely share this strategy. Apart from blaming the new landlords in the Tisza area for not maintaining the water drains and culverts, few stakeholders mentioned individual loss-reducing measures. Nor was there a sense that individuals and communities should be fully insured. This is true throughout Central Europe. For instance, after 1997 Polish floods, the prime minister of Poland made a public statement that uninsured victims had only themselves to blame for their financial losses and should not expect government compensation. This remark raised such a public outcry that the prime minister was forced to apologize (Stripple 1998).

Although the individualistic view of flood risk management has been conspicuously absent from the mainstream policy discourse in Hungary, it is beginning to assert itself as the country is becoming more integrated into European and global economies and as government authorities are recognizing that they cannot continue massive public support programs. Budget austerity is thus forcing the government to move toward individual responsibility and to adopt the market discourse that dominates in the United States and the UK. If uninsured disaster victims are guaranteed grants that enable them to rebuild their property in hazard-prone areas, and more people build in those areas, taxpayers will be subject to increasingly larger expenditures for bailing out victims of future disasters. This moral hazard argument led to reform of the U.S. natural disaster program and to calls for making private responsibility and insurance a cornerstone of risk management (Kunreuther and Roth 1998).

This policy of individual responsibility is justified on what at first appears to be an efficiency argument. With increased emphasis on incentives promoting loss-reducing measures, everyone stands to gain: the taxpayers because of decreased demand for postdisaster aid, and the Tisza residents if they are compensated for their loss-reduction expenses. The Hungarian stakeholders interviewed as part of this research were reluctant to accept this argument. They saw that local residents have few realistic measures to reduce flood damages. Besides switching to more flood-resistant crops or abandoning agriculture altogether in favor of small handicrafts such as rug weaving, the only remaining option is to leave the area. The relocation strategy is often advocated in wealthy countries, but it is problematic in Hungary, where more than 50 percent of the territory is at risk to flooding. As some stakeholders point out, the poor residents can only relocate to the cities, increasing urban problems and resulting in the abandonment of historic villages.

Holistic Development   The third view promotes the ecological preservation of the area and egalitarian policies toward the poor, including subsidized programs to help farmers change land-use practices, the renaturalization of the river by removing levees in some areas, and providing infrastructure for tourism. The advocates of this holistic development approach are strongly opposed to levees and other structural flood protection measures that, they claim, only push the risks downstream and endanger ecosystems. Fairness in this line of argument stands in opposition to the paternalistic fairness of the hierarchical discourse and the efficiency arguments of the individualist. Ecosystems should have standing in the policy debate, and the very poor should be given priority in a kind of equality for all. Commercial insurers are regarded with suspicion because risk transfer should not be an issue in an ecologically and socially just society.

These three perspectives—state protection, individual responsibility, and holistic development—form a contested policy terrain in Hungary. Each discourse constructs the problem and solutions in a way that reinforces the underlying worldview. Within this struggle, institutions and individuals may argue for the same policy, but for different reasons and based on different claims of fairness, which is a core concept behind the search for viable policy paths.

Public Perceptions

One can think of four fundamental concepts to justify fairness claims in allocating society's goods and burdens (see Rescher 1971). These are need, endowment, merit, and contribution. Distribution to those who have the greatest *need* or are the most vulnerable is the basis of such commonplace solutions such as rules for public housing, food stamps, and need-based financial assistance for higher education. In Hungary, stakeholder groups might argue for continuing public support for Tisza residents because they are vulnerable and need support. *Endowment* of talent, ability, or property, and *merit* are the fundamental notions behind meritocracy, most scholarships, and interest income. Because Hungarians living in the hills of Budapest are endowed with a safe location, stakeholder groups might argue for solidarity with those less fortunate, or they might argue that the residents of the Tisza merit support because of efforts they take to reduce their risks. Finally, reward according to effort and productivity, or sanctions due to deviant behavior—*contribution*—is the foundation of commission income, school grading systems, and the polluter-pays principle. If the Hungarian government is viewed as contributing to the risks because of its negligence in maintaining the protective levees, this may be an argument for public support to the victims. This latter claim has justified Hungary's strongly hierarchical flood risk management practices in the past.

To gain insights on the views of the Hungarian public with regard to flood risk management in the Tisza region, we surveyed 400 respondents with a face-to-face questionnaire (see Vari, Linnerooth-Bayer, and Ferencz 2003). The survey was carried out in four locations in order to include stakeholders at high and low risk to floods in both rural and urban areas. The sample size in each area was 100, selected to be representative in terms of gender and age.

The survey confirms that the majority of Hungarians believe that their government should retain primary responsibility for protecting the population and for absorbing the losses. The main causes of flooding were perceived to be lack of levee maintenance by the government, forest clearing in the catchment area, and insufficient levee height and strength. Culpability for the losses was not attributed to emitters of greenhouse gases, but rather to the central government for failing in its duty to provide protection, even zero risk.

The least important cause of flooding was considered to be local residents taking insufficient preventive measures or building in flood-risk areas. In contrast, many responses considered that the central government contributed to the problem. Respondents believed that responsibility should be mainly with the government rather than with property owners living in high-risk areas. The government was ranked number one or number two responsible party by 92 percent of the respondents, the neighboring countries by 51 percent of the respondents, the municipalities by 49 percent, and the property owners by only 10 percent of the respondents. An equally large majority was sympathetic with moving toward somewhat greater individual responsibility, meaning that many Hungarians may be in favor of combining state protectionism with local responsibility.

The strength of social solidarity in Hungary and the emerging view that individuals should also take more responsibility is illustrated by responses to a question that asked respondents if they fully agreed, partially agreed, or did not agree with each of the following statements:

• Solidarity requires that government compensate flood victims.

• Everyone should take more responsibility for flood risk, and those who can afford it should purchase private insurance.

• Locals should create a fund for helping flood victims.

• It does not matter what you do, flood victims will lose a lot.

Figure 12.1 indicates the percentage of respondents fully agreeing with each of the statements. Social solidarity receives more support in the high-risk areas (Upper Tisza and Szolnok), whereas a individual responsibility and private insurance receives a more sympathetic view in the low-risk regions and in cities (Zala and Székesfehérvár). Still, there is significant support for compensation across regions. Contrary to their economic interests, almost one-third of the respondents in the low-risk or no-risk areas agreed that solidarity requires that government compensate flood victims.

What motivates many Hungarians to express solidarity with flood victims? Half of the respondents claimed that flood protection is the responsibility of the government. If the river overflows the levees and floods the villages, the government is to blame, because it has not built levees strong or high enough. In another question, the respondents were queried about who should receive compensation and to what extent. Approximately three-quarters of the respondents agree that the government should compensate all victims regardless of their economic circumstances or role in preventing losses. Because the government bears the guilt, even wealthy vacation owners should receive compensation (only 7 percent of the respondents felt otherwise). Almost a fifth of the

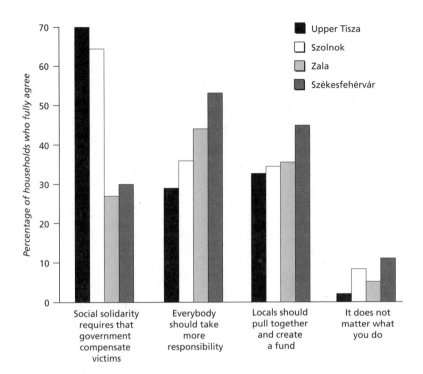

Figure 12.1
Percentage of respondents from four locations in Hungary fully agreeing with statements on responsibility on solidarity.

respondents base their support for loss sharing on the basis of solidarity with the poor and vulnerable.

Only four respondents supported individual responsibility. Yet these respondents also referred to broader responsibility and poverty as important fairness criteria. They insisted on a level playing field and that poverty should be given consideration in allocative decisions. They also appealed to responsibility of those imposing a risk. For this line of reasoning it is not the responsibility of the government to provide a risk-free environment for those living in river basins. Rather the, government should provide protection as a public good only to the extent that the benefits outweigh the costs. A World Bank sponsored study questioned whether the benefits of protection in this poor area justify the costs of maintaining and in some cases heightening the levees (Halcrow Water 1999). This line of argument, though almost entirely absent from the debate, would greatly reduce the significance of government contribution and liability.

In sum, stakeholder interviews and surveys confirm that the Hungarian public has varied views of the management of flood risks in the Upper Tisza region. The views depend to an extent on economic interests; those living in high and dry areas are less disposed to generous taxpayer support for the levee program and compensation to flood victims. But the views also depend on notions of a fair society—almost a third in the high-dry areas do support solidarity. The results showed less sympathy with more individual responsibility, or for extreme ideas on a more ecological and naturalistic path for the region. State protection appears to still command wide support in Hungary. However, in light of recent history, the minority views in favor of increased individual responsibility and more holistic development policies are revealing and important.

A Stakeholder Process to Develop a National Insurance Program

The empirical results from the stakeholder interviews and the public questionnaire formed the basis a pilot stakeholder workshop in 2003 that sought consensus on a Hungarian flood insurance program. This workshop also made use of a computer simulation model of flood losses in the Upper Tisza region. The purpose of this workshop was to test the feasibility of a model-based participatory forum. The loss-reduction issues were not dealt with explicitly in this pilot workshop, although a consensus did emerge among many of the key stakeholders that more attention should be paid to removing the levees in selected areas to release high water to natural reservoirs.

There are many potential models for the Hungarian flood risk insurance system. The U.S. National Flood Insurance Program (NFIP) offers public insurance that is mandatory for those holding a bank mortgage. The U.S. program is moving from flat-rate to risk-based premiums, to discourage households and businesses from locating to risk-prone areas. Households are eligible to purchase NFIP insurance only if they live in communities that have taken prescribed loss-reduction measures such as flood mapping and zoning. France's all-hazards system emphasizes social solidarity with deliberate flat-based premiums, resulting in cross subsidies across regions and hazards. The French system has recently included incentives for reducing risks, but overall it has accepted higher losses from lack of an incentive structure in return for national solidarity with disaster victims.

Three options for a nationwide insurance program arose from second interviews with the stakeholders. Increased support for insurance emerged especially from among the local mayors who had earlier opposed it. The change in attitudes originated from a realization that private insurance need not exclude solidarity: taxpayers can subsidize insurance premiums for the poor, provide the capital for reinsuring private insurers, and lower the premiums.

The three alternatives were formalized for use in a stakeholder workshop as follows (see fig. 12.2). Option A represents the reform of the current public-private system of government compensation and private insurance with less postdisaster relief to encourage households to purchase more voluntary, flat-rate insurance with cross subsidies. To motivate insurers to offer more comprehensive cover, the government would absorb losses by acting as an insurer of last resort. The government would also start to subsidize premiums for poor households. Option B

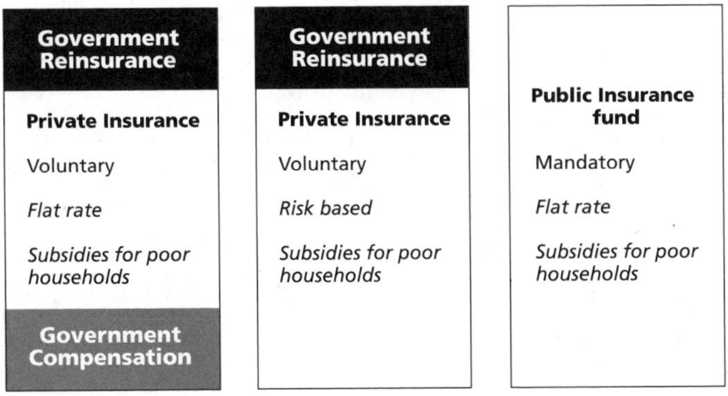

Government Reinsurance	Government Reinsurance	Public Insurance fund
Private Insurance	**Private Insurance**	
Voluntary	Voluntary	Mandatory
Flat rate	*Risk based*	*Flat rate*
Subsidies for poor households	*Subsidies for poor households*	*Subsidies for poor households*
Government Compensation		

Figure 12.2
Alternative designs for cost and responsibility for a Hungarian Flood Insurance Program.

moves more responsibility to property owners by discontinuing postdis-aster government compensation and relying on voluntary private insur-ance based on risk. The government continues to absorb a portion of the losses by subsidizing premiums of poor households and reinsuring the private insurance companies. Option C reduces the role of private insurers by establishing a government fund and mandatory contribu-tions from property owners. This is a form of public insurance, because the government fully underwrites the risks. As in the other two options, the government subsidizes premiums for poor households.

These three options formed the basis of the pilot stakeholder work-shop that was held in the Upper Tisza region. Participants included the local mayor, a resident of a nonrisk area, the leader of a local envi-ronmental group, officials of the regional water management authority and the national authority for disaster management, and a representa-tive of an international brokerage firm. The workshop served as a forum for stakeholders to advocate their policy positions and consider the arguments of the other participants. Theorists argue that decision making based on "discussion among free and equal citizens" (Elster 1998, 1) can produce outcomes that reflect the public interest. Delibera-tion is supposed to provide a space for reasoned discussion and the opportunity for critical reflection. The idea of the stakeholder workshop was thus to explore the terrain where stakeholders can agree on a policy direction, but for different reasons. Although consensus will not necessarily emerge, deliberation and citizen participation can be an effective means of formulating citizen grievances, ideas, and views and feeding them into the policy process (Renn and Webler 1995).

The moderated workshop began with a discussion on flood risk man-agement, after which the three options for a flood insurance program were introduced. This discussion was aided by computer model simula-tions of the incidence of the policy options on the three main stakeholder groups (Ekenberg et al. 2002). Guided by the model simulations, the participants were grouped according to the option chosen and asked to negotiate a common view in their subgroup—a constructed consensus within a single perspective or worldview. The groups were then asked to defend their policy choice.

The arguments of the three stakeholder groups illustrate the competing claims of what is fair and at the same time reveal a possible compromise. According to the spokesperson for a continued mix of public and private involvement (Option A, in fig. 12.2), "There is no doubt that in the case of flood disasters the government has a key role and has to assume full financial responsibility. Flood protection lines have been built, and theoretically ... no water should come out through the levees." He went on, however, to state that his group strongly supports the idea that it is not only the government that should take responsibility for flood losses, but also the citizen. Thus insurance companies should be involved.

The one advocate of the more individualistic Option B in figure 12.2 held firm that the government should not provide any compensation or reconstruction in the traditional form, but taxpayers could be called upon in two important ways. First, insurance premiums for poor households would be subsidized, and second, a government emergency fund (a type of reinsurance) would cover claims in the case of very large or multiple catastrophes that go beyond the means of insurers. Finally, the advocates of government-led action (Option C, in fig. 12.2), who rejected private insurance, were not convinced of the incentive arguments of placing more responsibility on residents of high-risk areas: "The issue is not that I want to grow wheat at the wrong place, but it's rather that I won't be able to restart my life. This should not be managed on a market basis." But even this group recognized that increased private responsibility was inevitable in the increasingly privatized economy of Hungary.

After arguing for their policy perspectives, the workshop participants turned to a lively and heated discussion on a possible compromise. This deliberation led to an imaginative new system shown in figure 12.3, in which only households with private insurance would qualify for government assistance after a disaster, but the government would heavily subsidize poor households in their purchase of flood insurance. The stakeholder participants also agreed that the government would not provide reinsurance for private insurers. Similar types of insurance programs are being currently discussed in Italy.

Figure 12.3
Consensus design among local stakeholders for a National Insurance Program in Hungary.

The stakeholders continued to ground their arguments in irreconcilable views of what is fair. Yet two criteria were common to all the positions and served as the basis for the consensus: *contribution* to the problem by the nonrisk community (in this case, the government) and *poverty* of the at-risk community. This middle ground offers important win-win possibilities. The proposed compromise policy will cost the government dearly in the short term, but it will create a culture of responsibility and insurance in the region over the medium term. Secondly, the heavy subsidization of insurance premiums for poor households placated those who are concerned about social justice and sustainable development. It is questionable, however, whether the Hungarian insurers would accept the compromise requiring them to offer much expanded cover at flat-based rates. For, however, the final solution is not so important as the demonstration of a participatory, model-based *process* that respects and builds on the conflicting stakeholder perspectives and achieves consensus on a policy path.

The UNFCCC and an International Risk-Transfer System

Most measures adopted under the UN Framework Convention on Climate Change (UNFCCC) and the Kyoto Protocol address national greenhouse gas emissions reduction targets (Müller 2002). But climate negotiators have also instructed parties to consider actions to meet the needs of developing countries with respect to the adverse impacts of climate change. Article 4.8 of the UNFCCC calls for consideration of the establishment of insurance as an important adaptation measure to extreme events. Although the climate change community has made several proposals for postdisaster humanitarian assistance, including the UNFCCC Climate Impact Relief Fund, there is little understanding in the negotiation process of the role that insurance can play in the efforts of developing countries to adapt to risks of extreme weather.

We suggest that public-private insurance systems, such as that proposed by the Hungarian stakeholders, could fulfill the intent of article 4.8. However, the system suggested by the Hungarian stakeholders cannot be transplanted to highly exposed poor countries, such as Honduras or Bangladesh, without support from the international community. Many developing countries face risks so devastating that disaster relief and recovery can overwhelm the collective resources of the country. Moreover, private insurance is neither available nor affordable in most of the developing world. Of all losses due to natural catastrophes in 2002, only 4.8 percent were insured in Asia and 1.1 percent in Africa (Swiss Re 2003). Only 3.8 percent of losses from natural disasters between 1985 and 1999 were insured in Latin America and the Caribbean compared to 10–60 percent in the developed world (Aufrett 2003). Moreover, postdisaster humanitarian assistance contributes only a very small and declining portion of the relief and reconstruction needs of developing countries (Linnerooth-Bayer and Amendola 2000). Humanitarian assistance agencies and lending organizations are promoting a shift from postevent humanitarian assistance to predisaster proactive prevention and risk financing (Kreimer, Arnold, and Carlin 2004; Freeman et al. 2003).

Public-private insurance systems are unaffordable and unavailable to households and businesses in less developed countries. Several higher income developing countries and regions, especially those with high catastrophe exposure, are, however, considering national insurance systems. A Caribbean insurance pool has been proposed, for example (Pollner 2000). The Turkish Catastrophe Insurance Pool (TCIP) is the first national disaster insurance scheme to become operational in a developing country (Andersen 2001). Turkish households pay an insurance premium to a privately administered, public fund. As in Hungary, this premium incorporates cross subsidies, but it is partly based on the risk zone within which the household resides, the construction of the property, and risk-reducing measures.

The Turkish Catastrophe Insurance Pool circumvents the fundamental problem of unaffordable earthquake insurance by offering limited coverage, by strong national cross subsidies, and most importantly, by transferring part of the risk out of the country with World Bank support. The systematic representation of this insurance pool in figure 12.4 shows that the World Bank provides reinsurance in the form of contingent and low-interest loans to cover two layers: losses occurring before enough premium has accumulated and losses that are unexpectedly high. In turn, the World Bank can cover part of its risk exposure by engaging in risk-transfer arrangements in the international financial markets in its own name. In this way, the World Bank has substituted the unpredictable granting of postdisaster loans for a calculable annual commitment to Turkey's national insurance system (Kuzek, Campbell, and Khater 2004).

Figure 12.4
Cost and responsibility within the Turkish Catastrophe Insurance Pool.

The Turkish insurance pool scheme was designed by government officials in close collaboration with the World Bank, and it shares important commonalties with the views of Hungarian stakeholders. Although there is more emphasis on risk-based premiums, cross-subsidies are still central to affordable insurance coverage in Turkey's poor communities. An important difference is the lack of government compensation to insured or uninsured victims of earthquakes. In other words, the market-based insurance system is intended to substitute for taxpayer solidarity. Another important difference is the Turkish scheme of mandatory insurance policies, a condition unanimously rejected by participants in the Tisza study.

The Turkish system is encountering delays in its implementation because of the reluctance of the parliament to legislate for its continued operation, including mandatory insurance for Turkish households. The political obstacles suggest that a stakeholder process in Turkey might have flagged issues, such as mandatory policies, that have delayed full implementation of the insurance pool.

The political obstacles do not distract, however, from the important precedent set by the TCIP, where the international community ensures its viability. The Hungarian study and the Turkish experience suggest a role for the climate regime in providing proactive, pre-event support to higher income developing countries as a complement to the more traditional post-event humanitarian assistance. This argument has been put forward as a potential in implementing article 4.8 within the FCCC insurance process (Linnerooth-Bayer, Mace, and Verheyen 2003 for the UNFCCC). There are similar roles the international community can play for less developed countries. For example, the climate regime might provide: (1) reinsurance for micro insurers that lack the requisite capital for catastrophe cover, (2) reinsurance for weather and other hedging instruments, or (3) support for insuring public infrastructure (Linnerooth-Bayer, Mace, and Verheyen 2003).

Conclusion

Many countries highly exposed to disaster risks are considering public-private systems for reducing and sharing disaster losses, and these systems will gain importance as losses from weather extremes and other disasters continue to rise. The Hungarian pilot study reported in this chapter demonstrates that despite large differences in stakeholder views regarding a fair risk-reduction and insurance system, a participatory process to arrive at a consensus is feasible. Although the Hungarian experience cannot be transplanted to the global level for assisting developing and less developed countries adapt to weather extremes, there are important insights from Hungary that can inform research in this area.

Despite competing notions of what is fair, two criteria emerged as almost indisputable arguments for a nationwide pooling system in the Hungarian pilot investigation: contribution to the problem by the nonrisk community and poverty of the at-risk community. In many ways these arguments mirror the debate on reducing and sharing the global burdens from climate change. Other findings of the Tisza study include observations of general support among the Hungarian public for a public-private disaster insurance system that combines responsibility on the part of the at-risk community with that of the nonrisk community. Further, views of fairness among stakeholders and the public did not fully coincide with economic interests. The issues of fairness, defined by contribution and underlying vulnerability, emerged as important.

In developing new strategies for reducing financial vulnerability of regions or countries to extreme-weather events, it is important to distinguish two categories of vulnerability: those regions or countries that face disaster risks that can be financed through national pools and those that face disaster risks that are beyond the collective means of the population to recover in a timely way. Unlike Hungary, very poor and highly exposed countries cannot afford a mutual pooling program. For these countries, the international community might consider complementing post-event humanitarian assistance with pre-event support for risk reduction and financial risk transfer. The Turkish Catastrophe Insurance Pool, which combines international reinsurance contracts and capital market transactions with a national insurance pool, offers one model for this purpose. Other models are necessary for less-developed countries, and include international support for microinsurance schemes, weather hedges, and assisting governments in financing risk to critical public infrastructure.

Acknowledgments

The authors are grateful for helpful comments of two anonymous reviewers, as well as for the advice and support from Jouni Paavola.

IV

Conclusions

13

Multifaceted Justice in Adaptation to Climate Change

Jouni Paavola, W. Neil Adger, and Saleemul Huq

If one is profiting from injustice, it is hardly going to be in one's interest to pursue justice.
—Shue 1992, 376

This book presents a rich picture of the landscape of justice in adaptation to climate change. A first major theme is distributive justice: climate change impacts will not be evenly distributed across space. The preceding chapters underline that a myriad of past and present social injustices have engendered the complex patterns of vulnerability that prevail in the contemporary world. In the opening chapter and here we argue that vulnerability should be considered one of the most important criteria for decisions on adaptation measures. Many contributors to this book have also argued that climate change impacts are not all the same—some matter more from a justice viewpoint than others. That is, climate justice requires that impacts that constitute threats to life and health and those that impact economic assets should be addressed as distinct from each other.

We argue that security concerns are distinct from welfare concerns and hence adaptation is inexorably linked to mitigation. This is because some risks are best dealt with by preventing them in the first place. Concerns for the future generations and the nonhuman world can also be addressed by preventing dangerous climate change. This does not mean that adaptation can be ignored as an independent concern. We have already committed ourselves to a future that will require adaptation by numerous vulnerable households and communities whether they want to or not. The involuntary nature of their exposure to climate change, the vulnerability of those who face the greatest adaptation pressures, the fact that developed countries have caused most greenhouse gas emissions, and the capacity of developed countries to assist developing countries all suggest that developed countries should be considered responsible for climate change impacts *and* a duty to assist developing countries in adaptation. Responsibility should also be extended to other countries when they become significant emitters of greenhouse gases.

This brings us to procedural justice. Vulnerable developing countries are not equal partners in international negotiations on climate change. Because of past and present injustices, many lack capacity to advance their national interests in international negotiations. Heterogeneity of developing countries as a negotiating block also makes it difficult for them to act collectively in the international political arenas. But procedural justice is not only a problem that plagues international negotiations. Many governments across the world lack accountability and transparency and cannot be considered to offer fair opportunities for participation to their own citizens, particularly for ethnic and other minorities. The interests of citizens are frequently omitted where there is no opportunity for voice in national planning and decision-making processes. Therefore, justice in adaptation will require attention to recognition, participation, and distribution of power at all levels and across levels.

Distributive and procedural justice are often intimately interlinked. Reforms to the climate change regime, writ large, therefore need to address both aspects of climate justice to make a difference. Redistribution without empowerment can be short-lived, and empowerment without redistribution can be an insult. In what follows, we suggest one way for addressing the key justice dilemmas in adaptation to climate change.

Unavoidability of Social Justice in Climate Change

As we have seen, adaptation to climate change consists of individual and collective choices taken at different levels of decision making in the context of present and predicted climate change impacts, other social concerns and priorities, and the existing institutional framework that engenders a particular distribution of resources, wealth, and power. All adaptation decisions thus compete for attention and resources with other pressing choices in society.

As Henry Shue (1992) has argued, justice concerns are unavoidable in climate change. All decisions regarding adaptation are moral in the sense that they are informed by some values that guide the comparison of alternatives and choice between them. Some of these values are self- and welfare-centered, whereas others may be more sensitive to concerns that are distinct from economic welfare. Situations where different parties have different interests and are informed by different values are likely to result in environmental conflicts (Paavola 2005). In these kinds of situations, collective adaptive decisions are needed to strike a legitimate balance between conflicting interests (Adger et al. 2003a). An acceptable and legitimate compromise between the involved parties and interests is likely to require complementary contributions from a number of approaches. As Müller (2001) argues: "In the context of moral decisions, things are not simple and the key to resolving inconsistent conclusions is not to reject moral theories, but to try and find a morally acceptable compromise between them" (p. 275).

Different theories offer complementary understandings of social justice. Cosmopolitan theories consider justice as being universal, unchanged by time and place. Cosmopolitan theories have generated important insights, such as those of universal human rights as manifestations of social justice. Communitarian theories consider that justice emerges from the relationships between members of a community and that social justice is thus specific to a particular space and time (Bell 1993). Although the communitarian approach provides an explanation for the variety of ways in which justice dilemmas have been addressed in different communities and contexts, it is often criticized for moral relativism. Obviously, much depends on how one defines "community." For climate justice the pertinent community could, for example, be considered to include all humans living now and in the future (Norton 2002), as their fates are bound together by their actions regarding the use of global atmospheric sinks. Cosmopolitans have also argued for the consideration of all humans and nonhumans as members of a global community (Attfield 2005). But the communitarian viewpoint highlights that humans may be affiliated with many communities that have different notions of justice. Therefore, justice is negotiated and constructed in the context of conflicting views and interests (Bromley 2004; Paavola 2005).

It is also important to distinguish between distributive and procedural justice. Distributive justice relates to the incidence of benefits and costs, broadly conceived so as to encompass nonpecuniary advantages and burdens (Kolm 1996; Young 1994) as well as the consideration of nonhumans (Attfield 2005, 43–44). Procedural justice relates to the way in which parties are positioned vis-à-vis processes of planning and decision making, encompassing issues such as recognition, participation, and distribution of power (see Fraser 2001; Tyler et al. 1997; Young 2000). Distributive and procedural justice considerations are relevant both within a generation and between generations, but we will focus here on intragenerational justice.

Justice dilemmas involved in adaptation to climate change can be resolved in many ways. In the area of distributive justice, Aristotle's contributory principle, Bentham's rule of greatest happiness for greatest numbers, priority of those in need, Rawls' maximin rule, and equality of opportunity, resources, and welfare are examples of just some of the rules that are available for making fair decisions (Kolm 1996; Sen 1992, 12–30; Young 1994, 9–13). The fairness and suitability of these rules can vary across problems and contexts. For example, the contributory principle can be fair in collective undertakings for mutual gain because it provides incentives for the participation of those who can contribute and stand to benefit. However, there are many difficult choices where not everybody can win (O'Brien and Leichenko in chapter 5). Utilitarian cost-benefit logic may shed light on some such choices. When difficult choices pertain to areas of life where people find the use of cost-benefit logic unacceptable, equality or need may provide the basis for fair decisions.

These principles are often applied so that justice appears a matter of distributing one overarching good such as money or utility fairly between the involved parties. This requires commensuration of goods and bads and allows compensating one bad with another kind of good. For example, adequate compensation could be considered fully to resolve justice dilemmas related to the incidence of climate change impacts.

However, it is not at all obvious that this line of reasoning should be accepted (see Bromley 2004; Gowdy 2004; Paavola 2002a). Walzer (1983) has argued that complex equality requires the absence of domination of one group across "spheres of justice." This would entail that groups disadvantaged in income or wealth terms should not be disadvantaged in other spheres of justice. Thus international transfers should not be considered to resolve justice in the incidence of climate change impacts. Vital interests in health and safety ought to be considered as distinct from those related to levels of income (see Paavola 2002b) and to occupy their own sphere. Justice demands the protection of these interests to avoid repeating the injustice of income and wealth distribution. This could be done by reducing greenhouse gas emissions so as to avoid dangerous climate change, simultaneously with income and wealth transfers.

Distributive justice is unlikely to be able to provide a sufficient foundation for climate justice because of the heterogeneity of involved parties. Therefore, procedural justice is needed to underpin the legitimacy of climate change regime. Procedural justice is sometimes associated with the arguments of libertarian philosophers such as Robert Nozick (1974) or economists such as Friedrich Hayek (1976), according to whom we should accept outcomes of processes such as markets and voluntary action as just even if they would be unequal. These theories are problematic because they deny the significance of unequal starting points, postulate the legitimacy of their favorite procedures, and end up affirming the fairness of *status quo*.

The more empirical approaches of social psychology, organizational studies, and socio-legal studies have indicated that procedures influence the legitimacy of decisions irrespective of outcomes (Lind and Tyler 1988). Procedural justice has been both an important demand and a part of political practice for grassroots environmental justice movements (see Schlosberg 1999; Shrader-Frechette 2002). Scholarship on the politics of identity and difference has also generated important insights into procedural justice (see Fraser 2001; Lash and Featherstone 2002). The core procedural justice concerns in adaptation to climate change can be best represented by the following three questions:

1. Which parties and whose interests are recognized, and how, in planning, decision making, and governance of adaptation?

2. Which parties can participate in planning, decision making, and governance of adaptation, and how?

3. What is the effective distribution of power in planning, decision making, and governance of adaptation?

These questions are related to but do not reduce to each other. *Recognition* is the foundation of procedural justice (Fraser 2001) but it can take many forms that do not necessarily involve participation. For example, planning and decision-making guidelines can make consideration of a group's interests an integral part of the process. *Participation* requires recognition but it can again take many forms, from simply informing or hearing involved parties to giving them a veto in decision making. The solutions for participation, together with political-economic factors of predominantly distributive nature, generate a particular distribution of *power*. The relative power of involved parties determines to what extent they can make their interests count in environmental planning, decision making, and governance. Procedural justice can foster legitimacy when it assures those whose interests are not endorsed by a particular decision that their interests have been considered and that they have a chance to count in other decisions. Procedural justice also enables affected parties to express their dissent or consent and to maintain their dignity (Schlosberg 1999, 12–13, 90; Soyinka 2004).

As we have already noted, distributive and procedural justice are not independent of each other. If a group is not recognized and cannot participate in planning and decision making regarding adaptation, its interests are unlikely to inform adaptation plans and decisions. This is why adaptation plans and decisions can aggravate inequality and vulnerability rather than reduce them. Similarly, the interests of future generations and nonhuman species are not reflected in the outcomes of plans and decisions because they are not represented effectively (O'Neill 2001). Yet it is clear that the interests of future generations and nonhumans should be recognized and be given at least some degree of protection through environmental decisions.

Cornerstones of Climate Justice in Adaptation

We suggest that the principles of "avoiding dangerous climate change," "forward-looking responsibility," "putting the most vulnerable first," and "fair participation of all" would help the global community make progress toward just adaptation to climate change. All of these principles are implied in the United Nations Framework Convention on Climate Change (UNFCCC) in a rudimentary form. However, the operationalization of these principles requires their further clarification and elaboration.

The four principles are clearly complementary and would all be needed for fair adaptation. The principles of avoiding dangerous climate change and forward-looking responsibility address the issue of responsibility for climate change impacts from the complementary viewpoints of safety and economic welfare (see also Baer et al. 2000). The principle of putting the most vulnerable first addresses the question of how assistance ought to be distributed between adaptation measures and vulnerable groups. Finally, the principle of equal participation of all addresses procedural justice concerns in adaptation. In what follows, we substantiate these principles in greater detail.

Avoiding Dangerous Climate Change

The objective of avoiding dangerous climate change is explicit in the convention's article 2. However, the principle requires further elaboration to encourage binding action. This objective requires the limitation of global emissions of greenhouse gases to a level that does not surpass the capacity of natural systems, food production systems, and economic systems to adapt. The convention's precautionary principle, set out in article 3, seeks to safeguard present and future humans and nonhumans alike but does not resolve responsibility for past greenhouse gas emissions or assign responsibility for damages caused by emissions of greenhouse gases. Therefore, the principle of avoiding dangerous climate change should be considered a minimum solution for responsibility—the least we should do without excluding a more comprehensive solution.

The principle of avoiding dangerous climate change could be operationalized by setting "a safe maximum standard" (on the idea of a safe minimum standard in environmental management, see Ciriacy-Wantrup 1952; Farmer and Randall 1998) for greenhouse gas concentrations in the atmosphere. Current estimates of safe stabilization levels for CO_2 concentrations vary between 400 and 500 ppm (Mastrandrea and Schneider 2004; O'Neill and Oppenheimer 2002). The establishment of a safe maximum standard is part of a fair solution to climate change. Climate change affects natural systems, food production, and economies in varied ways, depending on the spatial distribution of climatic changes and the local features of natural, food production, and economic systems. It is not meaningful to compare and rank widespread and nonmarginal climate change impacts across economic assets, public health, cultural impacts of change, and threats to biodiversity. Using the conventional tort law conception of liability for damages would be problematic in this situation: the vital interests of poor inhabitants of developing countries would not attract a high price tag (Spash 2002; Baer in chapter 7). A safe maximum standard can protect affected parties from disastrous outcomes of abrupt or dangerous climate change. Any safe maximum standard reflecting the low capacity of vulnerable systems to adapt would require significant decarbonization of the world economy toward a path of sustainability for all.

Of course, there are remarkable challenges to the successful setting and implementation of a safe maximum standard. What is considered safe depends on one's situation, including one's level of vulnerability, and many parties feel they are already experiencing dangerous climate change. The difficulty of agreeing on a safe minimum standard is not just a matter of divergent interests. The perception of danger has an existential or subjective side to it which cannot easily be captured by external assessments (see, e.g., Dessai et al. 2004; Satterfield, Mertz, and Slovic 2004). This means that any determined level of safety will always remain essentially contested in the real world.

Even the setting and enforcement of an absolute CO_2 concentration limit would not prevent adverse climate change impacts. The almost doubling of CO_2 concentrations from the preindustrial levels (450 ppmv, for example) would precipitate significant climate change impacts across the globe even if it were not dangerous to all humans (see Thomas et al. 2004). The establishment of outer-bound levels of concentrations of greenhouse gases or temperature change would be the first, most urgent step in resolving responsibility for climate change and in avoiding dangerous and abrupt climate change. Historical responsibility and responsibility for the future climate change impacts of greenhouse gas emissions within the "cap" of safe maximum standard would still need to be addressed as well as present danger from observed changes in climate.

Forward-Looking Responsibility

Most ways of implementing responsibility for climate chance impacts can be shaped so as to give at least some weight for responsibility for historical greenhouse gas emissions. For example, if responsibility is implemented through emission reduction requirements or through safe maximum standards, the burden of mitigation can be made heavier for those emitters that have the longest record of highest historical emissions or the highest present day greenhouse gas emissions. A uniform carbon tax for example, can be tailored so that it falls on those who emit more in per capita terms or who have the highest cumulative historical emissions.

It is also possible to establish more specific legal responsibility that resembles strict liability in tort law. In tort law, certain inherently dangerous activities can be treated as strictly liable for all damages that they cause. This contrasts with the standard approach where a party is deemed liable for damages only if he or she is found to have acted negligently. But there has to be a general understanding that certain activities are inherently dangerous before they can be deemed to entail strict liability. Those industrialized countries that implicitly argue against strict liability emphasize that they had no knowledge of the consequences of emitting greenhouse gases and hence cannot be held liable for historical emissions that predate the Climate Change Convention.

Although some degree of ambiguity prevails with regard to responsibility for historical greenhouse gas emissions, the ratification and coming into force of the convention clearly signals that the consequences of greenhouse gas emissions are now fully acknowledged. Therefore, post-UNFCCC greenhouse gas emissions should be accompanied with a "forward-looking responsibility" that involves compensation for the engendered climate change impacts.

The easiest way to implement forward-looking responsibility for greenhouse gas emissions that maintain atmospheric concentrations below the safe maximum standard would be to agree to a uniform carbon tax under the convention process and to implement it through national legislation. Social justice concerns could be crafted to a carbon tax scheme through a tax-free per capita quota set, for example, at half of the current global per capita carbon consumption (Paavola and Adger 2006). Such a tax could address issues of responsibility and assistance through hypothecated transfers of funds (see Paavola and Adger 2006).

Revenue from the carbon tax could replenish a fund for compensating the impacts of climate change and for assisting adaptation to climate change. This tax-fund system would, besides address justice issues in adaptation to climate change, also provide incentives for economically efficient choices in both mitigation and adaptation. The tax would result in the adoption of all abatement solutions that are efficient at the set level of tax, thereby decreasing future greenhouse gas emissions, climate change impacts, and the present tax burden. A combined fund for compensation and assistance would also give incentives for proactive adaptation. By making funds available for proactive adaptation, the solution would reduce the need to compensate for residual impacts yet maintain funds available for relief. This is also why the fund should be a combined assistance and compensation fund. Sufficient funds should be made available to compensate predicted impacts, but they should be usable for proactive adaptation measures that seek to avoid the realization of climate change impacts.

Putting the Most Vulnerable First

The convention makes several references to the need to "put the most vulnerable first." It gives some indication of which countries should be considered vulnerable and have a priority in receiving assistance. According to the convention, low-lying and other small island states; countries with low-lying coastal, arid, or semi-arid areas or areas liable to floods, drought, and desertification; and developing countries with fragile mountainous ecosystems are potentially vulnerable to adverse effects of climate change. However, the convention does not define vulnerability in a way that would facilitate its use as a guideline for allocating assistance for adaptation between countries and measures. We propose to clarify the principle below in greater detail to facilitate its use in adaptation decisions.

Research on adaptation to climate change defines vulnerability as a function of exposure, sensitivity, and adaptive capacity (Adger 2003b; Smit and Pilifosova 2003; Yohe and Tol 2002). The convention's understanding of vulnerability best matches with the first part—exposure—of the triad of factors that determines vulnerability. The convention pays less attention to the sensitivity of vulnerable groups to climate change impacts and their capacity to adapt. Research and practice of natural disaster management emphasizes these two aspects of vulnerability. For example, Wisner et al. (2004, 11) define vulnerability as "the characteristics of a person or group and their situation that influence their capacity to anticipate, cope with, resist and recover from the impact of a natural hazard." This definition draws attention to factors such as assets, sources of livelihood, class, race, ethnicity, gender, and poverty that demarcate vulnerable groups (see also Bohle, Downing, and Watts 1994).

The concept of vulnerability is central for climate justice because it ties the concerns of adaptation policy and planning to those of moral philosophy (Dow and colleagues in chapter 4). The practice of egalitarians to consider equality as a reasonable starting point for analysis offers one way to highlight the significance of the concept of vulnerability to moral reasoning (Barry 1999; Shrader-Frechette 2002). Equality can be considered just if there are no compelling reasons that would indicate otherwise. In some circumstances, need and lack of capacity can be considered compelling reasons justifying deviation from the norm of equality. Vulnerability encompasses characteristics that are indifferent from those covered by need or lack of capacity. Therefore, risk and lack of adaptive capacity provide a justification for putting the most vulnerable first in matters of distributive justice.

Attempts to characterize and measure vulnerability (see Adger 1999, 2003a; O'Brien and Leichenko 2000; O'Brien, et al. 2004; Tol et al. 2004; Brooks, Adger, and Kelly 2005) provide useful lessons for operationalizing the principle of "putting the most vulnerable first." First, existing research indicates that vulnerability cannot be reduced to exposure to climate change impacts as implied by the convention. It is not meaningful to compare the vulnerability of Florida and the Caribbean Islands to Atlantic hurricanes by examining the probabilities of landfall hurricanes. Second, vulnerability cannot be reduced to income measures. Availability of means and resources to invest in adaptation is only one of the factors in vulnerability to climate change. For example, vulnerability is partly determined by the extent of people's dependence on risky activities and sources of income such as agriculture or fishing. The capacity of households and communities to adapt also depends on their physical assets such as health, education, and human-created and natural capital, as well as on institutional arrangements that either facilitate or constrain their attempts to reduce their vulnerability.

The best way to guide the allocation of assistance at the national level would be to use a vulnerability-based leximin rule (see Kolm 1996). The principle of leximin suggests that, "if, when the neediest are best taken care of, there remains some possible choice, then best take care of the second neediest, and so on" (Kolm 1996, 59). This rule would call for assisting the most vulnerable group first and moving then up in the vulnerability ladder. The use of this principle would not require the establishment of separate priorities between types of adaptive measures—the content of vulnerability reduction would change when the attention shifts to new groups along the vulnerability ladder. Of course, vulnerability rankings would remain contestable and their determination would require fair and legitimate procedures. Allocation of assistance between countries would also require principles other than lexicographic vulnerability ordering. This is because responsibility for climate impacts could arguably create a right to compensation for the likely damages. Vulnerability can inform the international distribution of compensation and assistance but it is also likely to be informed by other factors.

Fair Participation for All

The climate change regime interprets participation narrowly, focusing on the interactions between states in the Conference of the Parties and the subsidiary bodies of the convention. The convention enshrines the "one party, one vote" principle but it also acknowledges that there are background inequalities that influence the ability of sovereign states to participate in international negotiations and actions. The regime seeks to correct these background inequalities by providing assistance for the participation of developing country parties and by capacity building to reduce barriers for participation. Furthermore, the convention opens up the Conferences of the Parties to observers, thereby extending limited participation horizontally toward nongovernmental organizations and other stakeholder groups.

However, governance of adaptation to climate change rests on a multi-level solution that means that only some decisions and actions are taken at the international level, whereas others are taken at the national, sub-national, and local levels. Obstacles to participation vary between and across levels. Levels of economic development, state capacity, and many other factors influence to what degree *states* can participate in planning and decisions on adaptation at the international level. The participation of nonstate actors at the international level is primarily limited by institutional rules but it is also affected by political-economic factors. At the national and subnational levels, the participation of political, regional, ethnic, and other groupings is influenced by political cultures, institutional rules, and political-economic factors. Although there are formal obstacles for participation at all of these levels of governance, political-economic factors such as inequality and lack of capacity form more formidable obstacle for equal participation. Political-economic factors also constrain effective participation across levels, but the lack of formal solutions for facilitating cross-level participation in climate change planning and decisions is even more glaring.

Effective participation can be fostered by the already used solutions such as financial assistance and capacity building. However, it is also likely to require new solutions, particularly procedural ones. Some initial moves toward this direction have already been taken at the international level by the establishment of the Least Developed Countries Expert Group. The guidelines for the preparation of National Adaptation Programs of Action (NAPAs) target procedural justice at the national level by requiring public consultation in the national adaptation planning process. Possibilities exist for extending this kind of "procedural prescription" to new areas, such as topical focus groups that could extend representation sideways and downward.

Another possibility for extending the effective participation of local actors in the climate change regime is to create a quasi-judicial subsidiary body that would adjudicate complaints and grievances related to adaptation to climate change. A weak form of this kind of body has already been established in another area of environmental governance by the North American Agreement on Environmental Cooperation (NAAEC). Although judgments made by this kind of international body do not have the same force of law as decisions issued by the courts of sovereign states, they could establish the international standard of best practice. Findings according to which states are not in compliance with international agreements they have signed could also be considered a reason to suspend their benefits. This would give the judgments some teeth. But more than anything, adjudication would recognize the interests and grievances of local groups and generate systematic and reasoned resolutions that would serve as precedents to national actions in the future.

Conclusion

We have mapped and examined social justice issues involved in adaptation to climate change. We believe that social justice is an integral part of environmental governance, including the governance of atmospheric sinks and adaptation to climate change, and that social justice issues are best addressed explicitly and directly. We do not believe that making the equity dimension explicit escalates environmental conflicts. Quite the contrary, keeping social justice off the negotiating table denies the relevance and legitimacy of the concerns and interests of vulnerable actors in the process.

We have suggested that justice dilemmas involved in adaptation to climate change include questions regarding responsibility for climate change impacts, the level and burden sharing of assistance to developing countries for adaptation, distribution of assistance between countries and adaptation measures, and equal participation in planning and decisions on adaptation. To date, the climate change regime has largely omitted responsibility but it has made a clear, albeit very general, commitment to assistance. The climate change regime has so far failed to operationalize assistance despite taking some steps to this direction. Moreover, the regime has made only minor progress in eliminating obstacles of fair participation at the international level and across levels of governance.

More research is needed, particularly on procedural justice in adaptation to climate change. The obstacles and procedural solutions for equal participation at the international level clearly need more attention. But even more importantly, analysis is needed on the challenges of cross-level interactions, such as those involved in local-national and national-international interactions in adaptation planning, and on solutions that could overcome them. One way to start addressing these issues would be to examine the lessons offered by the already adopted solutions: the Least Developed Countries Expert Group and the guidelines for the preparation of National Adaptation Programs of Action (NAPAs). In the area of distributive justice, approaches that address justice in terms of several distinct "numeraires" would merit more attention in order to tie the adaptation agenda more tightly to that of human development and development efforts in general.

We propose that the principles of avoiding dangerous climate change, forward-looking responsibility, putting the most vulnerable first and equal participation of all would be a step toward fairer adaptation. The first three principles address distributive justice involved in adaptation in a way that respects the diversity of affected parties and their situations. The principle of avoiding dangerous climate change can provide a degree of absolute protection to all vital interests, the principle of forward-looking responsibility gives effect to efficiency concerns and the principle of putting the most vulnerable first justifies progressive redistribution to those who are most in need. The last principle provides a guideline for resolving dilemmas of procedural justice, suggesting that all affected parties have rights that have to be respected by recognition and participation.

References

Adams, R., B. Hurd, and J. Reilly. 1999. *Agriculture and Global Climate Change: A Review of Impacts to U.S. Agricultural Resources.* Report for the Pew Center on Global Climate Change, Washington, DC.

Adeola, F. 1996. "Military Expenditures, Health, and Education: Bedfellows or Antagonists in Third World Development?" *Armed Forces and Society* 22: 441–467.

Adger, W. N. 1999. "Social Vulnerability to Climate Change and Extremes in Coastal Vietnam." *World Development* 27: 249–269.

Adger, W. N. 2003a. "Social Aspects of Adaptive Capacity." In J. B. Smith, R. J. T. Klein, and S. Huq, eds., *Climate Change, Adaptive Capacity and Development.* London: Imperial College Press, 29–49.

Adger, W. N. 2003b. "Social Capital, Collective Action and Adaptation to Climate Change." *Economic Geography* 79: 387–404.

Adger, W. N., N. W. Arnell, and E. Tompkins. 2005. "Successful Adaptation to Climate Change across Scales." *Global Environmental Change* 15: 77–86.

Adger, W. N., T. A. Benjaminsen, K. Brown, and H. Svarstad. 2001. "Advancing a Political Ecology of Global Environmental Discourses." *Development and Change* 32: 681–715.

Adger, W. N., K. Brown, J. Fairbrass, A. Jordan, J. Paavola, S. Rosendo, and G. Seyfang. 2003a. "Governance for Sustainability: Towards a 'Thick' Analysis of Environmental Decisions." *Environment and Planning A* 35: 1095–1110.

Adger, W. N., S. Huq, K. Brown, D. Conway, and M. Hulme. 2003b. "Adaptation to Climate Change in the Developing World." *Progress in Development Studies* 3: 179–195.

Adger, W. N., and P. M. Kelly. 1999. "Social Vulnerability to Climate Change and the Architecture of Entitlements." *Mitigation and Adaptation Strategies for Global Change* 4: 253–266.

African Development Bank (AfDB), Asian Development Bank (ADB), Department for International Development, United Kingdom (DFID), Directorate General for International Cooperation, the Netherlands (DGIS),

Directorate General for Development, European Commission (EC), Federal Ministry for Economic Cooperation and Development, Germany (BMZ), Organization for Economic Cooperation and Development (OECD), United Nations Development Programme (UNDP), United Nations Environment Programme (UNEP), and the World Bank. 2003. *Poverty and Climate Change: Reducing the Vulnerability of the Poor through Adaptation.* Abidjan: African Development Bank.

Agarwal, A., and S. Narain. 1991. *Global Warming in an Unequal World: A Case of Environmental Colonialism.* New Delhi: Centre for Science and Environment.

Agarwal, A., S. Narain, and A. Sharma, eds. 1999. *Green Politics: Global Environmental Negotiations 1.* New Delhi: Centre for Science and the Environment.

Agrawal, A. 1995. "Dismantling the Divide between Indigenous and Western Knowledge." *Development and Change* 26: 413–439.

Ahmad, Q. K., B. G. Verghese, R. R. Iyer, B. B. Pradhan, and S. K. Malla, eds. 1994. *Converting Water into Wealth: Regional Cooperation in Harnessing the Eastern Himalayan Rivers.* Dhaka: BUP and Academic Publishers.

Alcamo, J., and T. Henrichs. 2002. "Critical Regions: A Model-Based Estimation of World Water Resources Sensitive to Global Changes." *Aquatic Sciences* 64: 352–362.

Alexander, S., and M. Ruderman. 1987. "The Role of Procedural and Distributive Justice in Organizational Behaviour." *Social Justice Research* 1: 177–198.

Allen, M., and R. Lord. 2004. "The Blame Game: Who Will Pay for the Damaging Consequences of Climate Change?" *Nature* 432: 551–552.

Anand, P. 2001. "Procedural Fairness in Economic and Social Choice: Evidence from a Survey of Voters." *Journal of Economic Psychology* 22: 247–270.

Andersen, T. J. 2001. *Managing Economic Exposures of Natural Disasters. Exploring Alternative Financial Risk Management Opportunities and Instruments.* Washington, DC: Inter-American Development Bank.

Anderson, C. W. 1990. *Pragmatic Liberalism.* Chicago: University of Chicago Press.

Andronova, N. G., and M. E. Schlesinger. 2001. "Objective Estimation of the Probability Density Function for Climate Sensitivity." *Journal of Geophysical Research* 106: 22605–22612.

Arler, F. 2001. "Global Partnership, Climate Change and Complex Equality." *Environmental Values* 10: 301–329.

Arrow, K. J. 1963. *Social Choice and Individual Values.* New York: Wiley.

Arrow, K. J., J. Parikh, G. Pillet, M. Grubb, E. Haites, J. C. Hourcade, K. Parikh, and F. Yamin. 1996. "Decision Making Frameworks for Addressing Climate Change." In J. Bruce, H. Lee, and E. Haites. eds., *Climate Change*

1995: Economic and Social Dimensions of Climate Change, Contribution of Working Group III to the Second Assessment Report of the Intergovernmental Panel on Climate Change. Cambridge: Cambridge University Press, 125–144.

Athanasiou, T., and P. Baer. 2002. *Dead Heat: Global Justice and Global Warming*. New York: Seven Stories Press.

Attfield, R. 1999. *The Ethics of the Global Environment*. Edinburgh: Edinburgh University Press.

Attfield, R. 2005. "Environmental Values, Nationalism, Global Citizenship and the Common Heritage of Humanity." In J. Paavola and I. Lowe, eds., *Environmental Values in a Globalising World: Nature, Justice and Governance*. London: Routledge, 38–50.

Auffret, P. 2003. "Catastrophe Insurance Market in the Caribbean Region: Market Failures and Recommendation for Public Sector Interventions." *Policy Research Working Paper* No. 2963, Washington, DC: World Bank.

Azar, C. 2000. "Economics and Distribution in the Greenhouse." *Climatic Change* 47: 233–238.

Azar, C., and H. Rodhe. 1997. "Targets for Stabilization of Atmospheric CO_2." *Science* 276: 1818–1819.

Azar, C., and S. H. Schneider. 2002. "Are the Economic Costs of Stabilizing the Atmosphere Prohibitive?" *Ecological Economics* 42: 73–80.

Baer, P. 2002. "Equity, Greenhouse Gas Emissions and Global Common Resources." In S. H. Schneider, A. Rosencranz, and J. Niles, eds., *Climate Change Policy: A Survey*. Washington, DC: Island Press, 393–408.

Baer, P., J. Harte, B. Haya, A. V. Herzog, J. Holdren, N. E. Hultman, D. M. Kammen, R. B. Norgaard, and L. Raymond. 2000. "Equity and Greenhouse Gas Responsibility in Climate Policy." *Science* 289: 2287.

Bangladesh Centre for Advanced Sudies (BCAS). 1998. *Bangladesh 2020*. Dhaka: Dhaka University Press.

Banuri, T., K.-G. Mäler, M. Grubb, H. K. Jacobson, and F. Yamin. 1996. "Equity and Social Considerations." In J. Bruce, H. Lee, and E. Haites, eds., *Climate Change 1995: Economic and Social Dimensions of Climate Change*, Contribution of Working Group III to the Second Assessment Report of the Intergovernmental Panel on Climate Change. Cambridge: Cambridge University Press, 79–124.

Barnett, J. 2001a. "Adapting to Climate Change in Pacific Island Countries: The Problem of Uncertainty." *World Development* 29: 977–993.

Barnett, J. 2001b. *The Meaning of Environmental Security: Ecological Politics and Policy in the New Security Era*. London: Zed Books.

Barnett, J. 2003. "Security and Climate Change." *Global Environmental Change* 13: 7–17.

Barnett, J., and W. N. Adger. 2003. "Climate Dangers and Atoll-Countries." *Climatic Change* 61: 321–337.

Barnett, J., and S. Dessai. 2002. "Articles 4.8 and 4.9 of the UNFCCC: Adverse Effects and the Impacts of Response Measures." *Climate Policy* 2: 231–239.

Barnett, J., S. Dessai, and R. Jones. 2003. *Climate Change in Timor Leste: Science, Impacts, Policy And Planning.* Melbourne: The University of Melbourne and CSIRO.

Barry, B. 1999. "Sustainability and Intergenerational Justice." In A. Dobson, ed., *Fairness and Futurity: Essays in Environmental Sustainability and Social Justice.* Oxford: Oxford University Press, 93–117.

Baumert, K. A., and M. Markoff. 2003. *Indicator Framework Paper.* Washington, DC: World Resources Institute. Available online at <http://cait.wri.org>.

Beauchamp, T. L. 2003. "A Defense of the Common Morality." *Kennedy Institute of Ethics Journal* 13: 259–274.

Beg, N., J. C. Morlot, O. Davidson, Y. Afrane-Okesse, L. Tyani, F. Denton, Y. Sokona, J. P. Thomas, E. L. La Rovere, and J. K. Parikh. 2002. "Linkages between Climate Change and Sustainable Development." *Climate Policy* 2(2–3): 129–144.

Bell, D. A. 1993. *Communitarianism and Its Critics.* Oxford: Clarendon Press.

Berry, S. 1989. "Access, Control and Use of Resources in Africa Agriculture: An Introduction." *Africa* 59(1): 1–5.

Blaikie, P., and H. Brookfield. 1987. *Land Degradation and Society.* London: Methuen.

Blaikie, P., T. Cannon, I. Davis, and B. Wisner. 1994. *At Risk: Natural Hazards, People's Vulnerability, and Disasters.* London: Routledge.

Bodansky, D. 1993. "The UN Framework Convention on Climate Change: A Commentary." *Yale Journal of International Law* 18: 451–558.

Boehmer-Christiansen, S. 2003. "Science, Equity, and the War against Carbon." *Science, Technology & Human Values* 28: 69–92.

Bohle, H. G., T. E. Downing, and M. J. Watts. 1994. "Climate-Change and Social Vulnerability—Toward a Sociology and Geography of Food Insecurity." *Global Environmental Change* 4: 37–48.

Bouma, G., and H. Kobryn. 2004. "Vegetation Cover Change in East Timor, 1989–1999." *Natural Resources Forum* 28: 1–12.

Brennan, T. A. 1993. "Environmental Torts." *Vanderbilt Law Review* 46: 1–73.

Brklacich, M., R. Matthew, B. McDonald, and B. Upreti. 2004. "Advancing Conflict, Cooperation and Environmental Change—Human Security Research." *IHDP Newsletter* 3: 11–12.

Bromley, D. W. 2004. "Reconsidering Environmental Policy: Prescriptive Consequentialism and Volitional Pragmatism." *Environmental and Resource Economics* 28: 73–99.

Brooks, N., W. N. Adger, and P. M. Kelly. 2005. "The Determinants of Vulnerability and Adaptive Capacity at the National Level and the Implications for Adaptation." *Global Environmental Change* 15: 151–163.

Brosius, J. P., A. L. Tsing, and C. Zerner. 1998. "Representing Communities: Histories and Politics of Community-Based Natural Resource Management." *Society and Natural Resources* 11: 157–168.

Brown, D. A. 2003. "The Importance of Expressly Examining Global Warming Policy Issues through an Ethical Prism." *Global Environmental Change* 13: 229–234.

Brozska, M. 1999. "Military Conversion: The Balance Sheet." *Journal of Peace Research* 36: 131–140.

Bryant, R. L. 1992. "Political Ecology: An Emerging Research Agenda in Third-World Studies." *Political Geography* 11: 12–36.

Bryceson, D. F. 2002. "The Scramble in Africa: Reorienting Rural Livelihoods." *World Development* 30: 725–739.

Burger, J., E. Ostrom, R. B. Norgaard, D. Policansky, and B. D. Goldstein, eds. 2001. *Protecting the Commons: A Framework for Resource Management in the Americas.* Washington, DC: Island Press.

Burton, I. 1996. "The Growth of Adaptive Capacity: Practice and Policy." In J. Smith, N. Bhatti, G. Menzhulin, R. Benioff, M. I. Budyko, M. Campos, B. Jallow, and F. Rijsberman, eds., *Adapting to Climate Change: an International Perspective.* New York: Springer, 55–67.

Burton, I., S. Huq, B. Lim, O. Pilifosova, and E. L. Schipper. 2002. "From Impact Assessments to Adaptation Priorities: The Shaping of Adaptation Priorities." *Climate Policy* 2: 145–159.

Cairncross, S. 2003. "Handwashing with Soap—A New Way to Prevent ARIs?" *Tropical Medicine and International Health* 8: 677–678.

CARE Bangladesh. 2002. *Reducing Vulnerability to Climate Change (RVCC) Project: Community Vulnerability Assessment in Southwest Bangladesh.* Dhaka: Care Bangladesh.

Carter, T. R. 1996. "Assessing Climate Change Adaptations: The IPCC Guidelines." In J. B. Smith, N. Bhatti, G. Menzhulin, R. Benioff, M. I. Budyko, M. Campos, B. Jallow, and F. Rijsberman, eds., *Adapting to Climate Change: An International Perspective.* New York: Springer, 27–43.

Chomsky, N. 1995. "Introduction." In M. Jardine, ed., *East Timor: Genocide in Paradise.* Tucson: Odonian Press.

Chossudovsky, M. 1998. *The Globalisation of Poverty.* London: Zed Books.

Ciriacy-Wantrup, S. V. 1952. *Resource Conservation: Economics and Policies.* Berkeley: University of California Press.

Clark, C. O., P. J. Webster, and J. E. Cole. 2003. "Interdecadal Variability of the Relationship between the Indian Ocean Zonal Mode and East African Coastal Rainfall Anomalies." *Journal of Climate* 16: 548–554.

Clarke, G. R. G., and S. J. Wallsten. 2002. *Universal(ly Bad) Service: Providing Infrastructure Services to Rural and Poor Urban Consumers*. Policy Research Working Paper 2868. Washington, DC: World Bank.

Clarkson, R., and K. Deyes. 2002. *Estimating the Social Cost of Carbon Emissions*. Government Economics Service Working Paper 140. London: HM Treasury. Available online at <www.hm-treasury.gov.uk>.

Clay, E., and B. B. Schaffer. 1984. *Room for Manoeuvre: An Exploration of Public Policy in Agriculture and Rural Development*. London: Heinemann.

Collier, P. 2000. *Economic Causes of Civil Conflict and Their Implications for Policy*. Washington, DC: World Bank.

Cooper, N. 2002. "State Collapse as Business: The Role of Conflict Trade and the Emerging Control Agenda." *Development and Change* 33: 935–955.

Corell, E. 1999. "Non-State Actor Influence in the Negotiations of the Convention to Combat Desertification." *International Negotiation* 4: 197–223.

Cornes, R., and T. Sandler. 1996. *The Theory of Externalities, Public Goods, and Club Goods*. Cambridge: Cambridge University Press.

Cutter, S. 1996. "Vulnerability to Environmental Hazards." *Progress in Human Geography* 20: 529–539.

Cutter, S. L. 2003. "The Vulnerability of Science and the Science of Vulnerability." *Annals of the Association of American Geographers* 93: 1–12.

Daily, G. C. 1997. *Nature's Services: Societal Dependence on Natural Ecosystems*. Washington, DC: Island Press.

Deaton, A., and J. Muelbauer. 1980. *Economics and Consumer Behavior*. Cambridge: Cambridge University Press.

Demeritt, D. 2001. "The Construction of Global Warming and the Politics of Science." *Annals of the Association of American Geographers* 91: 307–337.

den Elzen, M. G. J., and A. P. G. de Moor. 2002. "Evaluating the Bonn-Marrakesh Agreement." *Climate Policy* 2: 111–117.

den Elzen, M., and M. Schaeffer. 2002. "Responsibility for Past and Future Global Warming: Uncertainties in Attributing Anthropogenic Climate Change." *Climatic Change* 54: 29–73.

Denton, F., Y. Sokona, and J. P. Thomas. 2000. *Climate Change and Sustainable Development Strategies in the Making: What Should West African Countries Expect?* Dakar: Organisation for Economic Co-operation and Development and ENDA-TM.

Department of International Development (DFID). 1997. *Eliminating World Poverty: A Challenge for the 21st Century.* White Paper on International Development. London: DFID.

Dercon, S., and P. Krishnan. 1996. "Income Portfolios in Rural Ethiopia and Tanzania: Choices and Constraints." *Journal of Development Studies* 32: 850–875.

Derr, P., R. Goble, R. E. Kasperson, and R. W. Kates. 1983. "Responding to the Double Standard of Worker/Public Protection." *Environment* 25(6): 6–11, 35–36.

Dessai, S., W. N. Adger, M. Hulme, J. Turnpenny, J. Köhler, and R. Warren. 2004. "Defining and Experiencing Dangerous Climate Change." *Climatic Change* 64: 11–25.

Dickens, P. 2000. *Social Darwinism: Linking Evolutionary Thought to Social Theory.* Buckingham: Open University Press.

Dimento, J. F. C. 2003. *The Global Environment and International Law.* Austin, TX: University of Texas Press.

Dobson, A. 2003. *Citizenship and the Environment.* Oxford: Oxford University Press.

Downing, T. E. 2002a. "Linking Sustainable Livelihoods and Global Climate Change in Vulnerable Food Systems." *Die Erde* 133: 363–378.

Downing, T. E. 2002b. "Protecting the Vulnerable: Climate Change and Food Security." In J. C. Briden and T. E. Downing, eds., *Managing the Earth: The Linacre Lectures.* Oxford: Oxford University Press, 5–34.

Downing, T. E., R. Butterfield, S. Cohen, S. Huq, R. Moss, A. Rahman, Y. Sokona, and L. Stephen. 2001. *Vulnerability Indices: Climate Change Impacts and Adaptation.* UNEP Policy Series 3. Nairobi: UNEP.

Douglas, M. 1985. *Risk Acceptability According to the Social Sciences.* New York: Russell Sage Foundation.

Duffield, M. 2001. *Global Governance and the New Wars: The Merging of Development and Security.* London: Zed Books.

Dungumaru, E. W., and N. F. Madulu. 2003. "Public Participation in Integrated Water Resources Management: The Case of Tanzania." *Physics and Chemistry of the Earth* 28: 1009–1014.

Easterling, D. R., G. A. Meehl, C. Parmesan, S. A. Changnon, T. R. Karl, and L. O. Mearns. 2000. "Climate Extremes: Observations, Modeling, and Impacts." *Science* 289: 2068.

East Timor Planning Commission. 2002. *East Timor: National Development Plan.* Dili: East Timor Planning Commission.

Edwards, M. 1999. "Security Implications of a Worst-Case Scenario of Climate Change in the South-West Pacific." *Australian Geographer* 30: 311–330.

Ekenberg, L., L. Brouwers, M. Danielson, K. Hansson, J. Johansson, A. Riabacke, and A. Vári. 2002. *Flood Risk Management Policy in the Upper Tisza Basin: A System Analytical Approach. Simulation and Analysis of Three Flood Management Strategies.* Laxenburg: International Institute for Applied Systems Analysis.

Elster, J. 1992. *Local Justice: How Institutions Allocate Scarce Goods and Necessary Burdens.* New York: Russell Sage Foundation.

Elster, J. 1998. "Introduction." In J. Elster, ed., *Deliberative Democracy.* New York: Cambridge University Press.

Enarson, E. 2002. *Working with Women at Risk: Practical Guidelines for Assessing Local Disaster Risk.* Miami: International Hurricane Centre, Florida International University.

Englebert, P. 2000. "Solving the Mystery of the AFRICA Dummy." *World Development* 28: 1821–1835.

Fankhauser, S. 1996. "The Potential Costs of Climate Change Adaptation." In J. Smith, N. Bhatti, G. Menzhulin, R. Benioff, M. I. Budyko, M. Campos, B. Jallow, and F. Rijsberman, eds., *Adapting to Climate Change: An International Perspective.* New York: Springer, 80–96.

Fankhauser, S., J. B. Smith, and R. S. J. Tol. 1999. "Weathering Climate Change: Some Simple Rules to Guide Adaptation Decisions." *Ecological Economics* 30: 67–78.

Fankhauser, S., R. S. J. Tol, and D. W. Pearce. 1997. "The Aggregation of Climate Change Damages: A Welfare Theoretic Approach." *Environmental and Resource Economics* 10: 249–266.

Farmer, M. C., and Randall, A. 1998. "The Rationality of a Safe Minimum Standard." *Land Economics* 74: 287–302.

Faulkner, F., and L. Pettiford. 1998. "Complexity and Simplicity: Landmines, Peace and Security in Central America." *Third World Quarterly* 19: 45–61.

Fischer, G., M. Shah, and H. van Veltuizen. 2002. *Climate Change and Agricultural Vulnerability.* Laxenburg: International Institute for Applied Systems Analysis.

Fischer, G., M. Shah, H. van Velthuizen, and F. O. Nachtergaele. 2001. *Global Agro-Ecological Assessment for Agriculture in the 21st Century.* Laxenburg: International Institute for Applied Systems Analysis.

Fitzgerald, V. 2001. "The International Political Economy of Conflict in Poor Countries." In F. Stewart and V. Fitzgerald, eds., *War and Underdevelopment. Volume 1: The Economic and Social Consequences of Conflict.* Oxford: Oxford University Press, 204–224.

Fjeldstad, O.-H. and J. Semboja. 2001. "Why People Pay Taxes: The Case of the Development Levy in Tanzania." *World Development* 29: 2059–2074.

Fletcher, T. 2002. "Neighborhood Change at Love Canal: Contamination, Evacuation and Resettlement." *Land Use Policy* 19: 311–323.

Fogel, R. W. 1986. "Nutrition and the Decline in Mortality since 1700." In S. Engerman and R. Gallman, eds, *Long-Term Factors in American Economic Growth*. Chicago: University of Chicago Press, 439–527.

Fogel, R. W. 1994. "Economic Growth, Population Theory, and Physiology: The Bearing of Long-Term Processes on the Making of Economic Policy." *American Economic Review* 84: 369–395.

Food and Agriculture Organization of the United Nations (FAO). 2002. *The State of Food Insecurity in the World 2002*. Rome: FAO.

Food and Agriculture Organization of the United Nations (FAO). 2003a. *Measuring Impacts of HIV/AIDS on Rural Livelihoods and Food Security*. Rome: FAO.

Food and Agriculture Organisation of the United Nations (FAO). 2003b. *FAO/ WFP Crop and Food Supply Assessment Mission to Timor-Leste*. 1 June, 2003. Rome: FAO.

Fraser, N. 2001. "Recognition without Ethics?" *Theory, Culture and Society* 18(2–3): 21–42.

Freedom House. 2003. *Freedom in the World 2003: The Annual Survey of Political Rights and Civil Liberties*. Lanham, MD: Rowman & Littlefield.

Freeman, P. K., L. A. Martin, J. Linnerooth-Bayer, R. Mechler, G. Pflug, and K. Warner. 2003. *Disaster Risk Management: National Systems for the Comprehensive Management of Disaster Risk and Financial Strategies for Natural Disaster Reconstruction*. Washington, DC: Inter-American Development Bank.

Fuglestvedt, J. S., T. K. Berntsen, O. Godal, R. Sausen, K. P. Shine, and T. Skodvin. 2003. "Metrics of Climate Change: Assessing Radiative Forcing and Emission Indices." *Climatic Change* 58: 267–331.

Galtung, J. 1969. "Violence, Peace, and Peace Research." *Journal of Peace Research* 6: 167–191.

Gibson-Graham, J. K. 2002. "Beyond Global vs. Local: Economic Politics outside the Binary Frame." In A. Herod and M. Wright, eds., *Geographies of Power: Placing Scale*. Oxford: Blackwell, 25–60.

Giles, J. 2002. "When Doubt Is a Sure Thing." *Nature* 418: 476–478.

Glantz, M. H. 1995. "Assessing the Impacts of Climate: The Issue of Winners and Losers in a Global Climate Change Context." In S. Zwerver, R. S. A. R. van Rompaey, M. T. J. Kok, and M. M. Berk, eds., *Climate Change Research: Evaluation and Policy Implications*. Amsterdam: Elsevier, 41–54.

Glantz, M., and D. Jamieson. 2000. "Societal Response to Hurricane Mitch and Intra- Versus Intergenerational Equity Issues: Whose Norms Should Apply?" *Risk Analysis* 20: 869–882.

Glasmeier, A. 2002. "One Nation Pulling Apart: The Basis of Persistent Poverty in the U.S." *Progress in Human Geography* 26: 151–169.

Gleditsch, N. 2001. "Armed Conflict and The Environment." In P. Diehl and N. Gleditsch, eds., *Environmental Conflict*. Boulder: Westview Press, 251–272.

Gleditsch, N., P. Wallensteen, M. Eriksson, M. Sollenberg, and H. Strand. 2002. "Armed Conflict 1946–2001: A New Dataset." *Journal of Peace Research* 39: 615–637.

Gleick, P. H. 2000. *The World's Water 2000–2001*. Washington, DC: Island Press.

Global Internally Displaced People Project (IDP). 2003. *A Global Overview of Internal Displacement by the End of 2002*. Available online at <www.idp-project.org>.

Goodall, B. 1987. *Dictionary of Human Geography*. New York: Penguin.

Goodhand, J. 2003. "Enduring Disorder and Persistent Poverty: A Review of the Linkages Between War and Chronic Poverty." *World Development* 31: 629–646.

Goodhand, J., and D. Hulme. 1999. "From Wars to Complex Political Emergencies: Understanding Conflict and Peace-Building in the New World Disorder." *Third World Quarterly* 20: 13–26.

Goodman, D., and M. Watts. 1994. "Reconfiguring the Rural or Feeding the Divide? Capitalist Restructuring and the Global Agro-Food System." *Journal of Peasant Studies* 22: 1–49.

Government of Bangladesh. 2002. *Bangladesh: A National Strategy for Economic Growth and Poverty Reduction*. Discussion draft. Dhaka: Government of Bangladesh.

Government of Bangladesh Bureau of Statistics. 2001. *Statistical Pocketbook of Bangladesh*. Dhaka: Government of Bangladesh.

Gowdy, J. 2004. "The Revolution in Welfare Economics and Its Implications for Environmental Valuation and Policy." *Land Economics* 80: 239–257.

Grubb, M. J. 1995. "Seeking Fair Weather: Ethics and the International Debate on Climate Change." *International Affairs* 71: 463–496.

Grubb, M., and J. Depledge. 2001. "The Seven Myths of Kyoto." *Climate Policy* 1: 269–272.

Gruber, L. 2000. *Ruling the World: Power Politics and the Rise of Supranational Institutions*. Princeton, NJ: Princeton University Press.

Grübler, A., and N. Nakicenovic. 2001. "Identifying Dangers in an Uncertain Climate." *Nature* 412: 15.

Gupta, J. 2002. "The Climate Change Regime: Can a Divided World Unite?" In J. C. Briden and T. E. Downing, eds., *Managing the Earth: The Linacre Lectures*. Oxford: Oxford University Press, 129–155.

Gurenko, E. N. 2003. *Introduction to the World Bank Insurance Practice: Key Lessons Learned and the Road Ahead*. A presentation at Financing the Risks of Natural Disasters conference in Washington, DC, 2–3 June, 2003. Available online at <http://www.worldbank.org/wbi/banking/insurance/natdisaster/pdf/Gurenko.ppt>. Accessed 9 November, 2004.

Halcrow Water. 1999. *Flood Control Development in Hungary: Feasibility Study. Final Report.* London: Halcrow Group.

Handmer, J. W., S. Dovers, and T. E. Downing. 1999. "Societal Vulnerability to Climate Change and Variability." *Mitigation and Adaptation Strategies for Global Change* 4: 267–281.

Hardin, G. 1968. "The Tragedy of the Commons." *Science* 162: 1243–1248.

Hassan, A. 1998. *Good Governance in the Somalia Context. Supporting Local Governance Where There Is no Government: UNDP's Experience.* New York: UNDP. Available online at: <http://magnet.undp.org>.

Hayek, F. A. 1976. *Law, Legislation and Liberty: The Mirage of Social Justice.* London: Routledge and Kegan Paul.

Hayes, P. 1993. "North-South." In P. Hayes and K. Smith, eds., *The Global Greenhouse Regime: Who Pays?* London: Earthscan, 144–168.

Hayes, P., and K. Smith, eds. 1993. *The Global Greenhouse Regime: Who Pays?* London: Earthscan.

Heidelberg Institute on International Conflict Research (HIIK). 2002. *Conflict Barometer 2002.* Heidelberg: University of Heidelberg.

Helm, C., and U. E. Simonis. 2001. "Distributive Justice in International Environmental Policy: Axiomatic Foundation and Exemplary Formulation." *Environmental Values* 10: 5–18.

Hill, H. 2001. "Tiny, Poor and War-Torn: Development Policy Challenges for East Timor." *World Development* 29: 1137–1156.

Horváth, G., S. Kisgyörgy, J. Sendzimir, and A. Vári 2001. *The 1998 Upper Tisza Flood, Hungary: Case Study Report.* Laxenburg: International Institute of Applied Systems Analysis.

Hulme, M. 1996. *Climate Change and Southern Africa: An Exploration of Some Potential Impacts and Implications in the SADC Region.* Norwich: Climatic Research Unit, University of East Anglia.

Hulme, M. 2003. "Abrupt Climate Change: Can Society Cope?" *Philosophical Transactions of the Royal Society A* 361: 2010–2021.

Hulme, M., R. Doherty, T. Ngara, M. New, and D. Lister. 2001. "African Climate Change: 1900–2100." *Climate Research* 17: 145–168.

Human Rights Watch (HRW). 1993. *Landmines: A Deadly Legacy.* New York: Arms Project of Human Rights Watch and Physicians For Human Rights.

Huntington, E. 1914. "The Adaptability of the White Man to Tropical America." *Journal of Race and Development* 5: 185–211.

Huq, S. 2001. "Climate Change and Bangladesh." *Science* 294: 1617.

Huq, S., and I. Burton. 2003. *Funding Adaptation to Climate Change: What, Who and How to Fund?* London: International Institute for Environment and Development (IIED), Sustainable Development Opinion paper. Available online at: <http://www.iied.org>.

Huq, S., A. Rahman, M. Konate, Y. Sokona, and H. Reid. 2003. *Mainstreaming Adaptation to Climate Change in Least Developed Countries.* London: International Institute for Environment and Development.

Huq, S., and H. Reid. 2003. "The Role of People's Assessments." *Tiempo* 48: 5–9. Available online at: <www.uea.ac.uk/cru/tiempo>.

Intergovernmental Panel on Climate Change (IPCC). 1992. *Climate Change 1992: The Supplementary Report to the IPCC Scientific Assessment.* Houghton, J. T., B. A. Callander, and S. K. Varney, eds. Cambridge: Cambridge University Press.

Intergovernmental Panel on Climate Change (IPCC). 1996. *Climate Change 1995: Impacts, Adaptations and Mitigation of Climate Change: Scientific-Technical Analyses.* Second Assessment Report. R. T. Watson, M. C. Zinyowera, and R. H. Moss, eds. Cambridge: Cambridge University Press.

International Panel on Climate Change (IPCC). 1997. *The Regional impacts of Climate Change: An Assessment of Vulnerability.* Cambridge: Cambridge University Press.

Intergovernmental Panel on Climate Change (IPCC). 2000. *Emissions Scenarios—A Special Report of Working Group III of the Intergovernmental Panel on Climate Change.* N. Nakicenovic et al., eds. Cambridge: Cambridge University Press.

Intergovernmental Panel on Climate Change (IPCC). 2001a. *The Scientific Basis, Summary for Policy Makers—Contribution of Working Group I to the Third Assessment Report of the Intergovernmental Panel on Climate Change.* J. T. Houghton, Y. Ding, D. J. Griggs, M. Noguer, P. J. van der Linden, X. Dai, K. Maskell, and C. A. Johnson, eds. Cambridge: Cambridge University Press.

Intergovernmental Panel on Climate Change (IPCC). 2001b. *Impacts, Adaptation, and Vulnerability—Contribution of Working Group II to the IPCC Third Assessment Report.* J. J. McCarthy, O. F. Canziani, N. A. Leary, D. J. Dokken, and K. S. White, eds. Cambridge: Cambridge University Press.

Intergovernmental Panel on Climate Change (IPCC). 2001c. *Mitigation—Contribution of Working Group III to the Third Assessment Report of the Intergovernmental Panel on Climate Change.* B. Metz, O. Davidson, R. Swart, and J. Pan, eds. Cambridge: Cambridge University Press.

Intergovernmental Panel on Climate Change (IPCC). 2001d. *Synthesis Report 2001—Contribution of Working Group I, II, and III to the Third Assessment Report of the Intergovernmental Panel on Climate Change.* R. T. Watson and the Core Writing Team, eds. Cambridge: Cambridge University Press.

International Campaign to Ban Landmines (ICBL). 2002. *Landmine Monitor Report 2002*. New York: Human Rights Watch.

International Federation of the Red Cross/Red Crescent Societies (IFRC). 2002. *World Disasters Report 2001: Focus on Recovery*. Geneva: International Federation of Red Cross and Red Crescent Societies.

Islam, M. S. 2001. *Sea-Level Rise Changes in Bangladesh*. Dhaka: Asiatic Society of Bangladesh.

Jamieson, D. 2001. "Climate Change and Global Environmental Justice." In C. A. Miller and P. N. Edwards, eds., *Changing the Atmosphere: Expert Knowledge and Environmental Governance*. Cambridge: MIT Press, 287–307.

Jardine, M. 1995. *East Timor: Genocide in Paradise*. Tucson: Odonian Press.

Jarosz, L. 1996. "Working in the Global Food System: A Focus for International Comparative Analysis." *Progress in Human Geography* 20: 41–55.

Jenkins, G. P. 1998. *Evaluation of Stakeholder Impacts in Cost-Benefit Analysis*. Development Discussion Paper No. 631. Cambridge, MA: Harvard Institute for International Development.

Johnston, R. J., D. Gregory, G. Pratt, M. Watts, and D. M. Smith. 2000. *The Dictionary of Human Geography*, 4th ed. Oxford: Blackwell.

Johnstone, N., J. Thompson, M. Katui-Katua, M. Mujwajuzi, J. Tumwine, E. Wood, and I. Porras. 2002. "Environmental and Ethical Dimensions of the Provision of a Basic Need: Water and Sanitation Services in East Africa." In D. W. Bromley and J. Paavola, eds., *Economics, Ethics and Environmental Policy: Contested Choices*. Oxford: Blackwell, 239–257.

Jones, P. G., and P. K. Thornton. 2003. "The Potential Impacts of Climate Change on Maize Production in Africa and Latin America in 2055." *Global Environmental Change* 13: 51–59.

Jones, R. N. 2000. "Managing Uncertainties in Climate Change Projections—Issues for Impact Assessment." *Climatic Change* 45: 403–419.

Jorgenson, D. W. 1985. "Efficiency versus Equity in Economic Policy Analysis." *American Economist* 29: 5–14.

Jorgenson, D. W. 1990. "Aggregate Consumer Behavior and the Measurement of Social Welfare." *Econometrica* 58: 1007–1040.

Jorgenson, D. W., and D. T. Slesnick. 1983. "Individual and Social Cost of Living Indexes." In W. E. Diewert and C. Montmarquette, eds., *Price Level Measurement*. Ottawa: Statistics Canada, 241–336.

Jorgenson, D. W., D. T. Slesnick, and P. J. Wilcoxen. 1992. "Carbon Taxes and Economic Welfare." *Brookings Papers on Economic Activity: Microeconomics*, 393–454.

Jorgenson, D. W., and P. J. Wilcoxen. 1990. "Environmental Regulation and U.S. Economic Growth." *Journal of Economics* 21: 314–340.

Kaldor, M. 1999. *New and Old Wars: Organized Violence in a Global Era.* Stanford: Stanford University Press.

Kaly, U., L. Briguglio, H. McLeod, S. Schmall, C. Pratt, and R. Pal. 1999. *Environmental Vulnerability Index (EVI) to Summarize National Vulnerability Profiles.* SOPAC Technical Report 275. Suva: South Pacific Applied Geoscience Commission.

Kasperson, J. X., and R. E. Kasperson. 2001a. *International Workshop on Vulnerability and Global Environmental Change.* Risk and Vulnerability Programme Report 2001–01. Stockholm: Stockholm Environment Institute.

Kasperson, J. X., and R. E. Kasperson. 2001b. *Global Environmental Risk.* Tokyo: United Nations University Press.

Kasperson, R. E., and K. Dow. 1991. "Developmental and Geographical Equity in Global Environmental Change." *Evaluation Review* 15: 149–171.

Kasperson, R. E., and J. X. Kasperson. 2001. *Climate Change, Vulnerability, and Social Justice.* Stockholm: Stockholm Environment Institute.

Kasperson, R. E., J. X. Kasperson, B. L. Turner II, K. Dow, and W. B. Meyer. 1995. "Critical Environmental Regions: Concepts, Distinctions, and Issues." In J. X. Kasperson, R. E. Kasperson, and B. L. Turner II, eds., *Regions at Risk.* Tokyo: United Nations University Press, 1–41.

Kates, R. W. 2000. "Cautionary Tales: Adaptation and the Global Poor." *Climatic Change* 45: 5–17.

Kates, R. W., and W. C. Clark. 1996. "Expecting the Unexpected." *Environment* 38 (2): 6–11; 28–34.

Kaul, I., I. Grunberg, and M. A. Stern. 1999. "Defining Global Public Goods." In I. Kaul, I. Grunberg, and M. A. Stern, eds., *Global Public Goods: International Cooperation in the 21st Century.* New York: Oxford University Press, 2–19.

Kaye, H. L. 1997. *The Social Meaning of Modern Biology.* New Brunswick, NJ: Transaction Publishers.

Keating, G. C. 1997. "The Idea of Fairness in the Law of Enterprise Liability." *Michigan Law Review* 95: 1266–1380.

Kelly, P. M. 2000. "Smoke and Mirrors." *Tiempo* 36/37. Available online at <http://www.cru.uea.ac.uk/tiempo/>. Accessed 30 July, 2003.

Kelly, P. M., and W. N. Adger. 2000. "Theory and Practice in Assessing Vulnerability to Climate Change and Facilitating Adaptation." *Climatic Change* 47: 325–352.

Kikar, G. A. 2000. *Synthesis Report for the Vulnerability and Adaptation Assessment Section: South African Country Study on Climate Change.* Proceedings of the presentation at the Workshop on Measuring the Impacts of Climate Change on Indian and Brazilian Agriculture, Washington, DC, 5–7 May: World Bank.

King, D. A. 2004. "Climate Change Science: Adapt, Mitigate or Ignore?" *Science* 303: 176–177.

Kironde, J. M. L., and M. Yhdego. 1997. "The Governance of Waste Management in Urban Tanzania: Towards a Community-Based Approach." *Resources, Conservation and Recycling* 21: 213–226.

Klinenberg, E. 2002. *Heat Wave: A Social Autopsy of Disaster in Chicago.* Chicago: University of Chicago Press.

Kohen, A., and J. Taylor. 1979. *An Act of Genocide: Indonesia's Invasion of East Timor.* London: TAPOL.

Kolm, S.-C. 1996. *Modern Theories of Justice.* Cambridge, MA: MIT Press.

Korsgaard, M. A., D. M. Schweiger, and H. J. Sapinza. 1995. "Building Commitment, Attachment and Trust in Strategic Decision-Making Teams: The Role of Procedural Justice." *Academy of Management Journal* 38: 60–84.

Koslowski, P. 1996. *Ethics of Capitalism and Critique of Sociobiology: Two Essays with a Comment by James M. Buchanan.* New York: Springer.

Kreimer, A., M. Arnold, and A. Carlin, eds. 2004. *Building Safer Cities: The Future of Disaster Risk.* Disaster Risk Management Series No. 3, Washington, DC: World Bank.

Kumar, K. S. K., and J. Parikh. 2001. "Indian Agriculture and Climate Sensitivity." *Global Environmental Change* 11: 147–154.

Kumar-Range, S. 2001. *Environmental Management and Disaster Risk Reduction: A Gender Perspective.* Paper prepared for the DAW/ISDR Expert Group Meeting on "Environmental Management and the Mitigation of Natural Disasters," 6–9 November 2001, Ankara, Turkey.

Kunreuther, H., and R. Roth, Sr. 1998. *Paying the Price: The Status and Role of Insurance against Natural Disasters in the United States,* Washington, DC: Joseph Henry Press.

Kuzek, D., K. Campbell, and M. Khater. 2004. "The Use of Probabilistic Risk Models for Managing Earthquake Insurance Risks: Example for Turkey." In E. Gurenko, ed., *Catastrophe Risk and Reinsurance: A Country Risk Management Perspective.* Washington DC: World Bank, 41–64.

Kyessi, A. G. 2005. "Community-Based Urban Water Management in Fringe Neighbourhoods: The Case of Dar es Salaam, Tanzania." *Habitat International* 29: 1–25.

Lash, S., and M. Featherstone. 2002. *Recognition and Difference: Politics, Identity, Multiculture.* London: Sage Publications.

Leach, M., R. Mearns, and I. Scoones. 1999. "Environmental Entitlements: Dynamics and Institutions in Community-Based Natural Resource Management." *World Development* 27: 225–247.

Leary, N. A. 1995. "Climate Change Costs: A General Equilibrium Analysis for the United States." In K. Miller and R. Parkin, eds., *Proceedings of an Institute on the Economics of the Climate Resource*. Boulder: National Center for Atmospheric Research, 399–434.

Leary, N. A. 1999. "A Framework for Benefit-Cost Analysis of Adaptation to Climate Change and Climate Variability." *Mitigation and Adaptation Strategies for Global Change* 4: 307–318.

Le Billon, P. 2001. "The Political Ecology of War: Natural Resources and Armed Conflict." *Political Geography* 20: 561–584.

Leichenko, R. M., and K. L. O'Brien. 2002. "The Dynamics of Rural Vulnerability to Global Change: The Case of Southern Africa." *Mitigation and Adaptation Strategies for Global Change* 7: 1–18.

Leichenko, R. M., and J. L. Wescoat. 1993. "Environmental Impacts of Climate Change and Water Development in the Indus Delta Region." *Water Resources Development* 9: 247–261.

Levy, M. 1995. "Time for a Third Wave of Environment and Security Scholarship?" *Environmental Change and Security Project Report* 1: 44–46.

Lewis, J. 1999. *Development in Disaster-Prone Places*. London: Intermediate Technology Publications.

Lewthwaite, G. 1966. "Environmentalism and Determinism: A Search for Clarification." *Annals of the Association of American Geographers* 56: 1–23.

Light, A., and A. de-Shalit, eds. 2003. *Moral and Political Reasoning in Environmental Practice*. Cambridge: MIT Press.

Lind, E. A., and T. Tyler. 1988. *The Social Psychology of Procedural Justice*. New York: Plenum Press.

Linden, H. R. 1996. "The Evolution of an Energy Contrarian." *Annual Review of Energy and the Environment* 21: 31–67.

Linnerooth-Bayer, J., and A. Amendola. 2000. "Global Change, Natural Disasters and Loss Sharing: Issues of Efficiency and Equity." *Geneva Papers on Risk and Insurance* 25: 203–219.

Linnerooth-Bayer, J., M. J. Mace, and R. Verheyen. 2003. *Insurance-Related Actions and Risk Assessment in the Context of the UN FCCC*. Background paper for UNFCCC Workshop on Insurance-Related Actions and Risk Assessment in the Framework of the UNFCCC, 11–15 May, Bonn: UN Framework Convention on Climate Change. Available online at <http://unfccc.int/sessions/workshop/120503/documents/background.pdf>.

Lipton, M. 1977. *Why Poor People Stay Poor: A Study of Urban Bias in World Development*. London: Maurice Temple Smith.

Little, P. D., K. Smith, B. A. Cellarius, D. L. Coppock, and C. B. Barrett. 2001. "Avoiding Disaster: Diversification and Risk Management among East African Herders." *Development and Change* 32: 401–433.

Lonergan, S., K. Gustavson, and B. Carter. 2000. "The Index of Human Insecurity." *AVISO* 6: 1–7.

Low, N., and B. Gleeson. 1998. *Justice, Society and Nature: An Exploration of Political Ecology.* London: Routledge.

Maganga, F. P. 2003. "Incorporating Customary Laws in Implementation of Integrated Water Resources Management: Some Insights from Rufiji River Basin, Tanzania." *Physics and Chemistry of the Earth* 28: 995–1000.

Marx, K., and F. Engels. 1961. "The Communist Manifesto." In A. P. Mandel, ed., *Essential Works of Marxism.* New York: Bantam Books, 1–13.

Masika, R., ed. 2002. *Gender, Development and Climate Change.* Oxford: Oxfam.

Mastrandrea, M., and S. H. Schneider. 2004. "Probabilistic Integrated Assessment of 'Dangerous' Climate Change." *Science* 304: 571–575.

Matthew, R., T. Gaulin, and B. Mcdonald. 2003. "The Elusive Quest: Linking Environmental Change and Conflict." *Canadian Journal of Political Science* 36: 857–878.

McMichael, A. J., A. Haines, R. Slooff, and S. Kovats. 1996. *Climate Change and Human Health.* Geneva: World Health Organisation.

Mendelsohn, R., W. D. Nordhaus, and D. Shaw. 1994. "The Impact of Global Warming on Agriculture: A Ricardian Analysis." *American Economic Review* 84: 753–771.

Meshack, C. K. 2003. Transaction Costs of Community Based Forest Management: Empirical Evidence from Tanzania. M.Sc. thesis, Environment Department, University of York, UK.

Messer, E., M. Cohen, and T. Marchione. 2001. "Conflict: A Cause and Effect of Hunger." *Environmental Change and Security Project Report* 7: 1–16.

Metz, B., M. Berk, M. den Elzen, B. de Vries, and D. van Vuuren. 2002. "Towards an Equitable Global Climate Change Regime: Compatibility with Article 2 of the Climate Change Convention and the Link with Sustainable Development." *Climate Policy* 2: 211–230.

Midgley, J., J. Hall, A. Hardiman, and D. Narine. 1986. *Community Participation, Social Development and the State.* London: Methuen.

Miletti, D. 1999. *Disasters by Design.* Washington, DC: Joseph Henry Press.

Miller, D. 1976. *Social Justice.* Oxford: Clarendon Press.

Miller, D. 1980. "Social Justice and the Principle of Need." In M. Freeman and D. Robertson, eds., *The Frontiers of Political Theory. Essays in a Revitalised Discipline.* Brighton: Harvester.

Modvig, J., J. Pagaduan-Lopez, J. Rodenburg, C. Salud, R. Cabigon, and C. Panelo. 2000. "Torture and Trauma in Post-Conflict East Timor." *Lancet* 356: 1763.

Mortimore, M., and W. M. Adams. 2001. "Farmer Adaptation, Change and Crisis in the Sahel." *Global Environmental Change* 11: 49–57.

Morton, J. 1999. "Population Growth and Poverty in Machakos District, Kenya." *Geographical Journal* 30: 37–46.

Moser, C. O. N. 1998. "The Asset Vulnerability Framework: Reassessing Urban Poverty Reduction Strategies." *World Development* 26: 1–19.

Moss, R. H., and S. H. Schneider. 2000. "Uncertainties in the IPCC TAR: Recommendations to Lead Authors for More Consistent Assessment and Reporting." In R. Pachauri, T. Taniguchi, and K. Tanaka, eds., *Guidance Papers on the Cross Cutting Issues of the Third Assessment Report of the IPCC*. Geneva: World Meteorological Organization, 33–51.

Müller, B. 2001. "Varieties of Distributive Justice in Climate Change: An Editorial Comment." *Climatic Change* 48: 273–288.

Müller, B. 2002. *Equity in Climate Change: The Great Divide*. Oxford: Oxford Institute for Energy Studies.

Munich Re. 2003. *Natural Catastrophes in 2002*, Topics, vol. 10, Munich, Munich Reinsurance Group.

Murray, C., G. King, A. Lopez, N. Tomijima, and E. Krug. 2002. "Armed Conflict as a Public Health Problem." *British Medical Journal* 324: 346–349.

Mwandosya, M. J., B. S. Nyenzi, and M. L. Luhanga. 1998. *The Assessment of Vulnerability and Adaptation to Climate Change Impacts in Tanzania*. Dar es Salaam: Centre for Energy, Environment, Science and Technology.

Narayan, D., and L. Pritchett. 1997. *Cents and Sociability: Household Income and Social Capital in Rural Tanzania*. Policy Research Working Paper 1796. Washington, DC: World Bank.

National Assessment Synthesis Team 2001. *Climate Change Impacts on the United States: The Potential Consequences of Climate Variability and Change*. Report for the U.S. Global Change Research Program. Cambridge: Cambridge University Press.

Neumayer, E. 2000. "In Defence of Historical Accountability for Greenhouse Gas Emissions." *Ecological Economics* 33: 185–192.

Nordhaus, W. D. 1991. "To Slow or Not to Slow: The Economics of the Greenhouse effect." *Economic Journal* 101: 920–937.

Nordhaus, W. D. 1994. *Managing the Global Commons: The Economics of Climate Change*. Cambridge, MA: MIT Press.

Norton, B. 2002. "The Ignorance Argument: What Must We Know to Be Fair to the Future?" In D. W. Bromley and J. Paavola, eds., *Economics, Ethics and Environmental Policy: Contested Choices*. Malden, MA: Blackwell, 35–52.

Nozick, R. 1974. *Anarchy, State and Utopia.* Oxford: Blackwell.

Oakerson, R. J. 1992. "Analyzing the Commons: A Framework." In D. W. Bromley, ed., *Making the Commons Work: Theory, Practice and Policy.* San Francisco: Institute for Contemporary Studies, 41–59.

O'Brien, K. L., S. Eriksen, A. Schjolden, and L. Nygaard. 2004a. *What's in a Word? Conflicting Interpretations of Vulnerability in Climate Change Research.* CICERO Working Paper 2004:04, University of Oslo: CICERO.

O'Brien, K. L., and R. M. Leichenko. 2000. "Double Exposure: Assessing the Impacts of Climate Change within the Context of Economic Globalization." *Global Environmental Change* 10: 221–232.

O'Brien, K. L., and R. M. Leichenko. 2003. "Winners and Losers in the Context of Global Change." *Annals of the Association of American Geographers* 93: 89–103.

O'Brien, K. L., R. Leichenko, U. Kelkar, H. Venema, G. Aandahl, H. Tompkins, A. Javed, S. Bhadwal, S. Barg, L. Nygaard, and J. West. 2004b. "Mapping Multiple Stressors: Climate Change and Economic Globalization in India." *Global Environmental Change* 14: 303–313.

O'Brien, K. L., L. Sygna, and J. E. Haugen. 2004. "Vulnerable or Resilient? Multi-Scale Assessments of Climate Impacts in Norway." *Climatic Change* 64: 193–225.

O'Neill, B. C., and M. Oppenheimer. 2002. "Climate Change—Dangerous Climate Impacts and the Kyoto Protocol." *Science* 296: 1971–1972.

O'Neill, J. 2001. "Representing People, Representing Nature, Representing the World." *Environment and Planning C: Government and Policy* 19: 483–500.

Oppenheimer, M., and B. C. O'Neill. 2002. "Dangerous Climate Impacts and the Kyoto Protocol." *Science* 296: 1971–1972.

O'Riordan, T., and A. Jordan. 1999. "Institutions, Climate Change and Cultural Theory: Towards a Common Analytical Framework." *Global Environmental Change* 9: 81–93.

Ostrom, E. 1990. *Governing the Commons: The Evolution of Institutions for Collective Action.* Cambridge: Cambridge University Press.

Overpeck, J. T., R. S. Webb, and T. Webb III. 1992. "Mapping Eastern North America Vegetation Change over the Past 18,000 Years: No-Analogs and the Future." *Geology* 20: 1071–1074.

Paavola, J. 2002a. "Rethinking the Choice and Performance of Environmental Policies." In D. Bromley and J. Paavola, eds., *Economics, Ethics, and Environmental Policy: Contested Choices.* Malden, MA: Blackwell, 87–102.

Paavola, J. 2002b. "Environment and Development: Dissecting the Connections." *Forum for Development Studies* 29: 5–32.

Paavola, J. 2004. *Livelihoods, Vulnerability and Adaptation to Climate Change in the Morogoro Region, Tanzania.* Working Paper EDM 04-12. Centre for Social and Economic Research on the Global Environment, University of East Anglia, Norwich, UK.

Paavola, J. 2005. "Interdependence, Pluralism and Globalisation: Implications for Environmental Governance." In J. Paavola and I. Lowe, eds., *Environmental Values in a Globalising World: Nature, Justice and Governance.* London: Routledge, 143–158.

Paavola, J., and W. N. Adger. 2002. *Justice and Adaptation to Climate Change.* Working Paper 23. Norwich: Tyndall Centre for Climate Change Research, University of East Anglia, Norwich, UK.

Paavola, J., and W. N. Adger. 2006. "Fair Adaptation to Climate Change." *Ecological Economics,* in press.

Page, E. 2000. "Theorizing the Link Between Environmental Change and Security." *Review of European Community and International Environmental Law* 9: 33–43.

Parmesan, C., and G. Yohe. 2003. "A Globally Coherent Fingerprint of Climate Change Impacts across Natural Systems." *Nature* 421: 37–42.

Parry, M., N. Arnell, T. McMichael, R. J. Nicholls, P. Martens, S. Kovats, M. Livermore, C. Rosenzweig, A. Aglesias, and G. Fischer. 2001. "Millions at Risk: Defining Critical Climate Change Threats and Targets." *Global Environmental Change* 11: 181–183.

Parry, M., C. Rosenzweig, A. Iglesias, G. Fischer, and M. Livermore. 1999. "Climate Change and World Food Security: A New Assessment." *Global Environmental Change* 9: 551–567.

Paterson, M. 2001. "Principles of Justice in the Context of Climate Change." In U. Luterbacher and D. Sprinz, eds., *International Relations and Global Climate Change.* Cambridge, MA: MIT Press, 119–126.

Patz, J. A., M. Hulme, C. Rosenzweig, T. D. Mitchell, R. A. Goldberg, A. K. Githeko, S. Lele, A. J. McMichael, and D. Le Sueur. 2002. "Regional Warming and Malaria Resurgence." *Nature* 420: 627–628.

Pearce, D. 2003. "The Social Cost of Carbon and Its Policy Implications." *Oxford Review of Economic Policy* 19: 362–384.

Pearce, J. 1998. "From Civil War to Civil Society: Has the End of the Cold War Brought Peace to Central America?" *International Affairs* 74: 587–615.

Pecher, I., S. Stoiko, and U. Kichura. 1999. "Conception for the Regeneration of the Upper Forest Boundary and for the Optimization of Hydrological Regime in the Ukrainian Carpathians, 1997." In J. Hamar and A. Sárkány-Kiss, eds., *The Upper Tisa Valley: Preparatory Proposal for Ramsar Site Designation and an Ecological Background.* Szeged: Tisza Klub, 207–213.

Pelling, M. 1999. "The Political Ecology of Flood Hazard in Urban Guyana." *Geoforum* 30: 249–261.

Pelling, M., and J. I. Uitto. 2001. "Small Island Developing States: Natural Disaster Vulnerability and Global Change." *Environmental Hazards* 3: 49–62.

Penalver, E. M. 1998. "Acts of God or Toxic Torts? Applying Tort Principles to the Problem of Climate Change." *Natural Resources Journal* 38: 563–601.

Perry, S. R. 1992. "The Moral Foundations of Tort Law." *Iowa Law Review* 77: 449–514.

Pielke Jr., R. A., and M. W. Downton. 2000. "Precipitation and Damaging Floods: Trend in the United States, 1932–97." *Journal of Climate* 13: 3625–3637.

Pielke Jr, R. A., and C. W. Landsea. 1998. "Normalized Hurricane Damages in the United States, 1925–97." *Weather Forecasting* 13: 351–361.

Pieterse, J. N. 1999. "Popular Development: Rethinking the Theory and Practice of Development." *Development and Change* 30: 183–185.

Pinkney, R. 1997. *Democracy and Dictatorship in Ghana and Tanzania.* London: Macmillan.

Platteau, J.-P. 2000. *Institutions, Social Norms and Economic Development.* Amsterdam: Harwood.

Polidano, C. 2000. "Measuring Public Sector Capacity." *World Development* 28: 805–822.

Pollak, R. A. 1981. "The Social Cost of Living Index." *Journal of Public Economics* 15: 311–336.

Pollner, J. 2000. *Managing Catastrophic Risks Using Alternative Risk Financing and Insurance Pooling Mechanisms.* Washington, DC: World Bank.

Portmore, D. W. 2000. "Commonsense Morality and not Being Required to Maximize the Overall Good." *Philosophical Studies* 100: 193–213.

Powell, M. R. 1999. *Science at EPA: Information in the Regulatory Process.* Washington, DC: Resources for the Future.

Pretty, J. 1995. "Participatory Learning for Sustainable Agriculture." *World Development* 23: 1247–1263.

Project Ploughshares. 2002. *Armed Conflict Report 2002.* Waterloo: Project Ploughshares. Available online at <www.ploughshares.ca>.

Rawls, J. 1972. *A Theory of Justice.* Oxford: Clarendon Press.

Rayner, S. 1994. *A Conceptual Map of Human Values for Climate Change Decision Making.* Paper presented at the Workshop on Equity and Social Considerations, IPCC Working Group III, Nairobi, Kenya.

Rayner, S., and E. L. Malone, 2001. "Climate Change, Poverty, and Intragenerational Equity: The National Level." *International Journal of Global Environmental Issues* 1: 175–202.

Rees, W. E. 2002. "An Ecological Economics Perspective on Sustainability and Prospects for Ending Poverty." *Population and Environment* 24: 15–46.

Reij, C., and A. Waters-Bayer, eds. 2001. *Farmer Innovation in Africa: A Source of Inspiration for Agricultural Development*. London: Earthscan.

Reilly, J., F. Tubiello, B. McCarl, D. Abler, R. Darwin, K. Fuglie, S. Hollinger, C. Izaurralde, S. Jagtap, J. Jones, L. Mearns, D. Ojima, E. Paul, K. Paustian, S. Riha, N. Rosenberg, and C. Rosenzweig. 2003. "U.S. Agriculture and Climate Change: New Results." *Climatic Change* 57: 43–69.

Renn, O., and T. Webler 1995. "A Brief Primer on Participation, Philosophy and Practice" In O. Renn, T. Webler, and P. Wiedemann, eds., *Fairness and Competence in Citizen Participation: Evaluating Models for Environmental Discourse*. Dordrecht: Kluwer, 17–34.

Renner, M. 2002. *The Anatomy of Resource Wars*. Worldwatch Paper 162. Washington, DC: Worldwatch Institute.

Rescher, N. 1971. *Distributive Justice: A Constructive Critique of the Utilitarian Theory of Distribution*. Indianapolis: Bobbs Merill.

Revesz, R. L., and R. B. Stewart, eds. 1995. *Analyzing Superfund: Economics, Science and Law*. Washington, DC: Resources for the Future.

Revkin, A. 2004. "Eskimos Seek to Recast Global Warming as a Rights Issue." *New York Times*, 15 December 2004.

Ribot, J. C. 1995. "The Causal Structure of Vulnerability: Its Application to Climate Impact Analysis." *GeoJournal* 35: 119–122.

Ringius, L., T. Asbjørn, and A. Underdal. 2002. "Burden Sharing and Fairness Principles in International Climate Policy." *International Environmental Agreements: Politics, Law and Economics* 2: 1–22.

Ringius, L., T. E. Downing, M. Hulme, D. Waughray, and R. Selrod. 1996. *Climate Change in Africa: Issues and Regional Strategy*. Report 1996: 08 Oslo: CICERO, University of Oslo.

Roberts, K. W. S. 1980. "Interpersonal Comparability and Social Choice Theory." *Review of Economic Studies* 47: 409–439.

Rogers, D. J., and S. E. Randolph. 2000. "The Global Spread of Malaria in a Future, Warmer World." *Science* 289: 1763–1766.

Roncoli, C., K. Ingram, and P. Kirshen. 2001. "The Costs and Risks of Coping with Drought: Livelihood Impacts and Farmers' Responses in Burkina Faso." *Climate Research* 19: 119–132.

Root, T. L., J. T. Price, K. R. Hall, S. H. Schneider, C. Rosenzweig, and J. A. Pounds. 2003. "Fingerprints of Global warming on Wild animals and Plants." *Nature* 421: 57–60.

Root, T. L., and S. H. Schneider. 2001. "Climate Change: Overview and Implications for Wildlife." In S. H. Schneider and T. L. Root, eds., *Wildlife Responses to Climate Change: North American Case Studies*. Washington, DC: Island Press, 1–56.

Rose, A., and S. Kverndokk. 1998. "Equity in Environmental Policy: An Application to Global Warming." In J. van den Bergh, ed., *Handbook on Environmental and Resource Economics*. Cheltenham: Elgar, 352–379.

Rose, A. Z., B. Stevens, J. Edmonds, and M. Wise. 1998. "International Equity and Differentiation in Global Warming Policy." *Environmental and Resource Economics* 12: 25–51.

Sagar, A. D. 2000. "Wealth, Responsibility, and Equity: Exploring an Allocation Framework for Global GHG Emissions." *Climatic Change* 45: 511–527.

Satterfield, T. A., C. K. Mertz, and P. Slovic. 2004. "Discrimination, Vulnerability, and Justice in the Face of Risk." *Risk Analysis* 24: 115–129.

Sauer, C. O. 1941. "Forward to Historical Geography." *Annals of the Association of American Geographers* 31: 1–24.

Sayer, A., and R. Walker. 1992. *The New Social Economy: Reworking the Division of Labor*. Oxford: Blackwell.

Schafer, J. 2002. *Supporting Livelihoods in Situations of Chronic Conflict*. Paper 183. London: Overseas Development Institute.

Schär, C., and G. Jendritzky. 2004. "Climate Change: Hot News from Summer 2003." *Nature* 432: 559–560.

Schlosberg, D. 1999. *Environmental Justice and the New Pluralism: The Challenge of Difference for Environmentalism*. Oxford: Oxford University Press.

Schneider, S. H. 1983. "CO_2, Climate and Society: A Brief Overview." In R. S. Chen, E. M. Boulding, and S. H. Schneider, eds., *Social Science Research and Climatic Change: An Interdisciplinary Appraisal*. Dordrecht: D. Reidel Publishing, 9–15.

Schneider, S. H. 1992. "Introduction to Climate Modeling." In K. E. Trenberth, ed., *Climate System Modeling*. Cambridge: Cambridge University Press, 3–26.

Schneider, S. H. 1993. "Pondering Greenhouse Policy." *Science* 259: 1381.

Schneider, S. H. 2001. "What Is 'Dangerous' Climate Change?" *Nature* 411: 17–19.

Schneider, S. H. 2002. "Can We Estimate the Likelihood of Climatic Changes at 2100?" *Climatic Change* 52: 441–451.

Schneider, S. H. 2004. "Abrupt Non-Linear Climate Change, Irreversibility and Surprise." *Global Environmental Change* 14: 245–258.

Schneider, S. H., and C. Azar. 2001. "Are Uncertainties in Climate and Energy Systems a Justification for Stronger Near-Term Mitigation Policies?" In *Proceedings of The Pew Center Workshop on the Timing of Climate Change Policies, 11–12 October, 2001*. Washington, DC: Pew Center, 85–136.

Schneider, S. H., W. E. Easterling, and L. O. Mearns. 2000. "Adaptation: Sensitivity to Natural Variability, Agent Assumptions and Dynamic Climate Changes." *Climatic Change* 45: 203–221.

Schneider, S. H., and K. Kuntz-Duriseti. 2002. "Uncertainty and Climate Change Policy." In S. H. Schneider, A. Rosencranz, and J. O. Niles, eds., *Climate Change Policy: A Survey.* Washington, DC: Island Press, 53–87.

Schneider, S. H., K. Kuntz-Duriseti, and C. Azar. 2000. "Costing Nonlinearities, Surprises, and Irreversible Events." *Pacific and Asian Journal of Energy* 10: 81–106.

Schneider, S. H., and M. D. Mastrandrea. 2005. "Probabilistic Assessment of 'Dangerous' Climate Change and Emissions Pathways." *Proceedings of the National Academy of Sciences* 102: 15728–15735.

Schneider, S. H., and T. L. Root. 1998. "Climate Change." In M. J. Mac, P. A. Opler, C. E. Puckett Haeker, and P. D. Doran, eds., *Status and Trends of the Nation's Biological Resources.* Reston, VA: U.S. Department of the Interior, U.S. Geological Survey, 89–105.

Schneider, S. H., and T. L. Root, eds. 2001. *Wildlife Responses to Climate Change: North American Case Studies.* Washington, DC: Island Press.

Schneider, S. H., and S. L. Thompson. 1985. "Future Changes in the Atmosphere." In R. Repetto, ed., *The Global Possible.* New Haven, CT: Yale University Press, 363–430.

Schneider, S. H., B. L. Turner II, and H. Morehouse Garriga. 1998. "Imaginable Surprise in Global Change Science." *Journal of Risk Research* 1: 165–185.

Scoones, I., ed. 2001. *Dynamics and Diversity: Soil Fertility and Farming Livelihoods in Africa.* London: Earthscan.

Scoones, I., and C. Toulmin. 1999. *Policies for Soil Fertility Management in Africa.* Report for the Department for International Development. London: International Institute for Environment and Development.

Semple, E. C. 1911. *Influences of Geographic Environment.* New York: H. Holt. Available online at <www.colorado.edu/geography/giw/>. Accessed 15 December, 2000.

Sen, A. K. 1977. "On Weights and Measures: Informational Constraints in Social Welfare Analysis." *Journal of Economics* 81: 112–124.

Sen, A. 1982. *Choice, Welfare and Measurement.* Oxford: Blackwell.

Sen, A. 1992. *Inequality Reexamined.* New York: Russell Sage Foundation.

Shackley, S., and B. Wynne. 1997. "Global Warming Potentials: Ambiguity or Precision as an Aid to Policy?" *Climate Research* 8: 89–106.

Shrader-Frechette, K. 2002. *Environmental Justice: Creating Equality, Reclaiming Democracy.* Oxford: Oxford University Press.

Shue, H. 1992. "The Unavoidability of Justice." In A. Hurrell and B. Kingsbury, eds., *The International Politics of the Environment: Actors, Interests, and Institutions.* Oxford: Oxford University Press, 373–397.

Shue, H. 1996. *Basic Rights: Subsistence, Affluence and U.S. Foreign Policy.* Princeton, NJ: Princeton University Press.

Shue, H. 1999. "Global Environment and International Inequality." *International Affairs* 75: 531–545.

Singer, P. 2002. *One World: The Ethics of Globalization.* New Haven, CT: Yale University Press.

Skoufias, E. 2003. "Economic Crises and Natural Disasters: Coping Strategies and Policy Implications." *World Development* 31: 1087–1102.

Smit, B., I. Burton, R. J. T. Klein, and R. Street. 1999. "The Science of Adaptation: A Framework for Assessment." *Mitigation and Adaptation Strategies for Global Change* 4: 199–213.

Smit, B., I. Burton, R. J. T. Klein, and J. Wandel. 2000. "An Anatomy of Adaptation to Climate Change and Variability." *Climatic Change* 45: 223–251.

Smit, B., and O. Pilifosova. 2001. "Adaptation to Climate Change in the Context of Sustainable Development and Equity." In J. McCarthy, O. Canziani, N. Leary, D. Dokken, and K. White, eds., *Climate Change 2001: Impacts, Adaptation & Vulnerability.* Cambridge: Cambridge University Press, 877–912.

Smit, B., and O. Pilifosova. 2003. "From Adaptation to Adaptive Capacity and Vulnerability Reduction." In J. B. Smith, R. J. T. Klein, and S. Huq, eds., *Climate Change, Adaptive Capacity and Development.* London: Imperial College Press, 9–28.

Smith, J. B. 1997. "Setting Priorities for Adapting to Climate Change." *Global Environmental Change* 7: 251–264.

Smith, K. R., J. Swisher, and D. R. Ahuja. 1993. "Who Pays (to Solve the Problem and How Much)?" In P. Hayes and K. Smith, eds., *The Global Greenhouse Regime: Who Pays?* London: Earthscan, 70–98.

Smithers, J., and B. Smit. 1997. "Human Adaptation to Climatic Variability and Change." *Global Environmental Change* 7: 129–146.

Sokona, Y., and F. Denton. 2001. "Climate Change Impacts: Can Africa Cope with the Challenges?" *Climate Policy* 1: 117–123.

Soyinka, W. 2004. *A Quest for Dignity.* Fourth Reith Lecture on Climate of Fear, University of Leeds, broadcast on BBC4, 24 April, 2004, 8 pm. Available online at <http://www.bbc.co.uk/radio4/reith2004/schedule.shtml>. Accessed 29 April, 2004.

Spash, C. L. 2002. *Greenhouse Economics: Value and Ethics.* London: Routledge.

Stern-Switzer C., and L. A. Bulan. 2002. *CERCLA: Comprehensive Response, Compensation and Liability Act.* Chicago: American Bar Association.

Stewart, F., and V. Fitzgerald. 2001. "Introduction: Assessing the Economic Costs of War." In F. Stewart and V. Fitzgerald, eds., *War and Underdevelopment:*

Volume 1, The Economic and Social Consequences of Conflict. Oxford: Oxford University Press, 3–38.

Stewart, F., C. Huang, and M. Wang. 2001. "Internal Wars in Developing Countries: An Empirical Overview of Economic and Social Consequences." In F. Stewart and V. Fitzgerald, eds., *War and Underdevelopment: Volume 1, The Economic and Social Consequences of Conflict.* Oxford: Oxford University Press, 67–103.

Stockholm Environment Institute. 2001. *Strategic Environmental Framework for the Greater Mekong Subregion: Integrating Development and Environment in the Transport and Water Resource Sectors.* Stockholm: Stockholm Environment Institute and Asian Development Bank.

Streck, C. 2001. "The Global Environment Facility: A Role Model for Global Governance?" *Global Environmental Politics* 1: 17–18.

Stripple, J. 1998. *Securitizing the Risks of Climate Change: Institutional Innovations in the Insurance of Catastrophic Risk.* Interim Report IR-98-098. Laxenburg: International Institute for Applied Systems Analysis.

Stripple, J. 2002. "Climate Change as a Security Issue" In E. Page and M. Redclift, eds., *Human Security and the Environment: International Comparisons.* Cheltenham: Elgar.

Swart, R. 1996. "Security Risks of Global Environmental Changes." *Global Environmental Change* 6: 187–192.

Swiss Re. 2003. *Natural Catastrophes and Man-Made Disasters in 2002,* Sigma 2/2003. Zurich: Swiss Reinsurance Company.

Szreter, S. 1997. "Economic Growth, Disruption, Deprivation, and Death: On the Importance of the Politics of Public Health for Development." *Population and Development Review* 23: 693–728.

Szreter, S., and M. Woolcock 2004. "Health by Association? Social Capital, Social Theory and the Political Economy of Public Health." *International Journal of Epidemiology* 33: 650–667.

Tanzania Association of Non-Governmental Organisation (TANGO). 2002. *Organisational Development Manual: Know Your NGO.* Dar es Salaam, Tanzania: TANGO.

Taylor, P. J., and F. H. Buttel. 1992. "How Do We Know We Have Global Environmental Problems? Science and the Globalization of Environmental Discourse." *Geoforum* 23: 405–516.

Thomas, C. D., A. Cameron, R. E. Green, M. Bakkenes, L. J. Beaumont, Y. C. Collingham, B. F. N. Erasmus, M. Ferreira de Siqueira, A. Grainger, L. Hannah, L. Hughes, B. Huntley, A. S. van Jaarsveld, G. F. Midgley, L. Miles, M. A. Ortega-Huerta, A. Townsend Peterson, O. L. Phillips, and S. E. Williams. 2004. "Extinction Risk from Climate Change." *Nature* 427: 145–148.

Thomas, D. S. G. 2003. "Into the Third Millennium: The Role of Stakeholder Groups in Reducing Desertification." In A. S. Alsharhan, W. W. Wood, and

A. S. Goudie, eds., *Desertification in the Third Millennium*. Rotterdam: Balkema, 3–12.

Thomas, D. S. G., D. Sporton, and C. Twyman. 2002. *Poverty, Policy and Natural Resource Use in Southern African Drylands*. Final Technical Report for Department for International Development. Department of Geography, University of Sheffield.

Thomas, D. S. G., and C. Twyman. 2004. "Good or Bad Rangeland? Hybrid Knowledge, Science, and Local Understandings of Vegetation Dynamics in the Kalahari." *Land Degradation and Development* 15: 215–231.

Thompson, M., R. Ellis, and A. Wildavsky. 1990. *Cultural Theory*. Boulder: Westview.

Tiffen, M., M. Mortimore, and F. Gichuki. 1994. *More People, Less Erosion: Environmental Recovery in Kenya*. Chichester: Wiley.

Tol, R. S. J. 2002. "Estimates of the Damage Costs of Climate Change. Part 1: Benchmark Estimates." *Environmental and Resource Economics* 21: 47–73.

Tol, R. S. J., T. E. Downing, S. Fankhauser, R. G. Richels, and J. B. Smith. 2001. "Progress in Estimating the Marginal Costs of Greenhouse Gas Emissions." Working Paper SCG-4, Research Unit Sustainability and Global Change, Hamburg University. Available online at <www.unihamburg.de/Wiss/>. Accessed 25 July, 2003.

Tol R. S. J., T. E. Downing, O. J. Kuik, and J. B. Smith. 2004. "Distributional Aspects of Climate Change Impacts." *Global Environmental Change* 14: 259–272.

Tol, R. S. J., S. Fankhauser, R. G. Richels, and J. B. Smith. 2000. *How Much Damage Will Climate Change Do? Recent Estimates*. Research unit stability and global change SCG-2, Centre for Marine and Climate Research. Hamburg University.

Tol, R. S. J., S. Fankhauser, and J. B. Smith. 1998. "The Scope for Adaptation to Climate Change: What Can We Learn from the Impact Literature." *Global Environmental Change* 8: 109–123.

Tol, R. S. J., and R. Verheyen. 2004. "State Responsibility and Compensation for Climate Change Damages—a Legal and Economic Assessment." *Energy Policy* 32: 1109–1130.

Tompkins, E. L., and W. N. Adger. 2004. "Does Adaptive Management of Natural Resources Enhance Resilience to Climate Change?" *Ecology and Society* 9(2): 10.

Toth, F., ed. 1999. *Fair Weather? Equity Concerns in Climate Change*. London: Earthscan.

Transparency International. 2003. *Global Corruption Report 2003*. Berlin: Transparency International.

Tripp, A. M. 1997. *Changing the Rules: The Politics of Liberalization and the Urban Informal Economy in Tanzania*. Berkeley: University of California Press.

Twyman, C., A. Dougill, D. Sporton, and D. S. G. Thomas. 2001. "Community Fencing in Open Rangelands: Self-Empowerment in Eastern Namibia." *Review of African Political Economy* 87: 9–26.

Twyman, C., A. Dougill, D. Sporton, and D. S. G. Thomas. 2004. "'Where Is the Life in Farming?': The Viability of Smallholder Farming on the Margins of the Kalahari, Southern Africa." *Geoforum* 35: 69–85.

Tyler, T. R., R. J. Boeckmann, H. J. Smith, and Y. J. Huo. 1997. *Social Justice in a Diverse Society*. Westview Press, Boulder, CO.

United Nations Conference on the Human Environment. 1972. Stockholm Declaration. United Nations Conference on the Human Environment. United Nations, Stockholm, Sweden.

United Nations Development Program (UNDP). 2001. *Disaster Profiles of Least Developed Countries*. Geneva: UNDP.

United Nations Development Program (UNDP). 2002a. *Human Development Report 2002*. Oxford: Oxford University Press.

United Nations Development Programme (UNDP). 2002b. "Country Programme Outline for Liberia (2003–2005)," Presented at the Annual Session, 17–28 June, 2002, Geneva. Available at <www.undp.org>.

United Nations Development Programme (UNDP). 2002c. *Ukun Rasik A'An: East Timor—The Way Ahead*, Human Development Report 2002. Dili: UNDP.

United Nations Development Programme (UNDP). 2003. *Human Development Report 2003*. New York: Oxford University Press.

United Nations Environment Programme (UNEP). 2000. *World Resources 2000–2001*. Washington, DC: World Resources Institute.

United Nations Environment Programme (UNEP). 2002a. *Global Environmental Outlook 3*. London: Earthscan.

United Nations Environment Programme (UNEP). 2002b. *Africa Environmental Outlook: Past, Present and Future Perspectives*. Nairobi: United Nations Environment Programme.

United Nations Framework Convention on Climate Change (UNFCCC). 1992. United Nations Framework Convention on Climate Change: Convention Text. Bonn: UNFCCC. Available at <www.unfccc.int>.

United Nations Framework Convention on Climate Change (UNFCCC). 1997. Proposed Elements of a Protocol to the United Nations Framework Convention on Climate Change, Presented by Brazil in Response to the Berlin Mandate. UNFCCC/AGBM/1997/MISC.1/Add.3.

United Nations Framework Convention on Climate Change (UNFCCC). 2003. Review of Adaptation Activities under the Convention. Working Paper No. 10. Bonn: United Nations Framework Convention on Climate Change.

United Nations High Commissioner for Refugees (UNHCR). 2002. *Refugees by Numbers 2002*. Geneva: UNHCR.

United Nations Population Division (UNPD). 2003. *World Population Prospects: The 2002 Revision*. Available at <http://esa.un.org/unpp>.

United Republic of Tanzania (URT), Ministry of Health and AMMP Team. 1997. *Policy Implications of Adult Morbidity and Mortality. End of Phase 1 Report Summary*. Technical Report No. 2. Dar es Salaam, United Republic of Tanzania, Ministry of Health.

United Republic of Tanzania (URT), Vice President's Office, Ministry of State—Environment. 2003. *Initial National Communication under the United Nations Framework Convention for Climate Change (UNFCCC)*. Dar es Salaam: United Republic of Tanzania, Vice President's Office, Ministry of State—Environment.

Uphoff, N. T., ed. 1983. *Rural Development and Local Organization in Asia*. London: Macmillan.

Vári, A., J. Linnerooth-Bayer, and Z. Ferencz. 2003. "Stakeholder Views on Flood Risk Management in Hungary's Upper Tisza Basin." *Risk Analysis* 23: 385–600.

Vaughan, D., and J. Spouge. 2002. "Risk Estimation of Collapse of the West Antarctic Ice Sheet." *Climatic Change* 52: 65–91.

Vellinga, P., E. Mills, G. Berz, S. Huq, L. Ann Kozak, J. Palutikof, B. Schanzenbächer, S. Shida, and G. Soler. 2001. "Insurance and Other Financial Services." In J. J. McCarthy, O. Canziani, N. A. Leary, D. J. Dokken, and K. S. White, eds., *Climate Change 2001: Impacts, Adaptation and Vulnerability*. Cambridge: Cambridge University Press, 417–450.

Verheyen, R. 2002. "Adaptation to the Impacts of Anthropogenic Climate Change—The International Legal Framework." *Review of European Community & International Environmental Law* 11(3): 129–143.

Wallensteen, P., and M. Sollenberg. 2001. "Armed Conflict, 1989–2000." *Journal of Peace Research* 38: 629–644.

Walzer, M. 1983. *Spheres of Justice: A Defence of Pluralism and Equality*. Oxford: Blackwell.

Wasson, M. 2001. "East Timor and Climate Change: Security and Sustainable Development." *Conference on Sustainable Development and the Environment in East Timor*, 25–31 January, 2001. Dili: Timor Aid, 38–41.

Webster, M., C. Forest, J. Reilly, M. Babiker, D. Kicklighter, M. Mayer, R. Prinn, M. Sarofim, Andrei Sokolov, P. Stone, and C. Wang. 2003. "Uncertainty Analysis of Climate Change and Policy Response." *Climatic Change* 61: 295–320.

West, J. J., H. Dowlatabadi, and M. J. Small. 2001. "Storms, Investor Decisions, and the Economic Impacts of Sea Level Rise." *Climatic Change* 48: 317–342.

Westing, A. 1980. *Warfare in a Fragile World: Military Impacts on the Human Environment.* London: Taylor and Francis.

Westing, A. 1997. "Environmental Warfare: Manipulating the Environment for Hostile Purposes." *Environmental Change and Security Project Report* 3: 145–149.

Wiegandt, E. 2001. "Climate Change, Equity, and International Negotiations." In U. Luterbacher and D. Sprinz, eds., *International Relations and Global Climate Change.* Cambridge: MIT Press, 127–150.

Wilcoxen, P. J. 1988. *The Effects of Environmental Regulation and Energy Prices on U.S. Economic Performance.* Ph.D. Thesis, Harvard University, Department of Economics.

Wilson, J. 1992. "The Moral Sense." *American Political Science Review* 87: 1–11.

Wisner, B. 2001. "Risk and the Neo-Liberal State: Why Post-Mitch Lessons Didn't Reduce El Salvador's Earthquake Losses." *Disasters* 25: 251–268.

Wisner, B., P. Blaikie, T. Cannon, and I. Davis. 2004. *At Risk: Natural Hazards, People's Vulnerability, and Disasters.* 2d ed. London: Routledge.

World Bank. 1999a. *Post Conflict Fund: Guidelines and Procedures.* Washington, DC: World Bank.

World Bank. 1999b. *The Transition from War to Peace: An Overview.* Washington, DC: World Bank.

World Bank, 2000. *Can Africa Claim the 21st Century?* Washington, DC: World Bank.

World Bank. 2002a. *World Development Indicators.* Washington, DC: World Bank.

World Bank. 2002b. *Tanzania at the Turn of the Century: Background Papers and Statistics.* Washington, DC: World Bank.

World Bank. 2003a. *The Economic and Social Costs of Armed Conflict in El Salvador.* Conflict Prevention and Reconstruction Unit. Washington, DC: World Bank.

World Bank. 2003b. *World Development Report—Building Institutions for Markets.* Washington, DC: World Bank.

World Commission on Environment and Development (WCED) Report. 1987. *Our Common Future: The Brundlandt Report.* Oxford: Oxford University Press.

World Economic Forum, Yale University Center for Environmental Law and Policy, and CIESIN, Columbia University. 2002. *2002 Environmental Sustainability Index.* Geneva: Global Leaders of Tomorrow Environment Task Force.

World Food Programme. 2003. *2003 Estimated Food Needs and Shortfalls for WFP Operational Activities*. Rome: World Food Program.

World Health Organization (WHO). 2002. *The World Health Report 2002: Reducing Risks, Promoting Healthy Life*. Geneva, World Health Organization.

Yeager, R. 1989. *Tanzania: An African Experiment*. Dartmouth: Aldershot.

Ylhäisi, J. 2003. "Forest Privatisation and the Role of Community in Forests and Nature Protection in Tanzania" *Environmental Science and Policy* 6: 279–290.

Yohe, G. 2000. "Assessing the Role of Adaptation in Evaluating Vulnerability to Climate Change." *Climatic Change* 46: 371–390.

Yohe, G., and R. S. J. Tol. 2002. "Indicators for Social and Economic Coping Capacity—Moving Toward a Working Definition of Adaptive Capacity." *Global Environmental Change* 12: 25–40.

Young, H. P. 1994. *Equity in Theory and Practice*. Princeton: Princeton University Press.

Young, I. M. 1990. *Justice and the Politics of Difference*. Princeton: Princeton University Press.

Young, I. M. 2000. *Inclusion and Democracy*. Oxford: Oxford University Press.

Index

Abatement, 42
Abrupt climate change, 29
Acceptable risk, 135
Adaptation
  and agriculture, 45
  anticipatory, 7, 46
  autonomous, 7, 45
  and behavioral changes, 6
  burdens, 6
  costs, 47, 69, 70, 94, 138
  costs and burden sharing, 73
  and ethical obligation, 96
  funding, 56, 63, 72, 132, 133, 148,
    149
  funding estimates, 143
  and mainstreaming, 11, 62
  options and priorities, 91
  passive, 45, 46
  planned, 45
  planning, 189, 194, 202, 217, 226
  prioritization, 70
  private, 12
  proactive, 46, 138
  research, 91
  strategies, 7, 70, 94, 109, 224
  strategies and equity considerations,
    92
  and sustainable development, 111
Adaptation Fund, 65
Adaptive capacity, 5, 28, 44, 82,
  107, 186, 192, 203, 205, 223
Adaptive resource management, 106

Adaptive strategies, 94, 224
Adverse effects, 55, 56, 58, 62
Agriculture, 224
  and Africa, 225
  impacts, 168
Air quality standards, 168
Alliance of Small Islands States, 11,
  74n3
Anarchy, State, and Utopia, 83
Angola, 122
Anthropogenic forcing, 25
Anticipatory adaptation, 46
Armed conflicts, 118
Arrow, Kenneth, 163, 175
Arrow's Impossibility Theorem, 163
Arctic. *See* Inuit
Atoll countries, 116
Avoiding harm, 95

Bangladesh, 18, 32, 70, 181, 187,
  196–199, 255
  impacts, 182–185
Bentham, Jeremy, 266
Biodiversity, 31, 32
Botswana, 228, 236
Bottom-up approach, 181, 192
Bretton Woods institutions, 126
Brundtland Commission, 188
Buenos Aires Decision, 58, 61
Building standards, 93
Burden sharing, 95, 243
Burma, 122

Burning embers, 27. *See also* UN
  IPCC Reasons for Concern

Cambodia, 89, 122
Capability, 82
  and vulnerability, 204
Capacity building, 95
Carbon tax, 41, 272
Caribbean insurance pool, 255
Cascade of uncertainties, 34
Chronic stresses, 85
Citizenship, 1, 83
Clean Development Mechanism, 43,
  65
Climate change
  defined, 55
  and responsibility, 115
  and uncertainty, 96
Climate change impacts, 169
  monetary estimates, 108
  distribution of, 155
Climate debt, 10
Climate insecurity, 115, 127
  and conflicts, 116
  and justice, 117
Climate justice, 79, 263
Climate variability, 2, 206
Coastal zone, 184, 187
Cold War, 125
Collaborative process, 89
Collective action, 1, 7, 264, 265
Collective adaptation decisions, 13
Colonialism, 3, 125
Common but differentiated
  responsibilities, 43, 56, 132
Common law, 135
Common-pool resources, 133
Communitarianism, 15
Community, 265
  management, 231
  participation, 198
Compensation, 109, 110, 111, 112,
  131, 134, 135, 137, 139, 148, 160,
  245, 248
  fault-based, 135

Complex equality, 15, 83, 243, 267
Computable general equilibrium
  models, 167, 169
Conference of the Parties (COP)
  and participation, 128, 275
  COP1, 67
  COP7, 181, 192
  COP8, 70
  COP9, 66, 67
  COP10, 61, 66, 67
Conflict, 18
Consensus, 252
Consent, 10, 81
Consumer behavior, 157
Consumer sovereignty, 157
Consumption, 87
Contributory principle, 266
Coping
  capacity, 192
  resources, 87
  strategies, 206, 233
Cost-benefit analysis, 31, 43, 160
Costs of adaptation. *See* Adaptation,
  costs
Critical stress, 86
Cultural divide, 30
Cultural heritage, 32
Cultural linguistic diversity, 87
Cultural theory, 243
Cumulative density function, 37
Cumulative emissions, 142
Cyclones, 183

Dangerous anthropogenic
  interference, 10, 42, 49, 56
Dangerous climate change, 32, 49,
  203, 263, 267, 269
  probability of, 23
Darwin, Charles, 100, 103
Deagrarianization, 225
Decentralization, 231
Deforestation, 87, 207, 210. *See also*
  Forestry impacts
Delaying tactics, 62
Deliberation, 252

Democratic decision making, 14
Dependency theory, 101
Desert, principle of, 82
Desertification, 58
Development, 224
Differential vulnerability, 79, 107, 182, 258. *See also* Vulnerability
Disasters, 93
Discontinuities, 26
Distributive justice, 3, 14, 16, 48, 54, 72, 128, 202, 204, 223, 273
  links with procedural justice, 264, 266
Diversification, 226
Double exposure, 108
Double vulnerability, 117
Droughts, 25, 58, 227
Duty to assist developing countries, 203

Earth system integrity, 3, 109
East Timor, 126–128
Economic globalization, 108
Ecosystem gods and services, 30
Effective participation, 54
Efficiency equity trade-offs, 155
Egalitarian liberalism, 109, 243
Egypt, 82
El Niño, 127
Emission reduction, 239
  luxury and subsistence emissions, 140, 144, 153n2
Emission scenarios, 168
Empowerment, 236
Environmental
  conflicts, 265
  determinism, 102, 103
  governance, 203, 218, 219
  security, 116
  stress, 86, 205, 212
Equity, 128
  normative judgments, 155
Essential emissions, 79
Ethical principles, 94, 175

Expected impacts, 69
Expert elicitation, 40, 91
Expert Group on Technology Transfer, 68
Externalities, 133
Extreme climate events, 26, 104, 239, 258
  frequency and magnitude, 84

Fair burden sharing, 44
Fair distribution of costs, 128
Fair outcomes, 14
Famine Early Warning System, 93
Farmers, small-scale, 88
Fault-based liability, 136
Financial transfers, 63
Fisheries, 184
  impacts, 168
  and livelihoods, 88
Five numeraires, 17, 27, 30, 31, 32
Floods, 25, 209, 210, 227, 240
  insurance program, 250–251
  prevention, 239
  protection, 8
  risk insurance, 251
  risk management, 252
  strategies, 244–246
Food aid, 8, 220, 227
Food security, 2, 184, 194
Forestry impacts, 168
Forward-looking responsibility, 271, 272
Fossil fuel, dependence, 11
Free riders, 134
Future generations, 268
Future inequalities, 115

Ganges-Brahmaputra-Meghna, 88, 183
Gender equality, 89, 186, 193, 216
Gini coefficient, 176, 213
Global benefits, 63, 64, 73
Global climate models, 84
Global emissions, 28

Global Environment Facility, 47, 59,
    63, 64, 66, 100
  Trust Fund, 73
Global environmental benefits, 47
Global food production, 86
Global managerial discourse, 111
Global markets, 6
Global warming, 4
Global Warming Potentials, 152n25
Globalization, 87, 117, 206. *See also*
    Economic globalization
Governance, 1, 67, 275
Grameen Bank, 198
Greenhouse gases, 61
  emissions, 115
  legacy, 79
  reporting requirements, 69
Greenland, 27
Group of 77 and China, 62
Growing seasons, 28, 234

Habitat shifts, 29
Harm, 134, 137
Hayek, Frederich, 267
Health. *See* Human health
Heat waves, 6
Hedging, 41
Heritage sites, 30
Hierarchy, 243
Historical emissions, 42
Historical responsibility, 9, 53, 136,
    139
HIV/AIDS, 87, 89, 93, 186, 207,
    216, 227
Holiday home, 13
Honduras, 93, 255
Human capital, 205, 211
Human Development Index, 85, 107,
    119, 176
Human health, 109, 174, 210
Human rights, 94, 95
Human security, 188
Hungary, 19
Hurricane, 25, 274
  damage, 51n1
  Mitch, 6, 93

Impacts
  assessment, 107
  functions, 168, 174
  nonmarket, 174
  spatial distribution, 94
Inaction, 7
Incremental costs, 63, 64, 73
India, 198
  agriculture, 108
  droughts, 183
Indifference curves, 161–162, 164
Indigenous communities, 117
Indigenous knowledge, 189, 191,
    193, 195
Individualism, 243
Individual responsibility, 249
Individual welfare, 156
Industrial revolution, 43
Inequality, 211, 275
  economic, 87, 206
Infrastructure, 212
Institutional circumstances, 105
Institutional failure, 3
Institutions, 206
Insurable risk, 242
Insurance, 6, 57, 58, 61, 74n3, 110,
    257
Insurance pools, 240. *See also*
    Turkey, Catastrophe Insurance
    Pool
Interdependence, 83, 84
Intergenerational equity, 29, 49, 56
Intergovernmental Panel on Climate
    Change, 104
  Reasons for Concern, 25, 26
  Second Assessment Report, 25, 36,
    105, 107
  Special Report on Emissions
    Scenarios, 23–24, 34, 36
  Third Assessment Report, 25, 36,
    106–107, 182, 239
Internally displaced people, 123
International law, 137
Inter-species equity, 29
Inuit and Inter-American Human
    Rights Commission, 74

Iraq war, 41
Irreversibilities, 49
Irrigation, 8, 105

Japan, 117
Joint implementation, 43
Justice
  communitarian theories, 204,
    265
  contested, 9, 12
  cosmopolitan theories, 204, 265
  libertarian theories, 14
  and peace, 129
  solutions, 129
Justice principles
  capability, 204
  desert, 80, 204
  equality, 80, 204
  liberty, 80, 204
  need, 80, 204

Kaldor-Hicks compensation
  criterion, 160
Kyoto Protocol, 2, 42, 65, 66, 110,
  254

Land degradation, 87
Land reforms, 111
Land shortage, 227
Landmines, 122
Least Developed Countries, 11, 16,
  56, 60, 104, 111, 181, 191, 194,
  199
Least Developed Country Fund, 16,
  60, 61, 65, 66, 132
Legitimacy, 231
Legitimate claims, 137
Liability, 64, 95, 131, 132, 134, 136,
  137, 139, 148
  North-South, 141
  scenarios, 148
  net, 140
Life expectancy, 211
Life-support commons, 131, 134,
  136, 137, 139, 149
Literacy rate, 211

Livelihoods, 206, 209, 226
  diversification, 111, 225, 230
  opportunities, 228
Loss pooling, 241

Maladaptation, 46, 62
Malaria, 186
Malnutrition, 85
Mapping, 86
Marginal abatement costs, 48
Marginalized groups, 48
Marine ecosystems, 87
Market discourse, 245
Market valuation, 32
Marrakech Accord, 9, 11, 47, 58, 59,
  64, 65, 66
Marx, Karl, 100, 103
Mekong, 88, 89
Middle East, 86
Migration, 8, 227
Millennium Development Goals, 11,
  19, 181, 185, 199
Miller, David, 83
Mitigation
  costs, 49
  defined, 155
  equity, 1, 2
  relationship with adaptation, 41
Mitigation-adaptation trade-off, 47
Mitigative capacity, 28
Mobile phone, 212
Monetary valuation, 156, 158
Moral hazard, 245
Moral responsibility, 139
Most vulnerable countries, 13, 71,
  81, 115
Most vulnerable first, 269, 272–274
Mozambique, 6
Multiple stresses, 85, 115

Namibia, 18, 231
National Adaptation Programme of
  Action, 11, 16, 18, 60, 132, 181,
  199, 276, 201, 203–204
  and Bangladesh, 196–199
  guidelines, 60, , 182, 189, 192, 204

National Adaptation Programme of
    Action (cont.)
 and procedural justice, 60
 process, 201, 217, 220
National Communications, 60, 68–69
National institutions, 201
Natural disasters, 58, 87, 96, 110,
    197, 205, 239
 losses, 255
 research, 93
Natural endowments, 82
Natural hazard reduction, 93
Natural resource use, 231
Negotiation, capacity, 72
Negotiating process inequities, 72
Neoclassical economics, 100, 103
Net economic welfare, 109
Netherlands, 82
Nile, 88
Niue, 70
No regrets, 41
Nonmarket goods, 166
North Africa, 86
North-South relations, 224
Norway, 107–108
Nozick, Robert, 83, 267

Oil-producing countries, 11
 OPEC, 12, 62, 63

Pacific islands, 82
Papua New Guinea, 117
Participation, 3, 14, 16, 99, 191,
    198, 268, 275–276
Participatory planning, 182, 191, 197
Participatory process, 194, 254
Particularly vulnerable, 56, 63, 64,
    69
Past injustices, 264
Pastoral livelihoods, 88
Perceived Corruption Index, 215
Physical vulnerability, 33
Pilot adaptation projects, 71
Policy coordination, 46
Policy integration, 197
Political ecology, 102–103

Political economy, 5, 100, 103, 115,
    125
Political instability, 124
Politics of identity, 267
Polluter pays principle, 132, 138,
    139, 149, 247
Population growth, 24, 29, 44
Post-conflict countries, 118, 119,
    120, 124, 128
Poverty, 86, 187, 194, 195, 197, 198
Power, 3, 268
Precaution, 3
Precautionary approach to
    adaptation, 93
Precautionary principle, 41, 56, 93
Precipitation, 84
Probabilities, 34, 51n2
Probability density function, 37
Procedural justice, 3, 14, 15, 16, 54,
    72, 79, 116, 181, 190, 191, 195,
    204, 217, 223, 264, 268
Psychological costs of uncertainty,
    84
Public bads, 133
Public goods, 133–134, 157
Public health, 203
Public policies, 6

Quality of life, 31

Rainwater harvesting, 8
Rangelands, 232
Rawls, John, 81, 110, 266
Rawlsian justice, 161
Recognition, 3, 112, 268
Refugees, 30, 122, 124
Reinsurance, 253
Representation, 67, 194
Residual damages, 138
Resilience, 6, 79, 81, 105, 191
Resource, access, 117
Resource dependent societies, 223
Responsibility, 9, 134, 139, 140, 146,
    203, 241, 264
Responsibility index, 140, 144
Right not to be harmed, 134

Rights, 116, 135
Rights-based regulation, 135
Rio Declaration, 137
Risk assessment, 49
Risk protection, 83
Risk susceptibility, 80
Risk transfer, 242
Room for maneuver, 7, 235

Safe maximum standard, 270, 271, 272
Savannah, 209
Scenarios, 24
Scientists, role of, 33
Sea level rise, 25, 46, 49, 59, 80, 104, 182
  impacts of, 87–88
Seasonal forecasting, 212
Security, 4, 109, 263
Self-determination, 95
Self-empowerment, 233
Self-identification, 99
Self-mobilization, 191
Sen, Amartya, 82, 163
Sensitivity, 204, 227
Shadow economy, 125
Shrimp exports, 187
Small island countries, 87, 196
Small Island Developing States, 53, 87
Smith, Adam, 100
Social capital, 89, 206, 211, 214
Social contract theory, 134
Social Darwinism, 101, 103
Social justice, 15, 79, 80. *See also* Justice
Socially constructed vulnerability, 114. *See also* Vulnerability
Social value assessment, 49
Social vulnerability literature, 106
Social vulnerability and women, 87
Social welfare, 165
  changes, 168
  equity, 166
  function, 155, 161, 168, 175
Sociobiology, 101

Solidarity, 243, 248
Solomon Islands, 117
Sovereignty, 10, 116
Species extinction, 25. *See also* Biodiversity
Spheres of justice, 267
Spontaneous adaptation, 104
Stabilization targets, 44
Stakeholders, 60, 191, 240, 244, 250, 251
State building, 221
Statistical rights, 137, 138
Stockholm Declaration, 137
Stockholm Environmental Institute, 89
Subjective probabilities, 40
Subsidiary Body for Scientific and Technical Advice, 57
Sudan, 122
Sundarbans, 184
Superfund legislation, 136
Surplus value, 101
Surprises, 23, 27, 28, 33, 94
Sustainable development planning, 94

Tanzania, 18, 201, 207, 208, 209
Technology transfer, 56, 57, 58, 67–68
Terrorism, 1, 41
Thermohaline circulation, 27, 117
Thresholds, 35
Tort law, 135, 270, 271
Toxic hazard, 138
Trade-off with growth and adaptation, 197
Traditional knowledge, 189
Translating services, 72
Transportation infrastructure, 89
Tropospheric ozone precursors, 168
Turkey, 19
  Catastrophe Insurance Pool, 255–257

Uncertainty, 5, 33, 139
  as a barrier to action, 91
  explosion of, 34, 35
Underdevelopment, 3, 115
Unexpected events, 94
Unfair outcomes, 115
United Nations Convention on
    Biological Diversity, 236
United Nations Convention to
    Combat Desertification, 236
United Nations Framework
    Convention on Climate Change, 9,
    53, 131, 203
  absence of adaptation definition, 55
  Adaptation Fund, 59. *See also*
    Adaptation, funding
  Annex I, 54, 68, 69
  Annex II, 54, 63, 69
  Article, 1, 55
  Article, 2, 10, 15, 32, 56
  Article, 3, 56
  Article, 4, 11, 56, 57, 58, 62, 63,
    64, 69, 71, 110, 241, 255, 257
  Article, 5, 56
  Article, 6, 56
  Article, 7, 57
  Article, 9, 57
  Article, 10, 57
  Article, 11, 57
  Article, 12, 57 Climate Impact
    Relief Fund, 255
  and developing countries, 72
  duties, 9
  liability, 271
  particularly vulnerable, 54
  Special Climate Change Fund, 59,
    65, 66, 132
  stabilization, 56
  subsidiary bodies, 54, 61
  ultimate objective, 56
  vulnerable countries, 54
United Nations Security Council,
    129
United States, 18, 48, 61, 73, 111,
    155, 167
  and adaptation, 156

  and agriculture, 107, 174
  Clean Air Act, 74
  Environmental Protection Agency,
    74
  resistance of, 61
Universal primary education, 186
Urban capital divide, 215
Utilitarianism, 13, 31, 107, 109, 136,
    151n12
Utility function, 157

Value, of human life, 30
Value judgments, 33, 40
Vector borne diseases, 85
Victimhood, 99
Violent conflict, 87, 115, 116, 122,
    125
Voluntary exchange, 156
Vulnerability, 12, 64. *See also* Most
    vulnerable countries
  and adaptation assessments, 71
  assessment, 85, 88, 89, 193, 194,
    202, 224
  asymmetry, 82
  communities, 195, 263
  defined, 5, 205, 273
  and distribution, 263
  dynamics, 85, 206
  hot-spots, 90, 91
  identification of, 84
  indicators, 85
  levels of, 171
  measurement, 274
  monitoring, 93
  moral imperative, 80
  peoples and places, 79
  and poverty, 86
  regions, 86
  socially determined, 106, 189
  sources, 17
  urban, 216
  and violent conflict, 118

War, 227. *See also* Cold War, Iraq
    War
  environmental effects of, 121

Water
  availability, 234
  resources, 87
  stress, 87
Wealth inequalities, 79
Weather-related disasters, 6, 239
Welfare aggregation, 160
Welfare change, 32, 171
Welfare economics, 18, 155, 156,
  173
Welfare equivalent, 158
West Africa, 225
West Antarctic Ice Sheet, 27, 43, 117
Who decides, 64
Willingness to pay, 172
Winners and losers, 4, 17, 97, 224
  defined, 98
  perceptions of, 97
  relative and absolute, 99
  theoretical perspectives, 97
World Heritage in Danger List, 74

Young, Iris Marion, 14